ELBOWS IN MY EARS

My Life with Little People,
Tigers, and Wardrobe Trunks

DANISE PAYNE

ELBOWS IN MY EARS
My Life with Little People, Tigers, and Wardrobe Trunks
by Danise Payne
PER002000 2. BIO002010 3. BIO005000
ISBN: 978-1-949642-97-1 (paperback)
978-1-949642-98-8 (hardcover)
978-1-949642-99-5 (ebook)

Cover design by Lewis Agrell

Cover photo by Bill Payne

Printed in the United States of America

Authority Publishing
11230 Gold Express Dr. #310-413
Gold River, CA 95670
800-877-1097
www.AuthorityPublishing.com

ACKNOWLEDGMENTS

In this book are my memories and experiences. My help with facts and lore came from various sources, and I give kudos to them all. If I left anyone off, I apologize, but thanks are there nonetheless.

My early writing was not refined. Jim and Joanne Foster encouraged me and gave gentle corrections. They offered insight into what lay ahead, and my vision took shape.

I received advice from the Henderson Writers' Group. Their numerous critiques and comments helped to smooth the road.

Years of rewrites followed until I found a match in an editor. Her abundant red marks in the track changes function gave birth to my written dream of passion. So, much thanks to Jevon Bolden. I am forever indebted and grateful for your patience and belief.

With the guidance of my project manager, Chela Hardy, *Elbows in My Ears* took tangible form. Whenever I had questions, she never ceased to answer.

For accuracy of details, I turned to those who know the history that dates back to the Colosseum in Rome—circus people.

The amount of facts held in The Robert L. Parkinson Library & Research Center in Baraboo, Wisconsin, will astound you! My phone calls to them revealed information I never knew. They helped my memoir become as tried-and-true as possible.

Robert F. Houston who provided data about black circus performers and John Cooper in Great Britain for his research of my status are two individuals to whom I tip my hat.

For circus-isms and logistics, I turned to Cowboy Clown, Mike Keever. And I would never have known how our circus train maneuvered without the one-on-one with our trainmaster, Charlie Smith.

Through it all, I give a loving thanks to my husband, Bill Payne. He helped my memory, and his great photos enliven the text. Thanks to all for the fulfillment of this book.

DEDICATION

I dedicate this book for the glory of God with love to my husband, Bill, who reminds me never give up on my dream; to my sisters and brother, Vanita, Robert, and Adriene, from whom I learned no one stands alone; to my Aunt Ernestine who supported me from day one; and especially with love to my parents, Alma and Bob Wilson, who taught me to persevere.

TABLE OF CONTENTS

INTRODUCTION

I am the daughter of an original Tuskegee Airman of World War II, and military protocol filled my childhood. By the age of seven, nonetheless, I wanted to perform. Nothing could stop me, for the Lord had ordered my steps and established me. To set me on my way, His still, small voice prompted me to acquire the know-how needed to succeed in a world that I never anticipated: at the age of sixteen, unicycle; at the age of twenty-three, juggling—-skills of a domain from the far side of the sun.

I would use this expertise in The Biz that greeted me. The road ahead would be fun, but not stress-free. There would be thorns of jealousy, disillusionment, exasperation, and panic in my side. I would need to remember that I was decked in armor. Equipped with faith and a funny bone, I became who I was to be. These are my remembrances with no pretense or embellishment. This is my story.

There was a time when I lived in a dream and rode unicycles and elephants, patted zebras, but avoided chimpanzees. A man walked with bears, and a woman hung by her hair. A three-foot-tall giant strolled with beasts four times his size. Who was that with wings on her back, a wand in her hand, and paint on her face? And oh, the toys: enormous, brilliant jack-in-the-boxes, a miniature car the shade of lemonade, and floats the color of a magenta sunset. I fell in love in that mystical, magical, wonderful world and found the love of my life.

In 1978, my diploma from Ringling Bros. and Barnum & Bailey Clown College cleared a path to the Red Unit of *The Greatest Show on Earth*, and my life transitioned from cinder-block houses that lined the streets of air force bases to a home the size of a bathroom. I learned to sleep confined with my elbows in my ears, yet circus captured my soul.

In 2017 legislators passed laws that prohibited performances with exotic animals in various cities. As a result, shows shut down, adapted, or pushed on intact. And so it happened that the owners of the greatest spectacle announced its closure after 146 years of bedazzlement. As it faded, premieres took the place of state-of-the-art circuses that sailed those used to greasepaint and glamour over murky waters. I am African American. How did that relate to me? A glance at history revealed a jagged tapestry of a colorful life.

The art form sprouted in Europe, and by the 1800s, people in the United States enjoyed circuses as well. The new outlet enticed the full-spirited to apply their hands at the trade and included Amelia Butler who joined James M. Nixon's Great American Circus in 1858.

Citizens hungered for entertainment, which opened the way to make money off the gullible ignorance of man at the expense of another. At times, it catered to the prejudices of the heart. In his museum, Phineas Taylor Barnum exhibited the odd, "freaks," such as a black man named William Henry Johnson who possessed an elongated forehead. Barnum billed him as The What Is It? or Man-Monkey—the link between ape and man. Another moniker for Mr. Johnson was Zip after the southern racist character Zip Coon.

In the early days, the massive Ringling Bros. and Barnum & Bailey Combined Shows presented grace, class, and style with circus acts, animals, and the physically abnormal. The payroll included African Americans. Men of color numbered among the crew as gandy dancers, a term associated with railroad workers. Non-circus individuals labeled them roustabouts. Circus gandy dancers formed a circle around tent stakes and pounded sledgehammers in perfect synchronization, one man after another. When finished, they tightened the guy ropes and raised the big top: "Heave it—weave it—shake it—take it—break it—make it. Move along," chanted the gang boss.

The American circus proved a gargantuan project. Performers included dancers, flyers, high-wire walkers, and clowns. But did the boss men allow blacks in the ring? In Europe, yes. For example,

Raphael Padilla, a black Cuban, propelled to stardom in the late 1800s of France as half the notable clown duo *Foottit et Chocolat*.

But in the United States by 1848, blackface comedy snared those of African descent into the role of lazy, happy, musical buffoons. Vaudeville continued that function into the twentieth century. Artistes smeared on cork and later greasepaint or shoe polish to depict a stereotype. They exaggerated their lips and wore woolly wigs, gloves, and tailcoats to portray the mammies, uncles, and aunties found in their mind's eye. The sentiment remained with the advent of film, but in due course faded to time.

Circuses flourished, but the big top's light dimmed on those with an ebony hue. Descendants of Africans, such as slack-wire artist Harrison Putney, a.k.a. The Great Layton, proved able, yet were relegated to minstrel shows. I would learn object manipulation, but before me, Ben Toledo and Rowland demonstrated phenomenal juggling skills. My training allowed me to pass through doors lit from the outside by Professor Charles Carr, handler of ten Shetland ponies and thirty dogs, on The Famous Mahara's Minstrels.

A few blacks did destroy myths and performed under canvas, closed as it may have been. Richard Potter, born in 1783, became the United States' first magician and worked with several companies.

Kudos to two individuals who knocked down strongholds on the life of sawdust. In 1885 Ephraim Williams pioneered as the first African American to showcase a circus when he co-owned the Ferguson & Williams Monster Show. He owned and toured several productions, among them a fifteen-car railroad extravaganza. Mr. Williams shone as an accomplished magician and trainer of one hundred Arabian horses. He played with success before white audiences. Established producers, however, resented his accomplishments. He persevered and died in the early 1900s—wealthy, yet faded into time.

In 1952 wild animal showman Clyde Beatty took Manuel Ruffin under his wings on his three-ring railroad production. He mentored and introduced the young man of color to the world. Manuel "Junior" Ruffin grew to a notable animal trainer of lions, tigers, and elephants; big top boss; trainmaster; and more.

The show biz tree branched in many directions, each with its own story. Circus life stood unique in that it offered a ride on a carousel around the outskirts of imagination. One by one, people of African descent strode through circus flaps into a fantasy. It was into that world I stepped in, in November 1978.

## CHAPTER ONE

CHUTZPAH

The very stuff that runs through the veins of a clown
The very stuff that's thrown and covers the ground
Whether your big top's a building with a concrete floor
Or a tent made of canvas with a flap for a door
Whether you powder on asphalt or track through the mud
You know you're a trouper when there's sawdust in your blood.

—D. Payne

How the massive creatures dwarfed the little man! He stood three-feet tall with the beasts' knees at his head, yet control belonged to him. A taller worker called out to him, "Piccolo, keep 'em in line!" The empty belly of the mile-long silver slug awaited the arrival of its bulky meal. Into their hay-laden cars the pachyderms trudged one by one. In the future, unbeknownst to me, whenever I would smell elephants, I knew I was home.

But one year before, my younger sister, Adriene, and I stopped in front of the Oakland Coliseum for a moment, then proceeded down a wide ramp. What lay ahead? We inched into the structure where the odor of animals permeated the air, then peered left and right into a fantasyland that waited to spring to life.

Overhead hung the high wire, trapeze bars, and spotlights. Elephant stands, band equipment, and brilliant banners decorated the interior. But something else caught my eye: four men with bright orange hair. They rested motionless on the sidelines clad in garments of vibrant purples, mustards, and scarlets. A lone black gentleman, who smiled in my direction, sat among them. With faces painted in white with dabs of blue and red, they resembled marionettes in search of a puppeteer. Their large shoes could have squashed any bug that sauntered by.

Adriene, who had come along for moral support, made a hasty retreat for the bleachers. I wrote my name on a sign-in sheet, then took a seat with thirty other young people who sat around the circumference of a ring. I was hoping for a slot in the 1977 class of Ringling Bros. and Barnum & Bailey Clown College—I was the only African American to audition that afternoon. A woman had told me about this tryout two days earlier. Up to that point, I had no idea what to do for a career. Circus never entered my mind. But it sounded fun. So, no more qualms. Not sure what to do with my future, I thought I'd give it a go and perhaps transform my life.

An older man stood. His impressive outfit of colorful fabric framed an oversized scarlet tie that dangled in the center of a golden shirt. He sported a pointed hat tipped to the side and an ever-present painted smile.

"OK, let's get this thing going. My name is Frosty, and I'm the boss clown here. I wanna welcome all of you. This here is Ringling Bros. and Barnum & Bailey Circus, otherwise known as *The Greatest Show on Earth*. We're gonna put you through some paces to see if you can be funny. Then, if any of you brought anything, I'm gonna let you show us what you can do." He paused and put his hands on his hips. "Any questions?"

No one said a word.

The elder clown turned and withdrew a banana the length of my arm, an enormous baseball mitt, and other objects from his box of toys at his feet. I considered my situation while he put these things on the ring.

My father, Bob Wilson, had been an original Tuskegee Airman during World War II. He had earned his wings in 1944 after eight weeks of ground school and forty-five hours of flight time. Daddy remained in the air force thirty years before retiring in 1971, a long time for military duty. Only a handful of families departed the service unscathed by the effects of life in a compound surrounded by barbed wire. After a career of "yes, sirs" and "no, sirs" my dad expected discipline and logic within his sphere of influence. Would clown match the standard for one of his kids?

Frosty's words interrupted my thoughts. "OK, guys, this is the deal. There's thirty-two of us hilarious people in this show. This is the Red Unit. There's two branches of Ringling. The other's called the Blue Unit. And each year they hold these auditions, see, for new faces. If you can cut the mustard through the school and get hired, you'll be apprentice clowns, 'First of Mays.' You'll work sixteen hours a day, with three performances on Saturday and the same on Sunday; two the rest of the time. That's six days a week. You don't get downtime 'cause the seventh is for travel to the next town."

The work schedule staggered me. But when he mentioned that everyone, including the animals, lived on the train, the prospect of fun with elephants obliterated my butterflies. I peeked again at the stands that the workers would use for the colossal mammals.

"OK, let's go. Hotterini! By the way, *hottay* and *hotterini* are my own words. If you make it to the show, you'll get used to hearin' 'em," the senior man with the painted face said.

He turned and introduced the orange-haired clowns, who rested on the perimeter, and they came to life as if in a spooky movie. They moved toward us wannabes as he continued, "Clowns perform on the spot, and we're gonna have you guys show how you think on your feet. You're gonna create certain scenarios for step number one of the tryouts. I wantcha to volunteer two by two and face each other in the ring a few feet apart. You're high-wire walkers, see. We wanna see what you'd do when you meet in the middle. OK, who's first? Hottay! Let's go."

I doubted this circus thing, but I wanted to show my stuff. Gravity, however, cemented me in place. Fellow candidates didn't waste any time and came forward in pairs. They moseyed to the center of the ring, crawled over each other on the invisible tightrope, and continued to the opposite side. I hesitated, then stood, and joined a tall, thin, young man with shoulder-length hair dressed in blue jeans and a T-shirt. We walked three feet away from each other and turned. With arms stretched to steady ourselves, we stepped onto the imaginary cable, strolled to the middle, and stopped. We stared at each other, and without thought, I jumped off the nonexistent wire into open space and scurried around him. What else would a clown do?

When we finished part one, Frosty took over. "To test your creativity choose props on the ring curb, see. Show how you'd use them."

I did. I improvised with the giant six-shooter to kill a fly, and the provided unicycle mixed ingredients of my feigned cake. Sheer chutzpah took over, and I put my exaggerated facial expressions to use.

Next, we separated into groups, and, with help from Frosty's fellow clowns, learned a skit—or their term, "a gag"—called "Dead and Alive!" Gestures proved important. We used the comic device of double takes in reaction to our partners' movements. Pieces of zany business, called shtick, made their way into normal motions. At one point in the piece, my colleague fell to the floor and remained on his back in a feigned state of unconsciousness. I tried to revive him and lifted his arm. His leg sprang up instead. I pushed his leg down and his arm shot up—back and forth. The pantomime made no sense, but showed how well we worked together. After everyone had a go at it, the time was nearing to present our own material for show-and-tell.

In hasty preparation for this moment, I had scrounged through my father's stuff in the garage—which had doubled as a makeshift theater for practice—and found four pipes, a bicycle tire, and a spare handlebar and stuffed them into a duffle bag. My unicycle would complete the shape of a bike. They served the purpose for my How to Construct a Bicycle sketch.

One by one, participants demonstrated their skills. I didn't budge until the end, then dragged my knapsack full of metal into the ring. Frosty eyeballed the spectacle and groaned. "This isn't gonna take long, is it?"

I stood in the center, removed each section from the big bag, and formed the crude bicycle on the floor. Then I picked up the unicycle. I glanced at my younger sister in the stands, who held up both hands and crossed her fingers.

Right foot on the right pedal, seat under me, up and on for two loops around the ring; then a dismount and bow. Adriene stood and cheered. A wider grin and my teeth would have fallen out. I had done my best, so I gathered my stuff and sat down.

When the auditions ended, Frosty thanked everyone and handed each of us an application. "Fill this out and mail it to the Clown College office as soon as possible." Adriene ran from the sidelines as the black clown approached and introduced himself.

"Hi, I'm Garry White. You did OK. We don't get many African American women at these tryouts. Do you realize that if you make it, you could be the first black girl clown with Ringling? You could be in *Ebony!*" he said. "Have you ever seen the show?"

"No. We've never seen any circus."

He invited us to return the next evening. We accepted with glee and blabbed all the way home and disclosed the particulars of the audition to our parents when we got there. Adriene slept like a baby that night, but I lay awake in bed, unable to turn off my brain.

Late the following afternoon, we made the two-hour drive back to Oakland. Garry waited outside the coliseum at the top of the incline. Though he dressed as he had at the auditions, his appearance struck me that time. There stood the figure of a man. His bulbous red nose rested above his mustache. Iridescent blue patches highlighted his maroon pants and sable tuxedo jacket. White gloves sans fingertips revealed his own. His bowler hat and sizable black-and-white shoes completed the look. With a jumbo, puffy, crimson bow tie, what a vagabond of a higher class!

"Hi, I'm glad you two made it. Come on. I'll show you a few things that most folks don't see. It'll give you an idea of what's involved if you make it to the show." Adriene and I followed down that wide ramp again and stepped into the backstage area. He pointed toward large navy drapes. "The blue curtain was out of the way for your tryouts. It's there now to separate us from the arena floor and the audience."

We headed down the hallway, and the pungent odor of animals again drifted from within the premises. Garry noticed our grimaces. "What's a circus without animals, right? We don't have time to check them out. Anyway, you'll see them during the show." The three of us continued, and my sister and I feasted our eyes on a cornucopia of wonder. Performers milled about in full makeup and costume, with others in bathrobes. Two clowns strolled by—one an African American, his head ornamented with a top hat.

"Hey, Dwayne," Garry called out, "this is Danise. She tried out yesterday." The men approached, and Garry turned to us. "Meet Dwayne Cunningham." Adriene giggled as the second funny man pumped her hand.

We encountered a dancer named Jacqui Shannon. After she walked by, Garry mentioned that she owned the distinction as the only African American showgirl on the unit. He led us onward, and we goggled at muscular men who spoke an Eastern-European language and at kids in white tights who played in the corridor. Wooden planks leaned against the gray walls. "Those are for the teeterboard acts." Gigantic ruby globes of some kind of metal rested on the side—for the bears to balance on, we learned—and a tiny yellow car with a red border design had squeezed in from the land of Dr. Seuss's Circus McGurkus.

We approached a door.

"This is the ladies' wardrobe." He turned and called out, "Mama, can we come in?"

"*Ja, ja!*" came a voice from inside.

"The wardrobe mistress is Miss Ellen. We call her Mama. She's from Germany and used to have a dove act back in the day."

When Adriene and I followed Garry into the chamber, we stepped into a carousel of Technicolor. Big, blue wooden boxes lined the space. These overflowed with impressive rose petticoats, orange wigs, and magenta, high-buttoned shoes. A formidable German woman with stark raven hair sat nearby. "Mama, this is Danise. She auditioned yesterday. I'm showing her and her sister around." The woman smiled and busied herself with a needle and thread.

"This is one of the busiest places for the dancers during the show," Garry said. "They'll rush in and change, then run out. Miss Ellen helps them dress and repairs rips and loose sequins. I wanted you to see the ladies' changing room 'cause girl clowns are sometimes in here." I glanced at Miss Ellen's empire of fabric and wondered, "Who designs such splendid creations?"

After that peek through the looking glass, we left the backstage with its hidden secrets. Garry escorted us to the public area. The aroma of popcorn tickled our noses. Oh, the hubbub! "Programs! Get your programs here! Take home a souvenir!" We proceeded past vendors outfitted in orange aprons who broadcasted their wares to snow-cone-slurping patrons. Lights in booths illuminated swirls of pink filaments wound around white paper cones: "Cotton candy here!"

We entered the arena, and Garry led us to seats on one end. "Enjoy the show!" he said, then disappeared into the crowd. I looked around again.

The bleachers spilled over with people whose demeanors rivaled those of children on Christmas morning. We sat above the artists' entrance. Dressed in black suits, the band below readied their instruments: drums, trombones, trumpets, an organ, and saxophones. The floor stood empty with those elephant stands still against the wall. We waited. Then, the houselights faded to black. Flickers of red, yellow, and blue from the kids' trinket wands and bracelets shimmered in the darkness.

A whistle sounded, and the spotlights highlighted a magical man who revealed a whole new world. The cast stood in place with arms raised as if in allegiance to the Creator. Oh, the glitter and the glamour, the elephants and the clowns, the music and that ringmaster! Fantasy captured my heart and propelled me into another dimension. I wondered at the spectacle and thought, "I could be a part of *this*?"

The next day I sat on my bed, and with a pen, transformed my life. The four-page form before me read, "Application for Admission to Ringling Bros. and Barnum & Bailey Clown College."

"In the top right hand, print large and legibly your family name and first initial": Wilson, D. The first page demanded easy answers. My birthplace was San Marcos, Texas. Parents: Bob and Alma Wilson. Marriage status: single.

The space below needed three full-face photos and two full-length ones that matched their precise measurements. The school preferred color pictures but no clown makeup. Additional information included social security number (prerequisite: American citizen) and any foreign languages spoken.

I came up for air and continued with questions such as "Do you suffer from claustrophobia?" No. "When was the last time you cried?" My brother, Robert, had escaped without injury from an accident that left our car smashed like an accordion.

"If you could be someone else, who would that be and why?" It didn't matter that they wanted to know. I dealt with all inquiries and named two favorite poets as requested. A list of phrases called for my interpretations. "Familiarity breeds contempt" proved the most difficult to decipher. At the end of the inquisition, which required three days to complete, my signature. I never realized the creation of laughter called for a deep dive into the search for Danise.

I said a prayer and sent off my application. A response arrived by mail: "You have auditioned one week too late to be considered for this year's class, but we will keep your information on file for consideration for the class of 1978."

A twelve-month span lay ahead.

The notion that one ran away and joined a circus didn't apply to Ringling Bros. and Barnum & Bailey. The action demanded thought, desire, patience, and chutzpah. Fortunately, I didn't want to flee *from* anything, only toward a new dawn.

Would my journey ever begin?

## CHAPTER TWO

AN AMERICAN EDUCATION

I'm a Texan, born military at San Marcos Air Force Base. Four years later the government transferred us to Bentwaters Air Force Base in England. We lived in a cottage of chalky plaster in the village of Great Glemham in Suffolk County near the bitter North Sea—a thirty-minute drive from the protocol of dress blues and khakis.

Our quiet lane meandered past a house here and there with neighbors of pale skin and rosy cheeks. Within a week a welcome came our way. At a knock, my mother opened the door to a family with boys who wore knickers and knee socks. "Hello. We're the Chandlers. We live down the road a piece," the patriarch said. His wife, Rose, would later invite us to a meal of minced beef, peas, and carrots covered with mashed potatoes that had been baked together to form the savory dish of shepherd's pie.

A few days later, another local opened her home for afternoon tea time. We entered her cottage and sat in the backyard and sipped the hot beverage served in dainty china cups and ate crumpets—small unsweetened cakes.

When Sunday rolled around, we strolled the narrow path to a quaint, old church of stone and took a seat inside. After the service, we met the vicar and other residents who attended, one of whom had the warmest of hearts. So comfortable was the gentleman with us that we Wilsons called him Uncle Fred. The jolly, older man sported tweed pants, a white shirt, and a tie. Round glasses sat on his nose above a mustache. He proved the king of the Hula-Hoop at outings. With raised arms and a toothy smile, he took his stance

9

in the middle of the large, plastic ring and shook his entire body to twirl the band forever. Uncle Fred and the round toy inspired a gag executed by my character in *The Greatest Show on Earth*.

After we had settled in, a new season began. I walked with kids of freckled faces and strawberry-blond curls to a one-room primary schoolhouse, which cracked the shell and exposed the little "me" within. Classmates influenced my speech. "Mom" became "mum"; "bathroom," "loo"; "truck," "lorry."

On the weekends, to take full advantage of the location, my parents loaded my older sister, Vanita, my brother, Robert, and me (my younger sister, Adriene, was born after we left England.) into the car to view castles with moats and walled cities. In the center of London, we waited outside Buckingham Palace for the changing of the guard. In Ireland, our automobile bounced down the lane and gave me a glimpse into my future.

Along the roadside in cool drizzle rested wooden caravans with rounded rooftops and sunburst wheels. My father slowed down and we gazed as my mother said, "Gypsies! They live in those wagons and travel around." In fact they were called the Travellers, Ireland's largest Indigenous ethnic minority known throughout time for get-up-and-go tinker work. The sight made its mark on my heart.

Four years of cloudy sunshine and chilly rain drew to a close when my father received orders to pack up and go. He mentioned later he dreaded a return stateside to walk the red carpet of discrimination. That would be new to me because I lived in a color-blind world; my parents never spoke of differences. That honor, reserved for society.

One morning the movers arrived. I stood back as they placed our belongings into large, wooden crates—an indication of overseas travel—with the precision of a deployment. When they finished, we packed a lunch of rolls of sausage enveloped in baked dough, ambled through the empty house, then drove to the public airport via guest vehicle. The armed forces shipped our Karmann Ghia to the States ahead of us. We boarded the commercial plane and said "cheerio" to Great Britain, our picturesque village of Great Glemham, my one-room schoolhouse, and the Chandlers and Uncle

Fred—companions who would remain so for life. Memories and tangible keepsakes accompanied us on the journey, as did a thick English accent for me.

Next stop, Chanute Air Force Base in Rantoul, Illinois, and an American education began. No more distinct cottages of Great Glemham. Instead, we lived in close proximity to our neighbors in one of the uniform duplexes with green carports that lined the treeless streets.

My entrance into American society came laden with the unfamiliar. My shade and pronunciation stumbled those with glaucoma of the heart. Young people introduced my ears to *blackie, nigger,* and *Oreo* (black on the outside, white on the inside). A trip across the ocean set me on another planet, and how did I talk funny? Different confronted me head-on. The daily verbal sonic booms enclosed me in a shell. "Sticks and stones may break my bones, but words will never hurt me" was a big fat lie.

How difficult to acquire playmates with such bombardments! I was nine years old. Enough! After school one day as a little soldier on a mission, I marched into the kitchen, found the Ajax, climbed the stairs, and slumped into the bathroom. Click! The door locked. I clasped the faucet. Ah, cool water released onto my right forearm. A dash of the cleansing powder and scrub, scrub. I wanted that black off.

I longed to be accepted in the United States as in Great Glemham, but I took note of the distinctions presented by my country. School—different; food—different; people—different; even my hair—different. I assumed every girl used a hot comb on nappy tresses after water caressed the strands. Caucasians flung their heads around, and their locks followed suit, or their ponytails swung back and forth. Mine stayed still. "Why didn't my hair bounce?" I wondered.

Nothing would change me, and the introvert took over. If I could have walked invisibly through the days, it would have been a done deal. Even the young needed to sing, "I exist."

What notes would begin my song?

Each tick of the clock pulled the world of little people, tigers, and wardrobe trunks closer, especially the day my parents drove us to St.

Louis to attend the musical *Applause*. It was my first play. Surrounded by enthusiastic spectators, we took our seats in the open-air venue.

When the star, Lauren Bacall, burst into the scene, her words "Welcome to the theater!" stormed through the air and thundered into my heart. "I'm going to be an actress when I grow up," I said to myself.

The mask of make-believe would offer protection from incongruity. From then on, the living room served as a space for shows and the carport for neighborhood presentations. The playacting for my family and the kids on base prepared me for my baby steps into the limelight. These occurred onstage for the first time in elementary school.

One week before the yearly assembly that took place in the gym, the teacher handed out one-liners. At showtime I remembered Lauren Bacall. I stepped forward on cue and said, "Suppose Alexander Graham Bell hadn't kept trying to perfect the telephone!"

One late afternoon, my father came home with transfer orders that indicated a move to James Connally Air Force Base in Waco, Texas. A week later, we piled cardboard boxes onto the floor of our single-story bland house. To store possessions, we padded silverware and toys in preparation for a bumpy ride in a moving van. Glasses and plates wrapped with care in newspaper would ride in a stack side by side. All nonperishables filled those containers of compressed paper. My father took beds apart, and along with other furniture, bundled the sections in blankets. I packed my precious white go-go boots last, then stood outside to wait for the familiar Mayflower van.

The long, green semi with a caricature of the pilgrims' ship pulled up, and the men bounded out and zoomed past. They entered the house and loaded our necessities on board—no need for wooden crates stateside. "See you in Texas!" they shouted and proceeded for Chanute's front entrance. Soon, we Wilsons headed out the gate and went south.

We relocated every four years, the norm for air force folks. But it also meant a severance from friends. As a result, a separation anxiety developed with a strange feeling of abandonment. I dreaded "so long" and harnessed a topsy-turvy assumption that life on the move would control the goodbyes. This carried into my adulthood. "Follow the get-up-and-go life of the gypsy, Danise, for preservation of self." Odd. To do the very thing that caused anxiety.

Texas, my birth state. Once again shade of skin factored into daily life. The civil rights movement had yet to take place; thus, we ran head into the phenomenon of segregation. Not at the facilities on base, but outside the perimeter—yes. All air force kids, regardless of ethnicity, attended schools in town not open to the neighborhood's civilian children of a darker hue.

Connally Junior High nestled in the middle of an African American farm community. Yet, every day buses carried their youth away, somewhere. "What did they think of me who passed with white students through forbidden doors?"

Closed in by the hallowed halls, we opened the textbooks, which mentioned little about my race and our accomplishments. By seventh grade, my surroundings had convinced me that only Caucasians could soar above the impossible. My eyes beheld a country that believed in my inferiority, that my roots stemmed from a link between apes and humans, tail and all. With each encounter of hate, life instilled the lie, for even I cheered Tarzan—the white caretaker of Africa, the Dark Continent.

But my father flew airplanes.

I didn't accept the view of less than. Instead, I read African American historical literature. Words found within the text blossomed value and a sense of worth. I turned a page and discovered that Alexander Graham Bell *couldn't* have perfected the telephone without the government license of Lewis H. Latimer, his African American chief draftsman. The Jenny coupler, a patented invention of a man of color named Andrew Jackson Beard, improved joining railroad cars together. The circus train I would later travel on connected by use of his innovation. Oh, such a long list of achievements by those who sprang from the land of Queen Tiye of Egypt!

The newly found knowledge infused logic where none existed. The difference in pigment and the sound of my voice almost did me in. But through the saving grace of television, a crevice developed in my thin shell, which allowed a sense of humor to bud that kept me through slanders. Thanks to *The Ed Sullivan Show,* I learned entertainers always won the crowd.

At the end of thirty years in the service, Daddy chose to retire at Mather Air Force Base in Sacramento, California. After his shift one afternoon in spring, he rode his bicycle home and called us together. "Wanna see what Mather looks like?" He held a picture book that depicted a utopian society—palm trees in the housing area, horses in stalls, and a lake for fishing. Oh, boy. I couldn't wait to head west. The days passed at a snail's pace after that, but when the usual time frame of four years ended, we said farewell to Texas.

Before the transition, my family packed the car to visit places that led to my wanderlust. Trips didn't follow the shortest path, however. East of the Pecos River, we barnstormed north through Oklahoma, Missouri, and Illinois, across to Kentucky and Tennessee, and into Atlanta from the northern part of Georgia to see Mom's kin. We seldom ventured into the racially hot states that bordered the Gulf of Mexico. One proved so rough for blacks in my parents' day that instead of *hell* for a curse word, Daddy said, "Alabama!"

Only once did we stay in a hotel along the way, and I never questioned why we slept in our car. We pulled onto the parking spaces of a Stuckey's or onto an empty patch of land. Our parents rolled the windows halfway down and inserted homemade screens to keep the mosquitoes out, yet let air in. My future owed thanks to those vacant lots of faded dreams.

After a zigzag route from Texas, we rolled in to Atlanta and relatives. One day my father created a *déjà vu* of my tomorrows. He exited Grandmother's house and strolled toward our Volkswagen Beetle. After he opened the door, he called each person to enter for an outing into town. As the first in, I flopped into the cubbyhole behind the rear seat. My roly-poly grandmother, prim and proper with tights to boot, waited in line to fill a spot. Her long, gray hair rested in an ever-present bun set in place by hairpins the length of my fingers. The waistline of her skirt floated above her middle. She stood next to six-foot-tall, thin Grandfather, the top of her head at his shoulders. The petite vehicle bulged after fifteen folks piled in. Dad climbed into the driver's seat and slammed the door. "All right, nobody breathe." My first Clown Car gag.

Soon, we bade goodbye to my mother's clan. Westward, ho! To California. We continued the drive out of the way down lonely stretches of concrete ribbon, which solidified my love for the road. Our little troupe turned a corner and passed a brown sign that boasted, "Historic Route 66." Later in my life, it would become a staple in my travels. We headed north to Gary, Indiana, where the maker of memories led to my father's Uncle Jim and his Aunt Roxie. They walked with guarded steps and sat with caution. They laughed with ease, but scolded with a strong constitution. Nonetheless, my shy attitude as a child accepted their assertive manner. Aunt Roxie and my maternal grandmother left remembrances of age from which sprang my final clown character.

# # #

We finally made it to California. We stopped at the front gate of Mather to check in, drove to Daddy's office, then down a long thoroughfare that wound past the flight line. The little book lied. Those in-the-middle-of-nowhere stables came into view on the left with a sign that stated, "For personal use." Across the street instead of a lake for fishing rested a little pond with muskrats and weeds. We didn't see any palm trees either, but the base was OK. Mather stood off by itself before construction of Highway 50. In due course, my parents bought a house in the nearby community of Rancho Cordova, and we stayed put because the Golden State offered a better education.

The first Sunday morning after we had moved off base, I woke to my father's voice: "Rise and shine and give God the glory!" His new version of reveille belted call to order, and I slipped onto the floor and dressed. After breakfast, off to the tiny United Methodist Church of Rancho Cordova. A man in a white robe with a green sash that wrapped around his shoulders greeted us at the door.

"Welcome. I'm Reverend [Herbert] Hirschfeld." We shook his hand and entered.

I glanced around, then slouched onto the pew. We were the only people of color. "Here we go again," I thought. But the congregation threw the curveball of acceptance, and we seasoned the melting pot. I grew to love this church. The pastor imparted lessons of faith that sustained the art of self-preservation. This carried into the Wilson household because at sunset we sat in front of my father who read scriptures that filled our spirits' bellies. My lifeblood flowed with power to move mountains, thanks to our gatherings at pale evening and to our minister who favored Fred Flintstone.

One sundown in the middle of the week, Mom entered my room. She sat next to me on the bed and said, "Let's talk." I pulled my legs to my chest and hugged my knees. She looked at the walls painted the tint of a sky that blushed. A picture of a black marine corps officer in dress blues kept watch from above the closet. My mother smiled and began. "Danise, you have two years left of high school. Think about what you want to do for a career. When you choose your next classes, I recommend home ec. That'll improve your cooking skills and teach you how to sew. Keep that in mind."

She clasped a handmade wooden box and opened it. Slats divided it into six sections—one labeled "milk" and another "church," for example. Each held paper cash wrapped by rubber bands. She pulled out a wad. "This is how I distribute the right amount to pay the bills or go to the commissary. Your father and I want to make sure you understand the value of money."

As a matter of fact, I remembered Dad's financial advice: "If you can't afford to pay for something, you shouldn't have it." Years later a hard-earned $1,200 purchased a bright-orange, used, 1972 Datsun 510 equipped with a radio. She spoke and I thought of my father. He had told me that as a young man, he swam across the Mississippi River, dared fate with jumps from cliffs, and rode a bicycle everywhere, which resulted in the nickname Bicycle Bob. He had awed me one day when he sat backward on the handle bars and pedaled down the street.

Mom caught my drift of attention and returned me to the road-map of childhood to adulthood. Her wise words met sad ears because "Peter Pan never grew up, must I?" filtered into my thoughts.

She paused and eyeballed my outfit, then echoed Dad's comments of the day before: "Always put your best foot forward because they're going to see only color." After she finished and left the room, I ambled to the closet shared by my older sister, Vanita, and younger sister, Adriene, and opened the door to the essence of me. Red-, white-, and blue-striped pants had infiltrated the fatigues-inspired, khaki-colored clothes that remained. Hot pants shorts draped from hangers.

I walked to the mirror that hung on the wall and stared at the image—a true representation of who faced it. My abstract-patterned blouse didn't match the hip-hugger, bell-bottomed pants or socks covered with patriotic stars that enveloped my feet. A copper thunderbird necklace dangled from my neck. The Vietnam War raged overseas, which had changed my ideals, and a typical American teenager smirked in the reflection.

My mother's spiel would sink in one day. But that dusk in the Indian summer of my youth in front of the looking glass, I placed my hands on my hips because individuality had stormed past the shadow of shyness. I dared the Establishment to turn a deaf ear. Sometimes, a headband encircled my hard-pressed (super-straight) hairdo. But at that moment, a big bouncy afro adorned my head, which cast the racial slurs of my adolescence to a back seat and pushed self-awareness up front. I stepped back and snapped my fingers at remembrances. Insults? Ha! "Say it loud, I'm black and I'm proud!"

Farewell to formative years that passed into yesterday. The next day to ease my parents' minds that their number-two little bird would make it off the ground, I sauntered up to them in the kitchen and unveiled my dreams. "I'm going to apply to the American Academy of Dramatic Arts in New York City. They have a great program with a full curriculum." I had already inquired, received their packet, and showed them the information. Then I explained my long-held plan for the arts. But my parents, concerned for the future, urged studies closer to home in a field that granted instant gratification, unlike drama. Thus, after high school, my center of higher education led to

California State University, Sacramento (CSUS, formerly Sacramento State College).

With dramatic arts out of the picture, a change in my major occurred five times. With no rhyme or reason, French entered the scene as the main course. But the sweetness of a dessert named limelight had taken over my palate.

The final semester, the distant odor of elephant and faint call of greasepaint dangled a tidbit of sawdust before my face. I sat in the rear of my French class and read the school newspaper hidden in my open language book. A short notice leapt from the page. "Hmm, juggling lessons are going to take place on the quad." The prospect of fun created a problem. The sessions would happen the last third of that required three-hour class. Later, an inexplicable urge to learn object manipulation prompted lies to the professor, who excused the absence.

On my way home, I drove to a sports shop and purchased three lacrosse balls—one green, one yellow, and one red—and the next day slinked off to grasp the art of throwing things. Might as well. An unseen force had impelled me to master a unicycle years before. My excursions from making the grade didn't stop recognition on the dean's honor list—twice. After five years, CSUS awarded my never-surrender ethic with a place in line among a sea of students dressed in black robes and mortar boards. At the call of my name, I crossed the platform and accepted a piece of paper bound in black—educated.

CHAPTER THREE

FAINT MELODY

The moment I earned a Bachelor of Arts degree in French, my air force-brat life ceased. The veil between child and grown-up evaporated. Protocol demanded the armed forces' version of a rite of passage: the requirement to hand over the services' ID. Twenty-three years of privileges vanished in one day. There would be no more entrance into the small store called the BX, movie house, or ceramic's shop. The event caused a trauma. How could the United States Air Force have forsaken its daughter? Men in blue uniforms declared me an adult and slammed the door on Uncle Sam's fraternity—shut out.

That night, I stood like a castaway at the foot of my bed. The normal scratchy, brown, base-issued blanket gave the impression of sod. Each of the four corners—pulled in the military tuck so taut a quarter would bounce—represented Uncle Sam's youth: square your shoulders and don't buck the system. I sunk onto the bed, enveloped myself in the covers, and drifted to sleep.

The next morning was a new day. Had my trip through college taken place for sheer formality? Never mind. With the ability to toss balls in the air and a plan, the first note on the ledger line materialized.

When my feet hit the floor, I set things in motion and thumbed through our local periodical, *The Sacramento Bee*. The entertainment section listed auditions for various theaters. Soon, I pounded the pavements and appeared in many presentations but desired The Sacramento Light Opera Association's Music Circus, which fell under the umbrella of Actors' Equity Association. The company utilized professionals and well-known stars as principals and presented musicals in the summer.

At their tryout notice for local artists, I clutched my resume and an 8" x 10" headshot, drove downtown, and parked. I entered a building and flopped onto the floor in a large room with one hundred young wannabes. To our right behind a long table sat the producers, directors, and choreographers, who introduced themselves. The pianist waited on the stage. When they called each name, we rose, surrendered our qualifications, stood next to the piano, and ballyhooed our way into or out of a job. My chutzpah opened the door to *Hello Dolly* with Jo Anne Worley of the television program *Rowan & Martin's Laugh-In*. Additional plays would follow.

The first day of practice, the unusual sight of a big top of canvas that enclosed the theater-in-the-round carried my eye to the logical name "Music Circus." Within the sidewalls, we performed on an elevated, round stage of excellent sightlines. Several ramps for entrances passed through the audience up the aisles. With no stage right or left, our backs always faced a section of the spectators. We focused on different directions and drew the viewers into the action. "Hello, tomorrow, hello."

The regional theater company didn't provide a salary for those not in the union, but they offered a work waiver, which granted experience. I needed a job, and once again I combed pages of the weeklies. An advertisement for the City of Sacramento Department of Parks and Recreation leapt from the print: "staff wanted" for a facility located in William Land Regional Park that recreated children's stories. The site, appropriately called Fairytale Town.

After a successful interview, my tenure began with a stroll under a large tin Humpty Dumpty that sat on the brick wall at the entrance. A pause beyond the oversized egg drew other signs from an alternate reality to my eyes. I held to the side as children bolted to a dark, covered stairwell that enticed them to climb and slide down an old lady's shoe. Cheers of glee attracted my attention to the left. How they played the swashbuckler on the Jolly Roger pirate ship! The walk to meet the supervisor, Karolyn, led past a pint-size train engine that believed in the impossible. "I think I can. I think I can."

Inside a small building, she informed the newbies that our duties would require us to sweep the yellow brick, crooked mile, which stretched throughout the property and clean Peter Rabbit's garden, equipped with live rabbits, for example. Within the enclosure, we would write, produce, and present puppet shows, plays, and variety shows in the tiny children's theater for those who would come on Saturday mornings.

At the end of my shift, I returned through the barrier that encircled those tangible dreams from childhood and drove around houses set in manicured yards of green bordered by rainbows of camellias that fashioned William Land Park.

Time flew by. One day I headed toward the playhouse unaware that I soon would become the first black woman clown with the Red Unit of Ringling Bros. and Barnum & Bailey Circus.

Clank! Clank! Sounds in the distance indicated one of the workers slid open the rusty metal doors, which allowed the audience to enter. They filed into the few rows of stands. Mostly children attended. They fit with ease on the short benches. Any adults rested with knees in their faces. Another employee, named Charlie, won the role of a ventriloquist for the performance. I played the dummy.

We waited behind the curtain until Karolyn spoke. "Ladies and gentlemen, welcome to Fairytale Town. Today we're going to present a variety show. Are you ready?"

The kids yelled in unison, "Yes!"

"OK, hope you enjoy the show."

Charlie stepped out and sat in a chair with me stiff as a board in his arms. When he plopped me on his lap, I opened my eyes and grinned. My wild facial expressions accompanied his wordplay throughout the show, which ended with cheers. We took our bows, and the curtains closed. Someone knocked on the door while we changed into uniforms to resume the day's assignments. Charlie reached for the knob and opened the portal to my tomorrow.

"Danise, there's a lady here to see you," he said.

"Hi, I'm Danise. How may I help you?"

The older white woman smiled and asked a thousand questions. "I enjoyed the show and so did the kids. You made a good dummy. Have you been performing long? What's your background?"

"I've been in the Music Circus and in plays at the Eaglet Theatre."

"Are you a drama major?"

"Not exactly. I minored in drama and majored in French."

Unsure of the reason for the interrogation, I mentioned my desire to pursue a film career in Los Angeles and a theatrical one on the Broadway stage. Money saved from Fairytale Town would allow the move.

"Oh. Well, you have great facial expressions." She paused. "Have you ever considered being a clown?"

The visitor proceeded with information about auditions for Ringling Bros. and Barnum & Bailey Clown College at the Oakland Coliseum. She didn't know when they would take place, however. At the end of her words, she left.

I glared at the door after her exit. My desire centered on a profession of a serious nature. To be a buffoon was a slap in the face. Her footsteps led her away, and my day dragged on.

I had never considered such a vocation. Images of a clumsy fool rolled in my brain as a tumbleweed blown by the wind—over and over. By midday, however, the greater strength of sheer fun—never mind the opportunity—defeated the insult of clown.

A thought occurred to me, "What would that be like?" At the conclusion of the eight-hour shift, I zoomed home and called the coliseum. They replied, "The tryouts take place this weekend—two days away." No sweat. I already knew how to juggle and ride a unicycle—useful skills.

In the garage, I practiced my "How to Construct a Bicycle" skit with the use of objects from Daddy's stuff. On the floor, I lay each metal pipe to form the shape, next the handlebar and front tire, and finally the cycle where the rear seat and tire would go. Of course, who can ride a bike of unconnected parts? I tried again and again with feigned frustration, then lifted the wheel and rode off in triumph. After practice runs, good to go. One problem persisted: only my younger sister, Adriene, conspired on my scheme. I had to tell my parents, but how?

My siblings would follow the norm. Vanita, a nurse; Adriene, a teacher; and Robert, a naval officer. What would my folks say about a daughter who wanted to join a circus?

Friday, the night before auditions, I knocked on their bedroom door.

"Come in."

My father sat in bed while he read *The Sacramento Bee*. My mother lay with the covers up to her nose.

I ground my teeth. "Hi."

No response. Mom peered from the blankets and waited.

A river of words gushed forth. "I'm going to Oakland tomorrow to try out for Clown College to be a clown with Ringling Bros." And time stood still.

Dad lowered the paper, shot a quick look in my direction, and resumed reading. Mom stared speechless.

"Well, good night," I said and left. And that was that.

I can only imagine their thoughts about a daughter hell-bent on God-knows-what.

A cock-and-bull story to my supervisor the following day allowed a drive home to prepare. I shook the dust off a navy-blue duffle bag my father had used in the early days of his career, then jammed in the metal parts for my skit. The knapsack, juggling balls, and unicycle rode in the trunk of the car. Adriene agreed to go for moral support, so once ready we left for Oakland.

As we approached the coliseum, the size took away my breath. Before us stood a large, round building encircled by an expanse of concrete. We drove through a gate and parked.

My underarms itched, a sign of nervousness. For reassurance of my ability to ride the unicycle, I retrieved it from the trunk and faced the stretch of parking as a ship to the open sea. Pure panic resulted from botched tries, however. I wrinkled my eyebrows, turned to my sister, and snarled, "I'm good enough to be a stupid clown!"

We gathered my things, trudged down a wide ramp, and passed through a massive door that swallowed us. Adriene and I continued into the belly of the edifice toward a tryout that stemmed from the far side of the sun. This was a three-ring circus. We passed two and headed for the third on the distant end where everyone sat. When we placed my bag down, the clunk from the metal caught everyone's attention, which caused me to grimace. Adriene retreated into the stands and took a seat—she was the only one up there.

The audition—with improvisation, the use of giant props, and personal skills—passed without a flaw, and I returned to Fairytale Town with my dreams on fire. After the Clown College letter arrived about the necessity to wait a year, the urge to spread my wings and move to Los Angeles screamed in my ear. That pull to my film career included a break to try the circus, if accepted. Aunt Ernestine, my lifeline, housed me until a one-bedroom apartment in North Hollywood presented itself.

A friend from Fairytale Town, determined to realize her ambitions for fame, joined the quest, and we leased a two-bedroom. I stayed starvation with a tour guide position at Universal Studios, which granted proximity to the movies.

Months wore on. Time elapsed. No word from Ringling. "Wonder what's happening about the school?"

One of the other guides, a boisterous young man, tried out in Los Angeles. He hung a circus poster in the waiting room, and coworkers assured him, "You'll make it for sure." The mention of my stab at it garnered the following: "You? No chance! You're too quiet." The glimmer of hope faded to black.

One Wednesday night I asked God for a sign to put my mind at rest. The next Sunday His still, small voice led me past my regular church in North Hollywood. I drove to a different house of worship in downtown seen on the way home from a visit with my aunt. I parked, entered the cathedral-like building, and sat in the rear with fifteen other people.

The service began with a hymn. Afterward, the pastor, dressed in a white robe that hung to his feet, stood and called to us. "Everyone's in the last pews. Please move to the first few rows. You won't want to miss anything." The sixteen of us hesitated then made our way up front. Once we had done so, he introduced a guest speaker who approached the pulpit. The attractive, older man with thinning, white hair smiled and said, "I grew up on Ringling Bros. and Barnum & Bailey Circus. . . ." My heart skipped to the beat of a faint melody. "I lived with lions and bears and chimpanzees."

My breath stuck in my throat while he spoke of his life with the show. What a confirmation! I listened, convinced my hip pocket held Clown College.

Doubt never entered my brain again. After work one day, my roommate flung open the door of our apartment as I neared.

"Come in."

She grabbed my arm and plopped me in a chair.

"What?"

"You had a call from the circus, and they want you to respond!"

I jumped up, screamed, grabbed their number from her hand, and ran to the phone.

"Hello, Ringling Bros. and Barnum & Bailey Clown College."

"Hi, my name is Danise Wilson, and I'm returning Ron Severini's call."

"Yes, this is Ron. Are you still interested in attending?"

"Yes!"

"Good, because you've been accepted to this year's class."

My ears took to his words as a bee to honey. After our conversation, suspense ended and escaped from the depth of my inner self. The world spun counterclockwise in sync with an impromptu dance of excitement that carried me from kitchen to living room. I telephoned home and shared the news, but after a day or two reality set in. I possessed no cash to get there and didn't want to borrow from my parents, which would have resulted in Dad's philosophy: "If you don't have the money, you don't need it." I bit the bullet and gave Vanita a ring. She agreed to lend me the funds to go. God bless my older sister.

Four days later, the mailman delivered an envelope dated August 1978. The return address bore a likeness of two elephants, a horse, and a clown who held the words "Ringling Bros. and Barnum & Bailey Combined Shows, Inc." The letter inside stated the following:

Danise Wilson,
 Mr. Irvin Feld, President, and Mr. Kenneth Feld,
 vice president of Ringling Bros. and Barnum & Bailey
 Combined Shows, Inc. and producers of The Greatest

Show on Earth are announcing the names of those applicants as students of the Class of 1978 of Ringling Bros. and Barnum & Bailey's World-Famous Clown College.

The Clown College Admissions Board has judged your application, and this letter is confirmation that you will be a member of the 1978 Class, this year celebrating its 11th anniversary.

Our sincerest congratulations to you, for you have been selected from over four thousand applications handled this year.

You will thoroughly enjoy and get great satisfaction from your eight-week participation in this unique training course for potential circus clowns, the only professional one in the entire world. The fantastic opportunity is being offered to you to learn the true art and craft of professional circus clowning, and the possibility of being offered a well-paying job as a clown to perform with the world's largest, most respected, and oldest (one hundred and eight years) entertainment organization, truly, an American Institution of great magnitude. This season, its gigantic touring units are traveling to eighty cities, coast to coast.

You will find your classmates to be dedicated, talented, stimulating, and congenial. Your instructors are the most professional, experienced and capable to be found anywhere in the world. We all look forward to knowing you better. Pertinent Clown College information is being mailed to you.

Sincerely yours,
Ron & Sandy Severini
Deans of Clown College

Twelve months after the audition, I zoomed home to prepare for *The Greatest Show on Earth.*

CHAPTER FOUR

ONE STEP CLOSER

Mix one-third cup uncertainty with four tablespoons skinny. Add one teaspoon goofy to four ounces fear of authority. Combine with one cup likes to have fun. Stir in a pinch of outgoing swirled with introvert. Season all the above with one-half tablespoon hates to say goodbye. Bake at 375 degrees until golden brown, and you have me. That "me" bounced into Clown College.

Cardboard boxes with my belongings cluttered our apartment. After I stuffed them into my orange Datsun 510, an all-too-familiar childhood scene replayed with "cheerio" to another friend. In the rearview mirror, she and my movie career faded into the distance.

Through the window ahead, a potential life with elephants. Vivid imaginations shortened the eleven-hour drive to eight hours from Los Angeles to my parents' house in Rancho Cordova, a straight shot north on Highway 99.

My mother opened the door and surrendered a telltale hug. This flight would propel her little bird aloft. I sprinted down the hall and found the packet that contained the preparation details for an out-of-the-ordinary life. My tuition-free education would take place in Venice, Florida. Payment requirements included lodging at the Venice Villas Motel, food, a clown makeup kit, and a circus cinema series. For $645, plus airfare there and back, I would learn the secrets of hilarity and high jinks.

Mom entered the room, sat, and together we read the list of required items. She looked at me. "You have a unicycle, but what kind of balls do you need?" She didn't know of my juggling escapade at Sac State, but I strolled to the closet and pulled out the three used for the class on the quad. "We'll get your notebook and pencils, and your dad's got rags for makeup removal." She read further. "What kind of 'strenuous acrobatic activity' are they gonna make you do that requires sturdy bras?" She sighed with concern—thanks to rumors of sleazy circus people.

Later I asked my father's thoughts. "What do you mean, what do I think? You rode your bike across Europe." How true. I never asked permission for any far-out scheme—that included the European adventure two years earlier, fueled by wanderlust. His hands flew up in surrender.

# # #

White, billowy clouds enveloped the silver wings of the plane. Thirty-five thousand feet of nothing stood between me and the ground below. My ears popped when we descended into the airspace of the famous circus city Sarasota. I looked out the window and expected to see caged bears and red-and-white circus tents. But no, only the flat green of Florida.

Passengers in baggage claim grabbed oblong suitcases and carted them off. After the moving ramp spit my stuff onto the carousel, I retrieved my unicycle and duffle bag of necessities and headed out. The jitters hit hard during the longest half-hour cab ride of my life to the town of Venice. "What waited ahead?" I wondered. As we neared a string of flat apartments called the Venice Villas, I peered through the window. Young men had turned the street into a showcase for skills. A short guy with unkempt hair juggled six balls; two tossed elongated, plastic clubs to each other; and another zipped around on a tall unicycle that had a seat five feet up on the stem above the small wheel. Ah, the art of intimidation.

The taxi deposited me in their midst. The information packet indicated that my home would be number fourteen. I gathered my gear from the trunk of the car, paid the driver, and slinked past the showoffs. Inside the one-bedroom quarters, my roommate piped up. "Oh, hello. I'm Brenda Wells." We chatted awhile, then sauntered outside. Brenda joined their fun, but my limitation of pattern for spheres in the air and trouble with mounting onto one wheel without a grip on something rendered me impotent and on the sidelines.

"Hi, I'm Tina Stotts," said another trainee from behind.

The result of my about-face startled me. There stood the shortest adult I had ever seen.

She pointed to the others and asked, "Can you do that?"

"Not really."

"I heard of these auditions but don't know nothin' about circuses. They always need little people, though." She spoke of the ridicule she encountered and the lack of encouragement due to her size. "I wanna make it. I wanna prove I can do something."

A new education began that day. Tina, at three feet eleven inches, considered "midget" derogatory and "little person" softer to the senses. A fast friendship developed between us—misfits from the norm.

The alarm sounded at 6:00 a.m. the next morning—the first day of class. After we washed dishes, Brenda and I donned jeans, T-shirts, and sneakers. We grabbed notebooks and pencils and ran outside to meet the other apprentices. Everyone bided his or her time when from around the corner chugged an escapee from the world of cartoons.

A children's school bus with a fresh coat of white paint had arrived. Headlights outlined in blue with black eyebrows served as eyes; the bumper sported a smile; and in the middle of the grille—a red nose. The words "Ringling Bros. Barnum & Bailey" emblazoned the sides in orange, and navy tint beneath boasted the words "Clown College," accompanied by a clown face with a college mortarboard. To leave no doubt, the rear proclaimed "*The Greatest Show on Earth*." Everyone grinned then boarded.

"Hi, campers, my name's Colleen," one pupil said.

"And I'm Joan," another piped up, then added to the festive atmosphere with a ditty on her accordion.

The driver pulled away from the curb but screeched to a halt when he noticed someone in full stride. The doors opened and the person leapt on with his breakfast of spaghetti in a pot. "Hi, I'm Ray," he said.

We all chitchatted the short distance to a building with a cobalt roof, which is where the circus stayed in the off-season. That winter quarters served as our school.

When the bus came to a halt, everyone streamed off past a pole that bore two flags: the American colors above and the red Clown College banner underneath, which signaled the program of study. With a spring in our steps, we passed a painted wall that welcomed all to Ringling Bros. and Barnum & Bailey Circus and bounded through red steel doors—a gateway to a cloistered world.

I looked around. Stands lined each side and faced an empty floor, save for one ring where we took our seats. No desks and chairs at this school. Unicycles from the pint-sized to the tall leaned against the railings. A row of huge metal balls rested next to them. Curiosity caused the thought, "What lay in the hidden chambers?"

A chubby fellow with wavy sable hair walked toward us, accompanied by a woman of similar stature. "Welcome everybody. My name is Ron Severini," said the man I spoke with on the phone in Los Angeles, "and this is my wife, Sandy. We're your deans for this 1978 class. Congratulations. You fifty-eight students beat out more than four thousand who auditioned this year. We pulled you from all kinds of directions. Stand and introduce yourselves." We did. What a hodgepodge! Students ranged from seventeen to twenty-eight years and included an accountant and grapefruit sectioner. I stood by myself as the only non-white pupil, but by then I had grown accustomed to my island.

Ron continued with the schedule: It consisted of six days a week from 9:00 a.m. to 6:00 p.m. We would break for lunch and dinner, then return at 7:30 p.m. for movies of the silent screen era.

"You'll watch Buster Keaton to study his extraordinary pratfalls," Sandy said. "Everyone'll learn to speak with body language, thanks to Charlie Chaplin films. The roster's enormous, but we've narrowed it down and included a master of sight gags, Harold Lloyd. Treasure troves of bits, every one of them.

"At the end of the eight weeks, you'll put on a gala night performance for the owner of the show. Afterward, he'll offer employment with either Circus World or one of the two traveling units of the circus, Red or Blue. With that, you'll be first-year clowns—First of Mays."

"If *no* job, back to the world equipped with a fine-tuned funny bone," I said.

Tina turned in my direction and grimaced at failure. We gripped hands and made a pack to make it together.

Our dean continued, "I would now like to introduce the president and chief executive officer, Mr. Irvin Feld."

A short, round man with a no-nonsense disposition approached. "Hello and welcome. You are the best of the candidates we reviewed. During the term, we'll examine each of you and judge our needs. I hope the experience will be enjoyable. Learn a lot. Again, congratulations and good luck." When he finished his speech, we sat on the edge of the ring curb poised to yell, "Choose me. Choose me."

I possessed no knowledge of circus and never considered it a vocation. Who was Irvin Feld? What happened to the Ringlings, Barnums, and Baileys? Later in the day, a trip to the small library on the site removed blinders from my eyes. On the bookshelves, written secrets of this unknown world answered the questions.

Irvin Feld had pitched snake oil as a boy. He earned a paycheck later in life as a successful businessman and record producer who booked gospel artists and popular singers in arenas. When he met John Ringling North and suggested the adaptation of *The Greatest Show on Earth* from canvas to buildings, he entered the circus world. He loved the show and became its president in 1967 at the Colosseum in Rome. As CEO he returned the faltering entertainment production to its former glory.

Mr. Feld gave birth to Clown College in 1968 to have a steady crop of young talent. Those employed were experienced, yet up in years.

We met our mentors for every class, which included how to blow things up in a safe way and make them disappear with the use of magic. California State University in Sacramento couldn't stack up to these beans.

A lot of dealings took place. After personal interviews, we posed for Clown College ID cards, attended an introduction to the makeup class, and viewed a circus film called *The Restless Giant*. Ringling consumed our souls by the end of the first day.

At 5:00 p.m. we shuttled to the Villas and then to Jacaranda Plaza, the local shopping center. Venice gained greenbacks from members of *The Greatest Show on Earth*, likewise from the students. When we bounced down the roads through town, no one gave our distinct bus a second look. Passersby had grown numb to the ever-present, bumbling fools.

We entered a store and bought desired grub for the week. For me, bread and Vienna sausages. Two years earlier on my bike trip across Europe, energy stemmed from crackers, salami, cheese, and apples—so off to the fruits and vegetables. En route, an airborne orange caught my attention from the next aisle, then an apple followed by a grapefruit.

"Hey, Billy, toss me that potato, will ya?" someone said from the other side.

"Sure, lob me some lemons."

I turned the corner, and Billy Dusell and other students practiced the art of manipulation with the produce. He had caused my panic on arrival day by juggling six balls outside the Villas. I guessed the clerks had become used to flying crops thanks to Clown College once a year, because they ignored the goings-on.

After we returned to the apartments and stuffed items into cabinets and food into the refrigerator, I stepped outside.

A black maid dressed in a starched white uniform approached. "You here for Clown College?" She was the only other person of color I had seen since my arrival.

"Yeah, I am. I'm from California, and this is my first time in Florida. We went to Jacaranda Plaza today. I didn't see many of *us*."

She rolled her eyes. "No, child. And you *won't* either."

"Oh, uh, where can I get my hair done, then?"

"Not around here."

She gave directions to the black neighborhood that was over the bridge and off the main thoroughfare called Tamiami Trail. I made a mental note, took the bus and a hike another day, but found my race tucked out of sight, out of mind. To tour with the circus could prove a reflection of my childhood.

The next day we joined Joan with her accordion and Ray with his pot of spaghetti for our ride to school. We exited the bus as usual; but when we entered the building, we noticed that someone had removed the ring, which left an empty floor. Ron greeted us. "Good morning. Come in, set your gear down, and spread out. All right, everybody. Circus life is nonstop, and you're gonna need stamina. You're gonna strengthen your bodies with a half-hour warm-up session."

He stepped back as we put down our belongings. We stood at arm's length—fingertips to fingertips—and another instructor took over. Like a military drill sergeant, he led us fledglings in ceaseless jumping jacks, push-ups, and sit-ups, and barked, "You're gonna do this every day. Get used to it." The dark, dreary building reeked of sweat by the time the first activity of boot camp ended. No chance to recuperate. We split into groups and dispersed into the arena.

Tina and I gave the schedule a once-over. It showed where each lesson would take place and who would teach. We chose a movement class taught by a man named Barry Lubin. The previous day during introductions we learned that he had performed with *The Greatest Show on Earth*, branched out, and had become the icon of the Big Apple Circus as the clown, "Grandma." We approached him as he dragged a sectioned ring curb into place in the middle of the floor. Eight other students sauntered up as well.

"Hi," he said. "Come on and have a seat." We did so without a clue about what to expect. "You'll find out that it takes a lot more to be a clown than you think. I'm going to teach you how to use your face, one of your greatest tools for emotions." He stood in front of us and grinned, then sprung his eyebrows up and down, one at a time. And the ice broke. His professional expertise stimulated our creative juices, and we hung onto every word.

Barry pointed to one of the guys. "You, thanks for volunteering. Come up here and stand." The draftee took his place, and our first instruction in the art of laughter began. Barry called out feelings to convey by way of facial expressions, such as anger, shyness, and love.

We took turns and carried out the requests. My mug transmitted each at the speed of a Morse-code operator and earned me the nickname, Mobile Face.

Next we put on a mask and simulated the sentiments with body motions. Tina put on the covering and contorted her body to mimic the emotions at Barry's request. "Sad." She slumped over and shook her head. "Happy." Up and down in a blur. Barry also gave her suggestions on how to use size to her advantage.

Each day brought lessons not taught in outside schools, such as walking on rolling globes, riding unicycles—the tall ones were called giraffes—and how to take and give slaps. Shaving cream in aluminum pans splattered all over the place in pie-throwing class. We even learned how to drop our pants. The technique for that? It was all in the timing. Everything revolved around it.

The next morning we formed a line in front of Allan Jacobs and Fred "Garbo" Garver to toss objects. Juggling began with a pattern known as the three-ball cascade—the extent of my knowledge. Easy street. Thanks to the class on campus at CSUS, I smirked and threw from one hand to the other for a good five minutes. That piece of cake screeched to a halt when Garbo progressed me to pitching in succession to the person opposite. After a few tries, the activity called passing made sense. Logic bowed out when we climbed onto our partners' shoulders and executed the two-man high variation. We lobbed the balls vertical instead of horizontal.

The dawn of the next day unveiled new miracles. Students filtered into the building. Tina and I proceeded to opposite sides of the open space near the back door. She said, "Danise, can you help me strap these on?"

My friend clutched a pair of pseudo-appendages and had climbed onto a chair. She held my hand and placed her feet onto the footplates. Afterward she fastened the feet buckles, which secured her over the four aluminum posts that were attached to each of the two lower, flat, metal bases.

I hooked leg bands around her knees, and she straightened up and smiled at my eye level. "Size is a four-letter word."

Three-feet-tall Tina proved herself bigger than me: she took hold of ropes that hung from above, and after several attempts, walked on those painter stilts. Me? Not my cup of tea due to the lack of assurance on false legs.

I left her to practice and returned to the main floor where the rest of us removed the ring curb for space. In circles of eight, we learned the impossible. Each student performed the basic three-ball cascade, and in unison we hurled to the person directly across. What a mass of flying objects! Scarves, rings, cigar boxes—anything was juggle-able. Who knew that the manipulation of tangible spheres and circles produced such vast possibilities?

Later Tina sauntered over and picked up three balls. Toss and drop, pick up—toss and drop—over and over. She stamped her foot and sighed. As the sole person of color in many of my endeavors, I sensed a common desire in Tina to do what they could do. She swung her short arms in frustration and gritted her teeth. Within days, however, Tina Stotts grasped the secret of the three-ball cascade. And in an unsteady way, she juggled with the rest of us.

The shape of her arms hampered the twirl of clubs, so she practiced balls and rings. Might as well. The elongated, plastic pins involved no rhyme or reason. To toss, each required a spin. That made no sense, and they hit my head again and again. I stomped outside at lunchtime and plopped myself under a tree that nestled in the grass of the small vacant airport across from the building. The serene location dissipated my aversion to clubs.

Between bites of Vienna sausages, I wrote letters destined for home on the provided Ringling stationery until a new battle brewed within my mind. "Hmm . . . today's the day for acrobatics—the course that requires a sturdy bra."

When classmates returned to our university, I gathered my stuff and trudged to join them. We entered, and the dreaded trampoline lay in wait on the floor. While in high school, I fell off the uneven parallel bars, knocked myself out, and developed a fear of going upside down. The phobia of topsy-turvy followed me to Florida.

By the first day of trampoline instruction, we had decreased from fifty-eight students to fifty-two. Six dropped out.

"Everybody gather around," the coach said.

I have long forgotten his name, but he showed no pity. As everyone surrounded the apparatus, he climbed on and executed circles in the air.

"Does he expect us to do that?" I whispered to Steve Wolski.

"Hope so," he said. "That's easy."

The drill sergeant flipped off the invention for torture, then stood with his hands on his hips and feet apart. His voice sounded throughout the arena. "You need to learn to tumble, leap, flip, and fly, not just trip, fall, roll, and get up without missing a beat. Who's first?"

Steve vaulted onto the trampoline and sprung into the stratosphere. He had experienced the device before and completed every order. "Good job. Did you notice his form? Fix your eyes on a spot on the tramp to keep yourself steady. OK, good. Next."

Eager beavers obeyed and transformed into rebounding bullets. Even Tina, with the aid of portable steps, climbed up and bounced like a Ping-Pong ball. I slinked behind the person after me, waved each past, and moved back little by little until I was last and had no choice. "What are you waiting on? Let's go."

I grasped the frame. "Ugh" helped me up and on. Due to the elasticity of the canvas, each step propelled my knees high. I stopped dead center, looked down at the attached springs, and hoped not to ricochet off.

"Start bouncing."

I didn't.

"Have you ever been on a trampoline before?"

"Yes, as a kid," I answered.

"OK, go ahead. Jump up and down."

I did and smiled.

"Now, drop into the sit position. Then back onto your feet."

Done, again and again.

"This time as you sit, stay put, then flip."

Not part of my ability, and I continued to bounce and stand.

"Flip!"

Tears invaded my eyes while my stomach carried out the maneuvers. "I'm trying."

Fellow Ringling Bros. and Barnum & Bailey hopefuls observed zilch, zip, diddly-squat.

He-with-no-mercy grabbed the trampoline, cocked his head, and shook my bones with his ear-shattering words: "If you're not going to do anything, then get off!"

Everyone witnessed my clumsy dismount. Mother cow! (Another of my father's pseudo curse words.) Determination set in to master that hang-up by the end of the eight weeks.

After that utter humiliation, we broke for dinner then returned for the night's scheduled films. We filed into the Pie Car, Jr., the cafeteria at winter quarters—on the circus train, performers ate in a restaurant appropriately called the Pie Car—and took seats to watch happy, singing circus people determined not to let a train wreck stop the performances. Jimmy Stewart, as Buttons the Clown, helped the injured and the show went on in Cecil B. DeMille's *The Greatest Show on Earth*. In Tod Browning's *Freaks*, strange human beings danced in a forest, and little people lurked around in the movie's eerie circus world. Tina, spared any embarrassment, slept through it all.

The next day after a "Good morning campers" from Colleen, we headed into the building for the usual warm-up session. I glanced at the small enclosure at the top of the stairs to the right. Mr. Feld peered through the window of his office to scrutinize our goings-on. He received progress reports on each of us and determined who best fit his need. My midway evaluation came from an instructor:

> *Danise,*
> *You're doing great. You use your face and body movement very nicely.*
> *Keep up the good work. I think you'll be well received.*
>
> > *Signed,*
> > *Barry Lubin*

After exercises we put on sneakers and proceeded toward a chamber with tables that held sewing machines. We sat down to the greeting, "I'm Sally Gates, and this is Mary Carroll." Our fabric wizards. "We've laid out brown paper for you to create the patterns for your costumes."

They led us step by step, and we began our transformation into those-who-throw-pies. With scissors in hand we cut the replicas, then bought fabric, and fed the material to mechanical needles. The whir of the machines began the attachment of our souls.

Thanks to home ec in high school at the insistence of my mother, I could design and sew my desired baby character's clothes. She would wear blue-green rompers with mustard circles and a puffy-sleeved, lemon top underneath, plus an oversized baby hat.

Each day ended with Sally's words: "All right you cute, little, dimpled, dumpled darlings, it's time to clean up."

A lot of instruction filled our plates. One bright, early morning, our teachers dished up the meat and potatoes.

As fifty-two avid trainees entered the outer hall to the Pie Car, Jr. Tina noticed three telephones on the opposite wall: one at her eye level but the other two at mine. "Look," she said, "I wish it was easy like that everywhere." What a compensation for her size!

Our dean, in full professional getup, caught our attention. "Come on in and take a seat," he said. We glanced at him, and in anticipation, plopped our derrieres onto chairs behind long tables set with round mirrors. "The identity of a clown rests in the face. Without the paint, funny people walk in anonymity. Today you're going to experiment." Makeup 101 stood before us.

He distributed tubes of red, small tins of sapphire, others of ebony, and containers of Stein's Clown White. Those necessities would transform us from human beings into cartoons. Everyone received peach shade for the flesh, but I gave mine away—not my skin hue. Bare Bronze Sheer Foundation by Fashion Fair would become my substitute. Later, on the road, I discovered the cream base was unnecessary. Dark skin did not wash out under lights. Instead, a little dab of blush did the trick.

While we busied ourselves with those artist tools, a veteran named Bobby Kay spoke of the seriousness of laughter. He had entered the profession in 1923. "Clowns used to get sick and die and nobody knew why until someone came up with the idea to test the greasepaint," he said. "They found that it contained lead. The stuff you use now's different. Saved our lives."

"Kudos to unseen faces of the science world," I thought.

"Put everything into a kit for safekeeping when you're done today." The handlebar bag from my European bike trip served the purpose.

The final touch: the nose. Ron hung samples on a wooden cutout of a clown, which he dubbed the Clown College Nose Department. We crowded around and tried on different styles. I chose a clip-on, cherry-shaped one and attached brown-painted elastic for extra security. With everything in front of us, the man who conducted the audition in Oakland took over.

CHAPTER FIVE

AUGUSTE

Born Glen Little, Frosty had attended the first class of Clown College. He too wore full gear. I remembered his colorful outfit and the hat that tipped to one side.

"Hotterini. We're gonna teach the basics of application," he said, "but you'll design your own look. Don't copy your neighbor's, except for you, Matt and Mike (twins). It's like fingerprints, see. No one's should match anyone else's.

"Three makeup types exist. One's called 'whiteface' with white covering the entire face, ears, and neck. To break up the solid mass, add designs of different colors, like I did. Another's 'auguste,' spelled a-u-g-u-s-t-e but pronounced 'ow goost,' with white around the eyes and mouth only. It's German slang for *stupid*. Hobo clown Otto Griebling's makeup was an example of the third, termed a character look."

No matter the class, pen did not meet paper; instead, our learning tree bloomed through trial and error.

"You have your equipment. Experiment with the first style," Ron said.

Steve sat in the adjacent chair and laid out his cosmetics. I followed suit. With military-brat precision, I placed each component in line, then stuffed my hair into a cutoff top half of a pair of nylons, which served as a skullcap. I stared into the mirror in front of me, studied my image, and passed on whiteface. The other students applied the cream.

"What are ya doing, Danise? Put on your makeup," Frosty said. "Everyone's almost finished."

"Auguste suits me better."

"We're doing this together to coach. You gotta try each technique."

"But Frosty, I examined my face. White makeup on me is the reversal of the old-time minstrels."

I peeked at the others who had finished. With round faces covered in white, they resembled Humpty Dumpty. Frosty glanced in my direction and let an audible breath of air escape. "Let's go. Hotterini. Remove the makeup with your baby oil."

Each lifted a bottle and squirted it into his or her hands, which they rubbed together. Next they quickly smeared the greasy fluid over their faces. A rainbow of purple palettes resulted. With a swipe of a rag, it was off. Time for auguste.

Full speed ahead. I grasped and opened the tin of white and lifted it to my nose. Such an odd smell, similar to motor oil! The utensils rested in perfect order from first to be used to last. I picked up a thin brush, dragged it through the paint, and the spirit of Picasso took over. His wizardry drew an outline around the eyes and mouth. Next the right index and middle fingers brushed over the top of the substance. How smooth to the touch! The artiste dabbed it into place within the silhouettes. Pat, pat, pat—to even out and eliminate the surplus.

Salvador Dali joined the fun. He invaded the creation with three white lines under each eye, sapphire on the lids, and distorted the brows with ebony. An amalgamation of the two brushed the tip of my right index finger into Stein's red to paint the lower lip. The top remained covered with white for aesthetics. A tap on my face over and over with powder using a sock set the artwork. The use of a man's shaving brush and a wet rag dusted off the excess and removed any residue.

Last but not least, the cherry nose clipped in place. At the end of the process, grotesqueness met surrealism. A reflection stared from the looking glass. On top of my brown canvas, the unknown me had emerged and I smiled.

Ron's examination revealed a menagerie of augustes, whitefaces, and one hobo. After inspection we bounded into the arena to receive orange wigs, and like the noses, we each tried on one.

Bright, reddish-yellow hair with brown skin equaled orangutan in my mind. A blue, curly covering for my head would do but not the wild Afros sold at most supply stores. Later I found a shop, purchased a coiled, blond wig, spray-painted it navy, and attached brown-tinted elastic. It was a done deal. My brainchild remained hidden until graduation night. Before then, orangutan.

New experiences filled each day, but midway through the sessions the moment we had waited for rolled in. "OK," Sandy Severini said, "line up and take your sneakers and socks off. Did everyone wash their feet?" To complete the package, our deans saved the best for last—the mark of the American clown: shoes. We encircled Ron and Sandy.

"The only way to get the exact size is to measure the lengths of both feet, insteps, ankles, and area behind your toes." Different companies specialized in the footwear, and Ringling Bros. and Barnum & Bailey Clown College worked with several. I wanted a style worn by young girls, and Whistles Clown Shoes made them according to my specifications.

After Ron took dimensions and orders, we forked over the money—$225 for mine. Weeks later, long boxes arrived. We sat on the floor as kids on Christmas morning and chose the parcel with our name. Lids sprang open; tissue paper flew everywhere. Inside my packet rested toe-to-heel my most prized possession: black-and-white oversized oxfords. We spread out and walked across the floor under the eye of Ron, up and down the stands as swimmers with flippers. The telltale sound of clowns in full stride echoed throughout the open space: *clump-clump, clump-clump*.

Our instructors coached and prodded, reshaped and fine-tuned throughout the eight weeks of school. Their criticism and suggestions sharpened our grasp of the craft as stones to tools. They taught audience communication, arena movement, and come-in clowning, which funny people executed on the arena floor while the spectators entered and took a seat. We absorbed lectures on circus history, logistics, and public relations.

I discovered that the world of greasepaint possessed its own vocabulary for common things, similar to the military, such as Pie Car. Clowns earned the nickname Joey after Joseph Grimaldi, who was born in 1778 and considered the father of modern clowns, due to his comic talent, characterizations, and use of makeup.

One morning, we entered the arena and noticed the ring curb in place with the oversized baseball mitt from the audition, a huge bat made of foam rubber, a large catcher's mask, and several different-sized balls. We sat around the circumference and waited. Soon, the personification of the art—Master Clown Lou Jacobs—entered from the side.

Before that day I had researched his history in our library and found that he was born in 1903 in Germany. He represented American circus, however, and had been honored with his likeness on a United States' postage stamp. He hailed from the old school and had worked Ringling since 1925 with fellow clowns Otto Griebling, Emmett Kelly, Sr., and Felix Adler. Those men paid their dues the hard way—on the road. Mr. Jacobs would pass their shtick to us.

Batter up! We divided into teams and played clown baseball. With the pro next to home plate for pointers, I stepped up. The pitcher did a double wind-up, spun around, and the ball whizzed past my straight-laced swing. Lou took the bat.

"If you jus' do it like me, you'll be all right, see," he said. With a wide-legged stance, he swung in slow motion and missed.

The umpire, in a huge body chest protector, made his call: "Steeeeriiiike one!"

Our mentor handed off to another pupil. The student pitcher threw an oversized ball that time. It shot by the novice, who did a backward pratfall. "Steeeeriiiike two!"

I returned to the plate and wound the bat over my head, grimaced, and swung. What an interesting game! First base scooted from my reach due to attached fishing wire, which resulted in a chase. The next batter zipped past me and the mobile first base, and the last progressed to nowhere at low speed. No one ever won, but with Lou's advice, we learned everything from the Baseball to Camera and Carpenter gags.

The believability of the false owed thanks to the virtuoso prop builder, George Shellenberger. He created the illusion of reality in our newly found world of absurdity. Needed supplies sprang from his ability, such as a pair of shoes that allowed a clown to lean and touch the ground without bending at the waist. His realistic camera squirted water, fell apart, and exploded at the words of the photographer: "How 'bout a nice picture, pal?"

Bruce Warner, equally talented, aided in the mirage with the use of an electric knife to foam rubber. He carved the giant baseball bat and movable bases, for example. His expertise with the lightweight substance guided our creations.

Clown College courses covered every imagined possibility. Our conspicuous bus chugged down the freeway near the end of the eight weeks and deposited us at the entrance of an amusement park known as Circus World. The day's exposure to various activities would broaden our minds. Our contingent headed to the back of a building for a touch of brute passivity: elephant riding. And there they stood—the largest land mammals—motionless like oversized, wrinkled, leather bags. *Elephas maximus*. Indian elephant. The top of my head rested below their underbellies.

Clowns and showgirls adorned the pachyderms during the show; therefore, each student rode. With the help of the handlers, alley-oop! We straddled their massive heads, our knees resting behind their ears. I reached out and touched the animal's weather-beaten hide of bristle hair. It pricked. The trainer called out, and the gray columns that bore the bulk moved forward. We proceeded around a circle and melted into the rolling movement of their walk. Later I would learn the true ride on an elephant's back did not resemble that stroll.

Next up? Our choice of apparatus. The entire class wanted to fly through the air with the greatest of ease, so off to the tightrope—no line. I hesitated at the base of a rope-ladder that dangled from the heavens.

The expert beckoned from thirty feet above, and said, "Take your sneakers off and put on the ballet slippers. It's easier to feel the wire. Climb slowly. Don't look down, and you won't get dizzy."

I pursed my lips and said, "I am a military brat—the daughter of a Tuskegee Airman. I can do this."

Determination pulled me up the first rung, then the next, and at the summit onto a small platform barely large enough for the pro and me.

The coach held a thick belt. "This harness is a mechanic," he said. "It goes on your waist and is controlled by the man below to ease you to the ground in case you fall off." He buckled it around my middle, then reached and grabbed two loops of leather that hung over my head. "Hold onto these for balance." He gave no more explanation, but said, "When you're ready, go."

To walk on air would test the bounds of foolishness. I stared at the expanse of space and white-knuckled the circles of rope while my heart thumped. No tightrope stretched before me. I stepped out, and my feet caressed a thick cable that resembled the feel of a wooden pole along my instep. The safety loops and mechanic secured any panic. One foot in front of the other carried me to the center of the correctly termed high wire. I stopped and thought "How can anyone do this for a living with only a long pole in their hands?"

The tilt of my head gave me away to the instructor who shouted "Don't look down!"

Too late. I froze. Someone took a picture.

A gentle tug of the mechanic from the man below urged me onward. The careful placement of each foot inched me toward the opposite stand where a sigh of relief spewed from my mouth. I descended the ladder with no problem, then collapsed onto the ground. The height convinced my spirit to never again defy death thirty feet up. I sent my family the snapshot of the stroll. Wonder what they thought?

"OK, class of '78," Ron said. "For starts, today we have an invited speaker, Peggy Williams from the Red Unit. She's gonna talk to you about the trials, tribulations, and fun of circus life."

We lounged in a small classroom in preparation for her. Our dean stepped to the side, and a woman with an ever-present smile took over. Words from one of the first females accepted to Clown College inspired everyone, and she spoke at great length on the subject. We laughed at her story of a normal shopping day. "Girl's underwear works best as a skullcap for me 'cause it holds my hair the snuggest," she said. "I got to be pretty good at finding the right size until a sales clerk yelled, 'There's a lady admiring herself in the mirror with girl's panties on her head.'"

Loyalty and love for *The Greatest Show on Earth* beamed through her face and underscored her sentences, even when she mentioned the size of the rooms on the train: "You're gonna live in a closet."

That evening we filed into the arena after dinner and sat in the bleachers. No movie that night. Instead our guest teachers performed in order to cement the first four weeks of a thousand words. They came off the road or out of retirement to mentor and showcase professional hilarity and high jinks.

The program began with a ventriloquist routine. Jim Tinsman played the human counterpart and stepped into the ring with Barry Lubin, who sat stiff as a board in his arms. He took a seat and talked to his fake, wooden friend. For every question asked, Barry answered with a goofy smile. Tinsman took a drink of water, and Lubin spit a stream in perfect trajectory two feet away, then forced out three short jets. At Fairytale Town, another employee and I had performed such a skit. But Barry's uncanny resemblance to a rigid puppet, with his one-at-a-time moveable eyebrows, put my portrayal to shame.

The pros performed nonstop, and the revue wrapped up when history sprang to life with Lou Jacobs. He walked in with guarded steps and stood beside a microphone and coat rack on which hung his alter ego. He stared into a mirror and smeared on makeup that covered up to the eyebrows and stopped with the forehead void of character. Before this moment, we had only seen pictures of him as the clown, such as a cover of a 1946 issue of *Life* magazine with a tableau of Mr. Jacobs in mid-schmooze with a giraffe. Our silence deafened.

A large, round, red nose dangled by its elastic from the rack. He closed his eyes and placed the bulb on the center of his face. Steady, aged hands lifted a painted, cone-shaped top half. He set it in place. It looked natural with the remainder of eyebrows and tufts of crimson fur for hair that stuck out from the sides. Perched on top, a tiny hat. He donned a scarlet-and-white checkered jacket to cover suspenders, which held up pants of the same material. With persona completed, he contorted his face and pointed to the sky. We bolted upright and cheered to Sir Auguste.

He spoke in a gravelly, German-accented voice. "I've been clown-ing longer dan you've been on dis eart." He whistled, and from the sidelines shot two small, white dogs. "Dese are my new partners, Buffy and Pee-wee. Dey're still learnin' da ropes."

They scampered off when Lou put his fingers to his lips and blew again. A chubby, more experienced associate bounced into the ring. "Dis is Knucklehead." Music began after he dressed his faithful Chihuahua in a long-eared head covering.

Donned in a hunter's hat with a rifle in hand, he stalked his dog—the pseudo-rabbit. When Lou circled so did his quarry behind him. He turned the other direction, and the Chihuahua sat up on his hind haunches. *Bang!* The varmint rolled down dead in slow motion. He reached to pick up his catch, but the headdress slipped off and a chase ensued. Unable to seize the elusive prey, Lou sank to one knee and put his hands together as if in prayer. Knucklehead gave in and jumped into his arms.

Lou Jacobs *was* Ringling Bros. and Barnum & Bailey Circus. His performance trapped my breath, and a fuse sparked that night. Would sawdust replace the lure of Broadway?

During the course of the final week, Mr. Jacobs dragged an old duffle bag full of stuff onto the floor while we surveyed from the stands. He set it down. "I was cleaning out some tings from my garage dat I collected troo the years. You can haf 'em if you want." He turned and dumped out all kinds of objects.

We bolted from our seats to claim old rags, dirty powder socks, torn shirts, or worn jockstraps—any piece of the master clown. Outside the arena after lunch, he held a small box.

"What is it, Lou?" I asked.

"Open it. It's for you."

Inside that beat-up cardboard container sat an old, crushed, red hat covered with ruby, sewn-on sequins encircled by a yellow, felt band.

"Dis was one of da first hats I wore after I used a cone-shaped head back in da big top days of Ringling."

"Jeez, Lou."

"It's just an old hat."

I held more than "just an old hat." A tangible form of the history of clowning rested in my palms. Why me? Nonetheless, that gesture became the ribbon on the package called Clown College as the eight weeks drew to a close. What an inspiration to do my best!

Time to prove worthy of his gift drew near. Everything experienced and hoped for in our intense, fun-filled journey would end with a gala graduation-performance audition. Before that night, however, we grew careless from exhaustion and students hurt themselves right and left.

My roommate suffered a horrible accident. The phone rang one morning while she cleaned her ears with a Q-tip. She forgot about the cotton swab, leaned over the bed, and picked up the receiver. A bloodcurdling scream arose. Brenda punctured a hole in her eardrum and lost her equilibrium. To add insult to injury, a day later she sprained her foot.

Students fell from giraffes, regulation-sized unicycles, and rolling globes. Clown slaps that created the illusion of contact became actual whacks accompanied by shrieks of agony. The school colors had become black and blue!

As for me, two days before that grand finale I twisted my right ankle in rehearsal. I sobbed and sank to the ground, not from the trauma but from what was at stake. Everyone clustered around in sympathy, then whisked me to the hospital.

After examination the doctor said, "No weight on it for a week. Then try walking." The man in white didn't know the blood that flowed through my veins. Right then and there, I vowed to take part in the ceremony, grabbed the crutches, and hobbled out.

During those final few days fellow students practiced skills and gags. Whenever I stepped without the wooden supports, unbearable throbs of pain traveled from my foot up my leg and cemented this thought, "I will be in the performance, even if it means to walk on my hands."

Clown College neared completion, and my shoulders drooped. Friends had become siblings. Colleen's greeting, "Hi, campers," lifted tired spirits. We got a kick out of Ray Solimeno and his pot of spaghetti. Would Joan play her accordion into a contract? For sure, the juggling mighty mouse, Bill Dusell, nicknamed Bucky, would get the nod. I still loathed separation and would miss everyone, no matter who went where.

On the day of graduation, we waited in front of the Villas for the final journey in our cartoon-like bus with its painted smile and red nose. No enthusiastic welcome sounded. Each passenger stared out the windows as our funny vehicle drove the street past the little airport.

The big, red doors of our university greeted. We entered the arena the last time as students and sat around the ring the saddest bunch of clowns I ever saw. Ron and Sandy Severini had been supportive leaders.

The man who guided our endeavors took his place before us. "Well, this is it, class of 1978. Sandy and I want to thank you for your hard work in our first class as deans. I know some of you mentioned that you didn't have enough time to perfect skills, but do your best." He pointed to the foot of the bleachers that faced us and continued, "Mr. Feld and his son, Kenneth, the executive vice president, will sit at that table. The two pens and paper tablets are for their notes on you. Strut your stuff and don't worry. Your sixty-seven gags showcase everything you've learned in these eight weeks."

The familiar ground of tryouts created butterflies in my belly. A black drape hung across the arena floor. Standing behind it, we'd wait to go on. The highlighted difference between this audition and others in my past beckoned: the stage with no beginning and no end, no left or right—the circus ring.

Family, friends, staff, civic leaders, and circus executives received invitations to the event. I'm not sure if my parents approved of my decision to attend Clown College, but they came to support me.

I left my crutches at the Villas, and after Ron's talk, hobbled into our area. Bobby Kay encouraged everyone with a few words while we put on our makeup: "Don't forget behind the ears and on the neck."

While the audience filed in, we donned our school-designed costumes, circled, and sang our class song about a gray squirrel that holds his nuts between his toes.

It grew quiet, and Ron gave the nod and disappeared to join the spectators. After his short speech to the crowd, my roommate, Brenda, as ringmaster blew the whistle. First out, the band led by Michael Heatherton, nicknamed Tuba. Eight members sported pink jackets, blue hats, and tooted a range of instruments with me on glockenspiel. When we stepped into the spotlight, the healing warmth of chutzpah surged within my bones. Its power eliminated the ankle injury and pain, which never returned.

The Felds kept tabs on us by assigned numbers on our shoulders—mine, number fifty. Tina, with arms a blur, depicted the predicament of a pint-sized fisherman. Bucky executed a variety of juggling patterns as if his life depended on it. I ignored my fear of topsy-turvy and flipped and leaped in a routine called charivari. We tumbled and rolled over a vaulting horse, which doubled as a diving board, and landed on a thick indigo mat that simulated a pool. We drowned the onlookers in clowning and skills for three hours.

Ron granted me a solo to depict joining up with a circus. I accomplished my mission with a song that centered on a return to one's roots of sequins and tights. On my suitcase hung the sign "Ringling or Bust." It was this dance number that had caused my sprained ankle, but no mishaps occurred that time.

After the last presentation, we took a bow and left the ring. The granddaddy of auditions had ended, and a rush of relief exploded from my pores. With a quick change, the entourage of potential professionals reassembled in the Pie Car, Jr. to attend a dinner. Mr. Feld made the rounds and introduced himself to my proud parents, then moved on.

My father turned and faced me. "I didn't know you could juggle balls and flip like that, Danise."

I smiled. "I didn't either."

Clown College for 1978 was over. To celebrate, we removed sheets from beds later that night for an impromptu toga party at the Venice Villas' pool.

At dawn we rose early. Each opened his door and twiddled his thumbs. The morning air hung as a heavy curtain that weighed on the shoulders. When Ron called your name, you rode in a car to the arena for a rendezvous with Mr. Feld to learn your outcome.

"Tina, you're up."

My little sister waited next to me. "Good luck, Tina," I said.

"Danise, your turn."

I gulped and slid in beside her. He called four more for that first load. The automobile pulled away from the curb and drove that familiar path. No longer students: instead, we vied for a job. At our destination we ascended the steps to the narrow hall outside Mr. Feld's office and took a seat. No one spoke.

The younger Feld opened the door. He appeared close to my age and sported a cropped afro. "Come in, Tina." She clenched her teeth, jumped from the chair, and swung her diminutive arms. We crossed our fingers for good luck, then my friend turned and entered.

The walls closed in while I hung in there for what seemed like an eternity. I wondered, "Who's gonna be next?" In due course, the door opened again and out shot an exuberant little person.

"I made it! I made it. I'm going on the Red Unit."

I stooped and hugged her. "Oh, Tina, that's great."

"Danise, you can come in now," Kenneth said.

That which I drove from Los Angeles to achieve waited inside—success or failure, a new life or a return to uncertainty.

I rose from Tina's embrace and looked at the doorway that led to that room up the stairs off to the right. With a dry throat and one foot in front of the other, I walked into the dimly-lit space. The Felds sat next to each other on the far side of a wooden desk close to the window. The workplace stood bare.

Irvin Feld introduced himself and his son, Kenneth. I shook their hands and eased into the empty chair that faced them. Thin, wavy hair topped the short stature of the senior man, owner of Ringling Bros. and Barnum & Bailey Circus. His glasses resembled the bottom of Coca-Cola bottles and rendered his eyeballs too large for his round face. The cigar in his mouth wasn't lit. Thank goodness. The smell of tobacco on fire turned my stomach. He flipped pages while he read my application.

"How's your brother?"

His car accident—in response to the question, "When was the last time you cried?"—slipped my mind.

"He's fine."

"I see you like to travel."

"Yes, that's true. I rode my bicycle across Europe."

"Tell me more about yourself, Danise."

"I'm an air force brat and have two sisters and one brother. Vanita is a nurse; my younger sister, Adriene, wants to be a teacher; and my brother, Robert, wants to join the navy. I was a shy kid, but I loved to perform."

Conversation continued for a moment, then a pregnant pause filled the room. The junior Feld had no questions. So, the father glanced at me, put his palms face down on the desk, and smiled.

"Well, Danise, I'm gonna put you to work. Red Unit. Welcome to *The Greatest Show on Earth*."

The walls created by the slurs of racists and the taunts from bullies couldn't stop me now. Momma's little bird sprouted wings. I pumped the Felds' hands and soared out of there. Tina had remained in the hall with the other four students. I flung my arms wide open in her direction. "I made it, too. We'll be on the Red Unit together."

Out of fifty-two students, Mr. Feld hired twenty-seven: Joan and her accordion, to Circus World in Orlando, Florida; and our bandleader, Tuba, to the Blue Unit. Seven of us, including Bucky, the mighty mouse juggler, headed to the Red Unit to join Lou Jacobs and Peggy Williams.

A skinny, introverted, air force brat stepped into the outer realm of Wonderland. No Fairytale Town could replicate what would soon take place. I emerged the first African American woman clown on the Red Unit of Ringling Bros. and Barnum & Bailey Circus. More notes appeared on the ledger lines of my life, and a tune arose.

## CHAPTER SIX

FIRST OF MAY

I wanna see elephants, tigers, and chimpanzees
Give me llamas and zebras and zeedonks and fleas.
—D. Payne

A clown's best friend—the thrift store.

My father and I wound our way through the streets of Sacramento to find a cheap trunk. We stopped at every secondhand shop, and at the end of the day, entered through one last door into dusty, dry air.

A man in baggy pants, a gingham shirt, and a full-length apron that covered his potbelly glimpsed from behind a desk. "Hi, folks. Come on in. How can I help you?"

Dad spearheaded the search. "We're looking for a trunk."

"It has to be a wardrobe one," I said.

"Well, I dunno if I got one of them, but you're more than welcome to look around."

"Thanks."

At Ringling the oblong, sturdy chests sheltered a clown's personal getup, and many styles existed. The upright wardrobe type occupied the least amount of space on the train. We gazed in each nook and cranny that bulged with vintage purses hung from doorknobs, hats of former fashion in need of repair, and other stuff heaped to the ceiling. I glanced in the aisles, then lifted a pile of dusty old rags to reveal a hidden treasure. "Here's one!" The four-foot-tall gray box, in good condition except for a broken clasp, received my father's approval.

"How much will you take for this?"

"Well, let's see now." The owner looked it over. "Forty bucks?"

"How about ten?"

"What! This trunk's seen more than we have in its day."

"You didn't even know it was in here."

"Yeah, yeah. Thirty-five?"

"Twenty-five."

"Sold."

At home Dad replaced the fastener for my padlock. Then I cleaned the container that would shelter my alter ego's soul and stenciled "Clown" with yellow paint on the outside. Good to go. The week before my return to winter quarters blurred. My mother made a duplicate costume, and I rearranged my life for a trip down the rabbit's hole.

I reviewed my contract, a standard American Guild of Variety Artists (AGVA) document of two-and-a-half pages that noted the particulars, such as performance season dates, apprentice clown year one, and salary—$155 per week. In addition to the usual taxes, my room on the train and union dues required extra money.

With my official paperwork tucked away, we left for the airport two days before practice. Tears filled my eyes when we stepped up to the ticket counter. I still hated goodbye no matter the good time that waited with hello. My family glanced at those in line who eyeballed my trunk that boasted the emblazoned title of my new profession.

"Whatcha got in there? A dead clown?" the man behind us asked.

"Not yet," I said.

The airline agent surveyed the massive box, then glared at us. "That'll cost fifty dollars to check."

We loaded my belongings onto the conveyor belt, paid the money, and headed to the gate. At the call of my flight, I smiled at my family and walked away from years of sonic booms and khaki-colored clothing and flew into a reveille of rainbow hues.

In the lobby of Sarasota Bradenton International Airport, a brunette woman my height approached. "Hi, I'm Antoinette Concello.

I'm the aerial director in charge of showgirls. I noticed your gear. Are you new?"

"Yes, ma'am."

"I have room in my car if you need a ride to the building."

I had to decline. Frosty, as boss clown, would transport his people. He was a no-show, however, so for ten dollars and fifty cents a van service transported me to the circus arena in Venice. I entered through the familiar red doors and stood with trunk on the right and sleeping bag and suitcase on the left—the epitome of lost.

How different. Gone, the unicycles against the railing; no "Gray Squirrel, Gray Squirrel" theme song. Three rings filled the floor where our trampoline and mats once sat. Lessons from class reminded me that ring three was closest to the back door, a.k.a. performers' entrance; two—center; and one—farthest.

The cold, damp space buzzed. "Hup." sounded overhead. "Flying trapeze!" I said to myself. The flat *thunk* of their hands that grasped the bars underscored the hum. Beneath them, bears shuffled on hind legs toward a large door on the right. A loud guttural rumble that resembled a dinosaur didn't halt their steps. While they exited, the elephants entered.

A different world unfolded before my eyes. My performer's heart could tackle the task at hand; nonetheless, the unfamiliarity of the circus caused me to tremble. Relief filtered in when I recalled that the master clown, Lou, would be there. I darted my eyes left and right when a voice interrupted my travels through fantasy.

"Hi. Did Frosty drop you here?" It was Antoinette Concello again.

"No. I actually took a van. He never came."

"Well, let's take care of your gear."

After we hauled my trunk to the dressing space known as clown alley, she said, "We'll take the rest of your things to the train." My heart raced at her words and almost burst with anticipation. We loaded my paraphernalia into her car and drove from the lot. En route she talked about the show with command.

We soon turned off the asphalt road onto one of gravel, and the epitome of wonderful get-up-and-go came into view. It sported the words "Ringling Bros. and Barnum & Bailey Circus" the length of its silver body. She knew where I would live, for Ms. Concello said, "Your room's in car number forty-four with my showgirls. Number forty-five is the Pie Car. You'll probably spend a lot of time there on the runs, the trips to each town."

We lugged my suitcase and sleeping bag up the steep steps and deposited them into the quarters. I would learn how to sleep with my elbows in my ears. It *was* the size of a closet per Peggy's words in Clown College, hence the claustrophobia question on the application.

We returned to the arena with Frosty, still a no-see-um. Ms. Concello resumed her duties, and I stood around. A thin man my height with perfect, white teeth and stark blond hair approached. Thanks to pictures in school, I recognized him as the famous German animal trainer, Gunther Gebel-Williams. He spoke with an accent.

"You new, clownie?"

Correct—not stacked for showgirl.

"Yes."

In lieu of a welcome he looked at my chest, put his hands on my breasts, and said, "You got no boobs. Ver your boobs?" He sauntered away and left me stunned speechless.

"What would he have done if I had?" I thought.

My composure from that affront returned, and I headed to the changing room. One of the circus kids drew near. She had finished drinking at the fountain and with perfect trajectory in my direction executed an impersonation of a fireman's hose. The water from her mouth soaked my boobless shirt. She skipped away with a grin. I had only been on the premises fifteen minutes. A moment later, Tina and Mike from Clown College ran over and we clung together.

Tina and I made our way to the girl clowns where Peggy chatted with Miss Ellen, the German woman my sister and I met in Oakland.

"Dis is clean place," she said to me. "You will be clean?"

"No, no Mama," Peggy said. "She is. Look at her shoes."

Peggy lifted my oversized oxfords kept in a clear plastic bag for safety. Miss Ellen approved and left.

"Don't worry about her. She's Mama. Welcome. You're gonna love it here, you and Tina. That's your trunk over there, Danise. In winter quarters our alley's in this spot. In some towns, it'll be with

Miss Ellen in ladies' wardrobe where the showgirls change into production costumes."

"You'll find us wherever we are. Come, I'll show you," Kathy
Herb said.

We followed her from our sectioned-off area. She did an about-face
and pointed to the masking tape that bore the words "girl clowns."

"Like you found it this time, that'll be on the curtain in every
town." She indicated a concrete column and continued, "In fact,
to find anything look for the arrows that lead in the right direction
and go. See, Pie Car's over there. By the way, did you two get paid?"

"No."

"Today is rehearsal payday. Here, I'll take you. No masking tape
guides to that, ya know."

We walked to the pay wagon, stood in line, stepped up, and said
our names. In the envelope, my first wages: eighty-five bucks—cash.
We returned to our enclosed space, met Ruth Chaddock, and put
away our stuff. Once finished, the five women clowns wandered
out back behind the scenes. We called it the backyard. The adult
Toyland with miniature cars; overblown, brilliant jack-in-the-boxes;
and wagons painted in bright hues mesmerized me.

Soon, Frosty called us into the men's clown alley. As boss clown,
he supervised and informed his charges of their contributions to
the show such as track gags, performed on the circumference of the
hippodrome floor, and walkarounds, attention-getting antics that
divert from the goings-on in the ring.

"OK, everybody gather 'round. Hottay, let's go!" he said. "There's
lots of stuff we gotta do, see. First, I want to welcome all you, First
of Mays. I'm going to assign parts for you seven in come-in clowning
and the different gags. You're on your own for walkarounds."

We took seats among the others. The veterans stood and said their
names. Five women clowns were numbered among a contingent of
thirty-two with three African Americans: Skeeter Reece, Garry White
(he had invited my sister and me to the show in California), and me.
In addition to Lou, another older man named Duane Thorpe, a.k.a.
Uncle Soapy, sat by his trunk. Although he didn't travel with us, one

of our old hand instructors, Bobby Kay, would make an appearance from time to time.

Twenty-seven men's trunks appeared to be strewn in a haphazard way, but a pecking order actually existed. Lou's and Uncle Soapy's sat to receive the best lighting for makeup application. First of Mays' received the worse locations within the labyrinth. Greasepaint containers and all kinds of objects sprawled here and there, such as an enormous cowboy hat—a wearable prop for clown, Mike Keever.

A tall American flag on his trunk caught my eye. "It's there on purpose," Keever said. "We play a lot of towns, and sometimes you forget where your spot is. The flag makes it easier to find mine, especially when in a hurry." Smart idea. Men's clown alley resembled an overblown mouse maze that had survived a tornado.

The rest of the day belonged to us after Frosty completed his beginning-of-the-season spiel. Tina and I moseyed throughout the building for a bit until the whistle blew, and we took seats on the curb in the arena. A similarity between stage and sawdust existed: superstitions. Number one, never sit with your back to the ring.

Rehearsals began. We presented a new show for the 1979 season with many first-timers, and most didn't know who did what. Three hundred seventy-five people breathed life into the presentation.

Mr. Feld welcomed everyone. Then the performance director, Tim Holst, conducted introductions. Several longtime circus personnel served in management. Hair silvered with age topped the handsome features of Trolle Rhodin—general talent director and son of a circus man. A flyer from years gone by functioned as technical consultant, Harold "Tuffy" Genders. When Tim mentioned Antoinette Concello as the aerial director, he announced she had performed the triple somersault back in 1937.

To connect the mass of people, he introduced the acts one by one. While "Getting to Know You" sounded from the organ, each group walked the inside of the circle and shook hands with the other artistes.

Tim continued the roll call with the strangest of all: those who painted their faces and dropped their pants. "OK, funny people of the Red Unit stand up—Bucky Dusell, Tina Stotts, Danise Wilson

. . ." We stood, and led by Lou Jacobs, clown alley—another use for the expression—made itself known.

I glanced and saw no freaks. Around the circumference sat Europeans, some from Iron Curtain countries; North and South Americans of different hues; men capable of supporting five on their shoulders; and women short enough to stuff in a box. Everyone looked normal to me. In the ring, however, had congregated a collection of oddballs born to make the world smile.

The Red and Blue Units comprised *The Greatest Show on Earth*. Both played the Big Route with major stops, such as New York City and Los Angeles; and the Rodeo Route, which crisscrossed the country with two- and three-day stands of smaller towns. As the Red toured one direction, the Blue worked the other. A repeat of the same production on the alternative path saved time and money and guaranteed a different performance for all audiences. The length of the rehearsal period depended on the year. The second season demanded only a two-week practice. With a new presentation, we required four weeks of preparation and props able to withstand two years of travel.

The days that followed bustled with activity in anticipation of the road. During breaks I sat in the stands and observed. Performers rehearsed acts handed from generations, such as the Flying Farfan family—the aerialists on the trapeze the day I arrived. All kinds of inconceivable ways to earn bread and butter sprang to life. One woman from Mexico dangled in the air by her thick, dark hair and defied gravity while she tossed torches of fire.

My eyes caught sight of Pedro Carrillo and Luis Posso, billed the Carrillo Brothers. With arms stretched for stability, they walked a slanted cable as if on a Sunday stroll. The high wire beckoned forty-two feet above ground. No net. Like gazelles, they jumped onto the small platform and looked at me. Pedro took hold of a long balance pole and ran back and forth with ease. He placed a chair midway of the wire and stood on the seat to dare fate.

When Luis ambled to the middle, plopped down, and dangled his feet, I peeked through my fingers in time to see his partner come from behind and leap over. The daring duo almost lost their footing with a mistake of the jump rope. Not really. They smiled after they executed the feigned misstep sure to draw gasps from the audience.

After them, Lou's daughter, Dolly, who was close to my age, graced the air with an aerial gymnastic ballet poised in two rings suspended by ropes—the Roman rings. Artistes from the young to the elderly worked like bees with a stamina from a higher source. The massiveness of the circus operation caused my head to spin. I needed a break, but curiosity about the animal performers stopped my retreat. Chimps, bears, elephants, and dogs—each with individual presenters—waited in the wings. The presence of God's creatures in the ring enlivens a circus. Without them, love's labor is lost.

Crew members caused a commotion on the floor when they pulled cages in and attached them one behind the other. The man with the hands that trespassed—Gunther—entered the ring. "I definitely gotta watch this—from afar," I thought, thanks to his touchy-feely welcome. I retook a seat. Years ago, Irvin Feld had leased the entire Circus Williams in Germany to acquire him.

Surrounded by a mesh-wire barrier, he called his tigers from the pens. One by one they sat on supports. Instead of the stereotypical whip and chair, he used his voice to put them through maneuvers. The cats stood in a line, lay down, and rolled over in unison, or bounced on hind haunches. He moved among them with authority, and they became one. Without doubt gifted in his craft with charisma that no other possessed, Gunther Gebel-Williams walked larger than life.

I recognized a man with a fedora who surveyed the star. My interest in zoology would spark a conversation later. He was "Doc" Henderson, the master veterinarian who had been with the show since 1941. His expertise ensured animal welfare on *The Greatest Show on Earth*.

On the sidelines showgirls climbed what looked like a thick rope strung from the rigging. They put a foot in a loop, hung topsy-turvy, and practiced aerial ballet for the production number of Web. They and the clowns served as fillers. What a new world!

CHAPTER SEVEN

MY CORNER OF THE SKY

After the last day of Clown College, George Shellenberger and Bruce Warner returned to their original jobs in the Prop Department. With their help, the alley built fake realities. I hammered and glued and made the foam rubber breakaway wall through which a little person would slam his motorcycle.

Frosty cast me in several gags, and I beamed with enthusiasm. He assigned a part for me in The Fruit Vendor gag with Chuck (Chucko) Sidlow, who portrayed a con man vendor.

Minus my oversized baby hat with a purse in hand, I took my place as the lady dupe and strolled by him and his red cart that displayed fruit and vegetables of hardened latex. We spoke to ensure a smooth flow, but we also used body language for folks out of verbal reach.

"Veggies! Get your veggies here!" he said. "Hey, lady! How about some produce?"

"OK, here's a grocery bag."

He offered the oranges. I shook my head and pointed to the grapefruit.

"OK, here ya go, lady."

He picked up the rigged one and squirted water on me.

"Hey!"

"How about a cabbage? Need any cabbage today?"

I nodded and handed him the carryall. He inserted the home grown product attached to elastic and yanked it out as I ambled away.

"Hey! Where's my cabbage?"

After more back and forth business and a few chases, I grabbed a rigged watermelon made from that lightweight rubber and cracked it over his head for the surprise ending known as the blowoff. We took a bow together.

I liked that spontaneous in-your-face style of performing. Laughter filled my spirit.

The big production numbers, which included Opening and Menage—short for menagerie but pronounced "manage," the act with elephants—required separate schedules. On the first day of those rehearsals, choreographers Jerry Fries and Bill Bradley stood in front of the microphone. Bill piped up. "Showgirls and clowns space yourselves on front and back tracks." (The area covered with a rubber mat that enclosed the hippodrome floor.) Then Jerry said, "We need a few clowns in the rings."

Next they placed each act by group, noted the spacing, and then demonstrated how to do-si-do. Under their tutelage, we learned to dance circus-style.

Practice proceeded like this: sit and stand and walk and run and sit and stand and walk and run and sit . . . with a daydream or two inevitable. My mind wandered off somewhere in Spec—short for spectacle, the grand pageant before intermission. I missed a cue and bounced up and down alone in the ring.

The rough work schedule blurred winter quarters. As a bubbly First of May, however, I wanted to volunteer for everything. Later Peggy cautioned, "Save your energy, Danise. It's gonna be a long season."

The body needs to adjust from a time clock of eight hours to drawn-out days filled with constant motion. I didn't listen and paid the piper. Harsh, frequent coughs heaved my chest. Chills arose from deep within. Every sneeze exhumed the bug from me, but it propelled the virus to coworkers.

A trek along Tamiami Trail led to a store for medicine to stop the result of an avid nature. During the endless haul back, a car pulled up. The driver called out. "Hi, I'm Bill Payne, the lead alto saxophone player. Want a ride?"

I recognized him but hesitated, then slid onto the seat. Shyness plastered me against the door. We returned to the building and walked in to Tim Holst barking over the microphone.

"Danise, come to ring two."

I halted, and he repeated the demand that reverberated in the small arena.

"Danise, where's Tina? She wasn't at the morning rehearsal. You're supposed to make sure she's here. She's your responsibility, Danise."

Not in my contract. Tina's friend, yes—nursemaid, no. To eliminate another summons, I spoke with her that evening at the train.

"Don't ruin your chances. We made a pact to make it together and we did, but it's up to you to show up. Listen, Tina, Tim announced in front of everyone my duty is to take care of you, for some reason. I can't do that, you know."

We had come a long way as friends against the odds. But a riptide developed. She was on her own.

The next day I wandered to the train after clown practice ended and stopped short, mesmerized. "Wow, look at that." Men strapped in stilts and dressed in coveralls from head to toe masked the windows with brown paper. "We're paintin' it. We wear this stuff to protect our skin and to keep from breathin' vapors."

With a high-powered hose, they glided from car to car and airbrushed each in silver. The ease of the false legs replaced cumbersome ladders.

My baptism into this new world immersed me further into its hidden wonders within the week. Again my stroll carried me to the wheeled residence. And as if he had escaped the celluloid of Cecil B. DeMille's *The Greatest Show on Earth*, in full vestment our chaplain—on assignment from a higher authority—walked the length of our home. He held a silver chalice filled with water made holy by his words. A sprinkle here and a dash there on each coach accompanied the traditional circus blessing for safety away from winter quarters. God's blessing primed Ringling Bros. and Barnum & Bailey's lodgings for a season on the road.

The departments seized their responsibility and clicked the show together like puzzle pieces. Don Foote, the man behind the glitter and glamour, and his assistant, Mel Cabral, created fantastic, spangly things to wear for production costumes. These replaced our nondescript rehearsal attire comprised of cutoffs, jeans, and T-shirts. My metamorphosis began with a request to report to the sewing class room of Clown College—goodbye khakis and sea green.

"Please go into that closet and take off everything except your underwear and bra," Mel said.

"What?"

"When you exit, come over to me to be measured."

The other fabric wizards, with pins and scissors, anticipated my striptease show with indifference. I slinked from the wardrobe dressed only in my undies and waited spread-eagle. Without hesitation, Mel positioned the yellow strip with numbers on my waist and ankles, up my back, inside my legs, and around my neck. I tried on petticoats that fell in waves and sparkly tops so tight they trapped my inhibitions. When finished, the ensembles fit to a T.

The one for Web tickled my fancy. The flowing, maroon skirt and attached, green side-apron bulged due to layers of puffy undergarments; it finished with a pinkish-yellow, long-sleeved top of bust size fifty—Nerf balls. A stiff wig coiffured in a high French bun and adorned with a scarlet flower covered my pantyhose skullcap. Never mind the orange color. My feet squeezed into red, high-buttoned shoes. What an inspiration to clown!

Designed with men in mind, the outfit for Spec produced the opposite effect. It comprised a glittery, skin-tight jumpsuit and round-shouldered, bolero jacket with a huge collar. Pink feathers encased the helmet topped with a small pointed hat of gold. I looked like a little black boy.

In the men's alley one morning, Frosty issued a six-page handout to be memorized. I returned to the girls' alley, sat by my trunk, and flipped through the pages of dos and don'ts, such as instructions if sick or missing a number, restrictions on train cars, and approval needed before changes in gags. Protocol circus style.

On December 13 clowns performed for Mr. Feld. The formal examination to see if we cut the mustard proved nerve-racking; thus, we called it the Nurembergs, after the testimony that wrenched the souls of the Holocaust survivors during the Nuremberg trials of their Nazi captors. Someone warned, "He picks you apart right on the spot. If he doesn't accept your costume or presentation, it's back to the drawing board." The words caused a bad case of the heebie-jeebies.

Our leader led us into the arena that night. We stood in single file and faced the owner of the show, who sat in the front row. Save for other members of the cast who came to watch in support, the building remained empty and silent. The ordeal began with inspections. Clowns before me stepped up for a once-over from top to bottom, then took a seat in the stands. Several folks didn't pass the grade and needed new looks.

"All right, Danise. You're on," Frosty said. The air force brat took over, and I came to attention—stiff as a board. Irvin Feld stared through his thick glasses. The ever-present cigar dangled from his mouth. His eyes moved from my blue, curly wig to my black-and-white oversized oxfords.

Meanwhile Lou, who sat directly behind him, leaned to the left and caught my gaze. He put his thumbs in his ears and wiggled his fingers, contorted his face, and crossed his eyeballs—his way to say, "Do something." I forgot about Mr. Feld. The jitters left when I responded to Lou. Facial expressions from Clown College surfaced at the speed of lightning: happy, shy, shock, for example.

The man in charge sat unaware of the goings-on behind him. He stopped chewing his stogie to watch my mug, which zoomed through changes a mile a minute. My face snapped out of hyperdrive when Mr. Feld said, "OK, next." After thumbs up from the boss man, I joined the others in the bleachers.

At the completion of that evaluation, the band accompanied everything else, from track gags to walkarounds and chases: one clown burst through the curtain with a skeleton strapped to his back and bolted down the track with the bones in close pursuit. We also presented several ring gags, such as the Firehouse with Tina hidden under the fireplug and the incomparable, timeless Clown Car.

"Hottay, Lenny, get in," Frosty said.

Dressed in a fat suit, Leonard Wolen barreled into the Datsun 510. Painters had camouflaged our vehicle and windows to resemble a taxi to guard the how-did-they-do-that secret.

"OK, Keever, you're next."

And the cowboy clown—big hat and all—plowed in with a lasso he'd use to catch Lou.

"Danise, your turn."

I wedged in on top of the others, and my thoughts traveled back to Atlanta where Daddy had crammed family members into our Volkswagen Beetle for that trip downtown.

After seventeen of us squeezed in, Frosty said, "Hotterini, that's it!" Then he slammed the door.

Jim Tinsman scrunched into the driver's spot, turned the engine on, put it in gear, and sang "gotta fart," to the tune "Gotta Dance!" And he did. We lurched forward and zoomed down the track. I had a ball, even when we smashed into each other inside as the car careened at the curves. We screeched to a halt in the middle of ring two.

Lou, the cop, waited to bop everyone on the head with his foam-rubber billy club as each exited. Dressed like a jockey, I flopped from the vehicle with a rope attached to my two-person horse and twirled to face the door to pull out my bronco—*whack!* What controlled mayhem! The door opened one last time, and out squeezed Lenny in his fat suit for the blowoff and the end of Nurembergs.

We performed in full regalia to see how everything looked under the lights. In the end, Mr. Feld made his decisions, which set the clowns for the next two years. In addition to the Fruit Vendor gag, my performances included a wind-up baby doll walkaround and the production numbers from Opening to Spec, during which I rode a unicycle. The show had come together, and on December 28, 1978, we opened in the evening.

Tina, Peggy, Ruthie, Kathy, and I prepared. "Hey, Peggy, are there any Ringlings still alive?" I asked.

"Yeah, Henry Ringling North is vice president."

I had been little-girl-lost after my family left Great Glemham. On opening night had the tide changed due to that celebrated family's enterprise?

"Doors!" The cry echoed throughout the building and informed the troupe that the audience received clearance to stream into the arena. We removed plastic helmets from our trunks and donned white jackets. With our flag-topped poles, the women clowns joined the men and stepped into a fully-lit house for the Drill Team of come-in. While the public flowed in and took their seats, we marched around ring one and bumped into one another as practiced.

We ran off when the preshow ended to dress for Opening. Outside the curtained alley, hurried footsteps and the quiet shuffle of bears mixed with the excited whispers of performers. I gathered my one-piece, spangly jumpsuit from the blue, wooden wardrobe box and slithered into it. The hat for Opening, encased with thin, pink feathers, topped it off; and silver slippers caressed my feet. A face in the mirror stared. "Hello, clown." The life God groomed me for had begun.

The clowns joined the rest of the troupe behind the proscenium and listened for the cue. I glanced at the souls who would ricochet from boards attached to sawhorses and the brave ones who would spring off the dreaded trampoline. The line of performers—human and animal—stretched into the backyard. Everyone sparkled. All stood silent. The Carrillo Brothers rested in place. Gunther Gebel-Williams relaxed behind them with his elephants and riders. Film and Broadway would have to wait.

I turned to my little sister, who resembled a cake topping. "Well, this is it, Tina."

Led by Bucky, the mighty mouse juggler, the seven of us First of Mays gathered in a circle and hugged. The electric bulbs in the arena faded to black. With auburn hair, beard, and mustache, our dashing ringmaster, Kit Haskett, stepped through the curtain and blew the whistle.

Under the direction of the musical conductor, Keith Greene, the band played a march, and we sprinted into position. For me, into ring two already set for the tiger act. I took my place on the cats' stand and peered into the darkness. The trinkets kids waved twinkled like stars in the heavens and revealed a sold-out house—a "turnaway."

This is a one-word circus term to indicate that no more seats were available. The show would turn away any additional onlookers.

My heart pounded to the rhythm of the music. Silence. The drumroll began, and the spotlight came up on Kit, who was dressed in blue-and-silver, spangly tails.

His voice resounded, and he stretched certain words. "Laaaaadies and gentlemen. Children of aaall ages. Producers Irvin Feld and Kenneth Feld proudly present The 109th Edition of Ringling Bros. and Barnum & Bailey Circus. The Grrrrreatest Show on Earth!"

The lights came on, full up. The musicians played a flourish of notes called a fanfare. We raised our arms above our heads at an angle, and the packed house bolted to their feet and cheered. Awesome. No play on earth could produce such a glow that tingled the spine. Right then and there my corner of the sky emerged from sawdust, and my spirit trumpeted a song.

At the end of Opening the three clowns in ring two ran out as Gunther opened the cage door and the tigers bounced in. What a night! No mishaps, except for me. The state of nervousness knocked me off my unicycle—twice: the moment Spec began and then a repeat, a *déjà vu* of the panic in the parking lot before tryouts in Oakland. The other single-wheeled riders continued. I ran to the side barrier, held on, mounted, and rode like the wind one step ahead of the elephants.

We presented more shows over the next few days, then ended our premiere. Move-out night arrived. "Be sure to pack everything and lock your trunks, Danise and Tina. After that, you're done. The working men will haul them away and put them on the train, but you have fifteen minutes before they do," Peggy said.

My makeup came off in a flash with smeared baby oil. I put my gear away and jammed my oversized oxfords into the plastic bag to take with me on board, not wanting to let them out of my sight. A quick shower followed since none existed on the coach. When finished, I stepped into the arena and stood captivated. The crew lowered the clanging rigging with precision that mirrored the pack-up-and-go of the military. No time to gawk, though. Transportation to the train would soon leave.

Instead of the Clown College funny vehicle, a yellow school bus would make three runs: the first, three minutes following the show; the second, thirty minutes later; and the last, one and a half hours after Finale. Each ride cost twenty-five cents, and after I dug in my bag for a quarter, we headed off the lot.

I peered through the windows eager to be on the way. Soon, winter quarters in Venice, Florida, would be yesterday's town. The route card cost ten cents and listed the cities of the season in order. The first jumped from the sheet: St. Petersburg, Florida, also known as St. Pete.

CHAPTER EIGHT

THE SILVER SLUG

Before move-out night the trainmaster jostled the railroad coaches closer together, which allowed connection by those Jenny couplers I learned of years ago. When the bus approached, the positioned livestock cars nestled under bright lights on poles came into view, as did our living quarters at rest to the rear. I bounced off the bus and into number forty-four. The coach buzzed with activity as everyone put away stuff in preparation for the run. I entered my roomette and followed suit. Then I observed Tina, who lived across the hall, as she crammed belongings into the space under her bed. The cupboards lay out of reach. She finished and said, "I'm going to the vestibule," which left me alone with visions of wonder that danced in my head.

At 9:00 p.m. her voice rang out, "Here they come!"

I shot from my room to join her and bulldozed past three show-girls who sat on the floor and blocked the way. They weren't First of Mays and had witnessed the spectacle before.

Animal walk had begun. The procession of the four-legged performers from building to train mimicked the call of Noah. Tigers, horses, and camels would enter our wheeled ark. I leaned out and strained my eyes against the night. As phantasms from another realm, the elephants appeared out of the shadows as mounds of earth that lumbered over the bridge.

Gunther controlled them at the head of the line. He called to one, "Ceta, here!" followed by his created mishmash wordage, which resembled "udelay, udelay, cominzee here!" The massive creature responded. He ran and barked instructions: "Jenny, *schnell.*"

With blond hair, he reminded me of Tarzan. Thoughts of his you-got-no-boobs greeting that first day came to light, yet his God-given talent shown through. Apprehension toward him faded into the darkness, replaced by awe and respect.

His voice grew louder. "Piccolo, keep them in line!" Born Helmut Schlinker, the mighty-mouse assistant stood three feet tall, but he held the behemoths in a single file.

Trunk to tail the pachyderms plodded past our coach close enough to be touched. I closed my eyes against their quiet footfall—against the sound as a broom that sweeps the floor. Who knew heavy bodies to be silent?

Afterward I jumped from the vestibule and tagged along.

As they reached their hay-laden cars, Gunther gave a command, and they turned side to side. He started at the head of the herd and called each by name. "Ceta, in! Nellie, Nellie, come, come!"

One by one, they trudged up a narrow ramp. With each stride, their feet lifted higher to clear small crossbars.

"Pretty funny seeing these guys step over a little board like that, huh?" Pete Cimini, nicknamed Camel Pete, said.

"Yeah, why do they?"

"Elephants are sure-footed, and they don't like to walk on anything that might make them trip. The crossbars prevent missteps. You want to hear something else? They're not afraid of mice, either. They're aware of their own size and don't want to trample on anything smaller. They know they'd crush it."

I didn't learn *that* in my zoology class. When the last gray bulk wedged in, I returned to number forty-four fully convinced to ride one in the show some day, if allowed.

Drowsiness caused my eyes to close, but the intoxication of rail travel popped them open—back and forth—so letters bound for home filled time. At 7:00 a.m. a jolt of the train propelled me to my feet. Movement! Good thing Clown College taught to secure anything loose, a reminder of relocations from base to base. A bent nail in the wood beside the cabinets would keep them shut during the run.

Another lurch. I bolted to the vestibule. Someone had lowered a heavy, steel platform to cover the steps and closed the door, which split into two halves: the top section that was unfastened, and the lower that was always locked for safety while we proceeded. We inched forward. On board, high-wire walkers, musicians, a sway-pole artist, leopards, and me.

I looked to the right. The banner, up and down its length, shouted Ringling Bros. and Barnum & Bailey Circus. In the stillness of daybreak, the chug-chug of the engines separated us from winter quarters. My enthusiasm could have propelled us to St. Pete, but we headed out of the yard at a snail's pace. Fairytale Town, Clown College, and the little girl who hated goodbye faded into the distance. We were on our way.

I reentered my 3' x 6' x 9' and stretched out on top of my sleeping bag, nestled in the confines of my little world. The living quarters had housed one of the quintessential showgirls. With bright red wallpaper and beaded drapes, it had resembled an itty-bitty bordello. I had eliminated her decor in Venice with a can of white paint and self-adhesive shelf liner. A Ringling poster, a basket of dried flowers, and yellow curtains complemented the cubicle. My teddy bear, Sooty, sat on the shelf—a constant companion.

The wall received a map of the continental United States to trace our route: the first year, the Big Route, I penciled in red; the second year, the Rodeo Route, I would outline in blue. A picture of child actor Jackie Cooper in prayer on his knees said it all: "Please God, let me be a clown when I grow up!" The company supplied our unicycles, so my personal one rested in a cubbyhole beneath me. And the outside of the door displayed a flier that read "Danise's Hole-in-the-Wall."

Restlessness. I opened the portal to my sanctuary and called out, "Hey, Tina." No answer.

Across from mine her door stood open and framed my little sister, who had crawled into a ball on top of her stuff for some shut-eye.

We chugged toward St. Pete on freight tracks that required endless stops at road cross sections for the passage of other locomotives.

But en route I would slumber as a cradled baby at the gentle sway of Ringling's train that I fondly called the silver slug.

At the next sunrise, a sudden jerk of the train prompted me to saunter once again to the vestibule. We crept through train yards with rows and rows of rails, stationary cattle cars, and large black cylinders on wheels for oil transport. Onward. Behind the byways, we paralleled backyards where residents leapt from lounge chairs to wave. Our logo shouted loud and clear: the circus is coming!

The day progressed to twilight, and we arrived at our destination. With cameras in hand, those who lived in towns (who troupers called "townies") lined the way for the 7:15 p.m. animal walk.

# # #

In the morning after a bowl of cereal, I dressed, gathered my gear, and boarded the bus for the ride to the cold, lifeless, concrete shell of an edifice—like the one in Venice until Clown College began. Tina and I walked down the ever-present, wide ramp that bustled with activity and followed the arrows past the different dressing rooms and the menagerie to girl clowns. Everything sat as it had in winter quarters and would remain so for the season, a welcomed familiarity. I removed my oversized oxfords from the plastic bag, placed them in my mobile closet, and chitchatted until Tim called everyone to the stands. We moseyed in and sat.

He stood among a crowd on the track and shook the hand of a gentleman on his left, then leaned into the microphone. "For those of you who don't know, we film a television special each year. The audience will sit on one side of the floor in front of the cameras, but we'll perform as if it's a full house. We have a guest ringmaster you might recognize. He's been in a few movies. I'd like to introduce Danny Kaye."

What a surprise! Tall and slender, the actor stepped from the group and approached the front, said a few words, and our run in St. Pete began.

That morning's show served to rehearse, then film Mr. Kaye's part with our goings-on. All flowed as it should have until the number before intermission—Spec. Everyone took his or her place. After I sprinted to my tall, metal kite in ring one, put my hand into a loop, and stepped onto a seven-inch platform, a working man hoisted me thirty feet up.

Mr. Kaye, known for a fast lilt, put it to use with a song that promised a lively time at the circus with bears that dance to the music from a brass band. He completed one run-through, then the director took over. "Cut! Do it again!"

While they repeated the action in ring three, my composure slipped away at the opposite end. After forty-five minutes suspended in the air on a stand no larger than my two feet, I became a bit loopy and motioned to the crew member below to let down my kite. No chance. "I could jump," I thought, but what a long way to fall!

A heated discussion from the other side diverted my attention from stupid ideas. Our host grew exasperated with logistics and ordered the television company around. His words rang true; it took too long. After one hour and fifteen minutes we finished, and the man in dark coveralls lowered me to the floor.

The next day during a break, Tina and I rested in the stands when Danny Kaye strolled by. He looked up and asked, "Mind if I join you?" He climbed the risers and sat between us. We grinned like Cheshire cats and spoke of his movies until Tina had to leave, whereupon he turned and looked at me.

"What's your name again?"

"My name is Danise, Mr. Kaye."

"Call me Danny, all right?"

I sat side by side with a man whose films pulled a cheerful countenance from the depths of sadness. Our occupations mirrored each other; both stemmed from the fantasies of the heart. Yet, the remainder of my visit with the Hollywood icon proved the coin had two sides.

His words tested our Barnum and Bailey world. "Circus is odd, don't you think?"

"In a way, but that's what draws the crowds."

He stared at my blue, curly wig and the greasepaint on my skin.

"How can you stand all that stuff on your face?"

He had portrayed a court jester, Hans Christian Andersen, and Captain Hook, for example, with makeup, costumes, lights, movie sets, and all—the epitome of make-believe.

"We get used to the face paint and forget it's there."

"Yeah, well, I travel to film locations, but this is ridiculous. You journey for a year."

I cheered our silver slug. "On a train!"

My inner thoughts told me he wasn't buying this line of work. The need to stand up for my career surfaced.

"I've always loved your movies. But what's the difference?"

We sat face-to-face, and with a gleam of curiosity, he gazed at me. In silence he listened to the description of bizarre circus life—Clown College, visits to kids who wouldn't live another day, tours for the blind, for example. The movie star absorbed my defense of clown. The stillness of his expression broke, and his lips curled upward. With a twinkle in his eyes, he gave me a hug.

Later the entire alley surrounded him for a photo segment. He posed with a mop head for a wig, a chocolate candy wrapper on his teeth, and an orange peel on the nose. The cameras froze that image in time and captured walkarounds: Mitch and his cigar that exploded and Lou with his dog, Knucklehead, dressed as an itty-bitty elephant.

When I strolled by, Danny Kaye held my arm and pointed to the audience. A photographer took our picture, and it appeared in the trade magazine *Variety* captioned, "Danny Kaye and Friend."

The special concluded as our true ringmaster, Kit, sang about a Toyland menagerie. The televised presentation served as a peephole into an existence out of the ordinary and enticed the public to pay for a closer look. At the end of the week, we said goodbye to St. Pete and headed out.

Love for train travel began in winter quarters with the first jolt of the locomotives. On this run, I set out to acquaint myself with our special mode of transportation. Ours differed from the happy-go-lucky railroad cars that carried a flying elephant in the animated Disney movie. I melted into the real-life counterpart of Casey Junior's Dumbo train.

Size and setup of the berths depended on the status of the worker. Inside the women's coach resided a kitchen with a refrigerator, one stove, and one dryer. Our roomettes were too small for such individual luxuries, so we shared. Showgirls, however, forbade powder socks or bright, orange-and-yellow striped tights mixed in with their fishnet stockings.

I knocked on Tina's door. "Come on. Let's explore." We passed through the living quarters for the men clowns—similar to ours—and through coaches with staterooms of larger spaces for musicians and acts, such as high-wire walkers. We opened another vestibule door and called out, "Can girl clowns come in?" A necessity, the workingmen's home lay before us. A voice from inside gave the all-clear, and we stepped in. The crew—once called roustabouts—slept in a corridor lined with upper and lower, opened bunks. We had strolled far-off and called it quits after that, thankful for our small corners of the sky. We returned to our car, Tina to her residence, but I stayed in the vestibule and leaned out.

Between the engines that exhaled fumes the color of the night and the last cars that carried floats and wagons—their vibrant colors variations of magenta and mustard—stretched one mile of iron horse. We hugged the tracks in safety thanks to Charlie Smith, our trainmaster. Not a tall man, he walked with bowed legs and always wore a baseball-style cap. Clown College information revealed that he was born in 1915—the same year as my father. The company recruited him in 1956, and his expertise devised ways that quickened our move-out time. When I joined up (circus lingo for joined the show), he had captained our ship for more than twenty years.

I rested alone in my thoughts, but my initiation into this new lifestyle continued when Tina reentered the vestibule. "Come on, Danise, let's go to the Pie Car and see what's up."

We had passed through it during our excursion, but a meal sounded like a good idea. With two steps to the right, we would partake of a brand-new eating experience.

The Pie Car resembled a restaurant on wheels. A row of counter-top tables fixed to the wall lined the windows. Benches faced each. Opposite sat the open-air cook station from which an aroma from the day's fare greeted the nose. Antoinette Concello spoke true words. The coach served as a great place to gather, and we joined two men from our clown class for supper. For a modest fee, we dined on liver with onions, green beans, and corn. For dessert, food poisoning that began with a rumble in my belly. I shot from the dinette and headed to the toilets on our car. Four dancers blocked the way.

"Excuse me. I have to go to the restroom."

"Restrooms?" Jacqui retorted. "Oh, no, Little Bit." She always called me that. "We don't say restrooms. It's a donniker."

"A what?"

"It's called a donniker!" She remarked to the others nearby, "What a First of May."

I met Jacqui Shannon, one of the few black showgirls, after my audition in Oakland. A cutout picture from *Jet* magazine of her, Dwayne Cunningham, and Garry White had hung on my wall in Los Angeles for inspiration.

Relief waited at the donniker, a small enclosure with only a toilet. To reach the sinks in the hallway, one needed to bend the waist; fishnets hung overhead. "No more Pie Car food for me. Vienna sausages will do fine," I thought.

I returned to my room. In my study of the confinement, an idea occurred: "What about my hair?" The difference between white tresses and black remained with me since childhood. A decision surfaced: wash and press my own mop in the communal kitchen, which would send a cloud of cooking-hair smell down the hall and invite questions, or keep my locks straight with the chemicals of a permanent. I took the easy route with the latter.

My focus then switched to the language barrier. I wanted to make a go at this career, so obtaining knowledge of circus jargon took precedence. I dug in the cubbyhole beneath my bed for the Clown College lingo list from Peggy Williams, scanned the first page, and found the new word for restroom under "D." *Donniker*. My eyes darted to the top of the series. *Annie Oakley*, a complimentary ticket or free pass. *Ballyhoo*, the spiel shouted in front of the sideshow to attract attention. *Calliope* (pronounced "cally-ope" by circus folk), a musical instrument that consisted of steam whistles played like an organ. The endless pages and the rock of the train offered a lullaby, and my eyes closed on the day. We moved into West Palm Beach and returned to a normal show.

Travel with pachyderms had propelled my departure from Los Angeles. To ride required chutzpah. No better time existed to ask for the adventure. One day I sought out Garry White, our tour guide after the Oakland auditions. We had become friends, and I figured his performance getup would fit since we appeared to be the same size.

"Hey, Garry, how about letting me take your place on your elephant." The stagers had assigned him as a rider for the season.

"Sounds good to me. I could use a break. You think you can handle it?"

"Sure. I watched Menage from under the stands the first three days."

It looked easy enough, but my gamble rested on Tim Holst. As performance director, he approved changes. Maybe he wouldn't notice our switch on the sly.

"OK, Danise. We have to clear it with Gunther, though."

We found the man with the trespassing hands who chimed in. "You ride, clownie?"

"No, but I'd like to."

"OK, Vee see 'bout dat."

No begging needed. Garry surrendered his production costume. During the Red Unit's next performance, when Menage rolled around, I donned the bulky ensemble of maroon sequins and huge hat with a pink feather—which fit—and headed into the hallway. Gunther took me to my mount, Jenny. The mobile building didn't budge when my hand patted her trunk. "Nice elephant." I stood next to that gentle giant and looked up at her beady eye. Upon instruction she lowered her front end.

Gunther touched the leather strap around her head. "Hold onto this and put your left foot onto her left front knee." I did so. He said her name, "Jenny," and gave a command. My heart pounded as she nonchalantly raised her leg, which propelled me up and onto her back. My legs dangled behind her ears. It made no difference to her who perched up top, one rider or another. I looked around.

A line of jumbos and their human performers waited until the cue. Our spangly outfits broke the monotony of the gray that swayed in the dark. We topped the animals as decoration sprinkles on a sober cupcake.

The curtain opened. No time to change my mind. We catapulted down the hippodrome track, dashed around the curves, and screeched to a halt on the front track at ring three. My grimace and death grip to the bridle shouted pure unadulterated panic. Clown College behemoth-walk-around-in-a-circle had ended.

With a big toothy grin, Gunther ran beside me every step of the way. "In case you fall off!" he said.

My only concern involved Jenny when she sat on the tub, which she hated. Meanwhile, Gunther shot to the other side of the floor, and with a mishmash of words, put the elephants through their paces. All the pachyderms sat up except the one beneath me. Instead she shifted her weight from foot to foot, which caused me to roll from side to side as a boat in a storm.

Ringling's Tarzan sprinted back and uttered his created expressions. "Jenny, Jenny. Udelay, udelay. Up!"

A trumpeted squeak of protest reverberated through the thick hide, into my attire, and settled within my legs. Before she heaved her bulk up, Jenny touched her forehead to the ground. I didn't know to recline but held onto the halter in a vertical, bottom-higher-than-head position. At that moment, my location changed. I found myself atop a large, gray balloon heavy-laden with helium. An unseen giant released us, and in slow motion we rose backward until I rested in a blast-off-to-the-moon pose—reverse of the previous stance. With her front legs now raised, Jenny's "up" rendered a clear view of the ceiling. I glimpsed up and thought, "Wow, I never looked at the rigging before!"

I raised my arm above my head at an angle as if to say ta-dah—a circus pose called to "style." But luck ran out when a sequin on my sleeve hooked to the huge hat plume. "Can't hold on with my hand in the air."

Unlike the seasoned showgirls who rode with hands on hips, my posture smacked of a cowgirl who white-knuckled for a rough ride.

I panicked and thought, "Gotta break loose before the dash down the track." I yanked and tugged to no avail.

At that time, Tim strolled by and stopped next to Jenny and me to observe. He glanced in my direction and stared but never said a word while I tried to look Garry-like. The pachyderm lowered herself at half speed at the end of Menage. Fortunately, I broke free from the feather before the herd bolted down the track, through the curtain, and abruptly halted. I dismounted and grinned at my blaze of glory.

"Vell, clownie?" Gunther asked.

"That was fun!"

My legs shook for several hours and throbbed for three days.

After the day's work and a short ride to the train yard, I collapsed in my hole-in-the-wall.

CHAPTER NINE

STEAL AWAY NORTH

Leftover adrenaline rendered me awake enough to study the route card: Jacksonville, Florida; Birmingham, Alabama; Greensboro, North Carolina; and Richmond, Virginia. One hundred fifteen years earlier, those cities carried slavery in the Heart of Dixie, but freedom greeted those of African descent if you stole yourself away and headed north. The former ideology of the Southern states presented African American history on a platter of bold impudence.

Our train followed the route of the Underground Railroad, which led to my own mini-African American, history tour. A sojourn beckoned to the locations of events I learned about through my independent study years ago at Connally Junior High. My people in bondage had put messages in song to indicate the arrival after sundown of Harriet Tubman. She had conducted the broken-spirited away from hell on earth. Negro spirituals rang in my heart and drew me to visit places the female Moses had set her feet upon while leading others to deliverance. When we reached Jacksonville, Florida, the old mentality of the South reared its ugly side one day.

I climbed the stands during a break on a typical three-show Saturday to eat lunch. The residue of snow cone juice and cotton candy likened the bleachers to an obstacle course. With his cap cocked to the side, a local policeman in a baggy uniform interrupted my hurdle over the previous leftovers.

"Whatcha doin' there?"

"I'm looking for a clean place to eat."

His eyes shone like black marbles. His words rained like cold fire. "No, you're not. You're lookin' for somethin' to steal."

"I am not! I don't steal."

He slid his stubby hand to his weapon, withdrew it from its holster, and pointed it in my direction. "Git outa here."

And yet, again, another bully in my life. That one, though, a dangerous animal with a gun. I couldn't punch him as I had done to the tormentor in high school. So I hesitated, then retreated to Tim Holst, determined to do him in. It turned out, he had hassled Skeeter as well. They fired him the next day. Hellfire and damnation! Next stop—Birmingham, Alabama.

The train chugged toward the state my father used for a curse word, then settled in the yard. When our nondescript yellow school bus carried us to the building through the metropolis, my stomach churned. I sat aware of the spider's web that had been its past. At our destination, we dispersed and slipped behind our respective blue curtains. Soon Frosty called the clowns to the men's alley. We sat in front of him ready to vanquish any residue of hate in a cockamamie world. But it was a different day and time. He paused, put his hands on his hips, and melted my unease with his statement. "You get a treat tomorrow. You guys are going to eat breakfast with someone special—Red Skelton. His compliments. Hotterini." In fact the only occurrence in Alabama was the meal with the notable variety entertainer, and it took place on February 11—my birthday.

We eager beavers arrived at the designated hotel early that morning. Dressed in civvies, we sprung into the banquet room. Chairs surrounded a long table and another displayed a cornucopia of scrambled eggs and biscuits, grits and bacon. Delights of orange juice, coffee, and herbal teas met the eyes. We waited with cameras in hand. Soon a gray-suited, large man with a broad smile filled the doorway. "Hi, I'm Red Skelton. Call me Red!"

Everyone bolted to say hello to the big-hearted, happy soul.

We engulfed him, and Red greeted each of us. "You're Danise!" he said when he shook my hand. I figured he had received a photo of the alley. Since I was the only black, woman clown on the unit, it was an easy guess. Lou stepped forward. To witness two mighty men of their craft meeting eye to eye and hand in hand electrified the air.

When the group took seats with our host at the head of the table and Lou next to him, Red unveiled several tape recorders. "I brought these so I can learn something in case you all reveal secrets."

The opposite occurred. He blabbed, and we gained the knowledge. He spoke about mishaps in a burlesque show.

"The production closed due to something I said."

In the scene, he walked with a woman on a cloudy day. The actress wore a mid-calf length skirt (considered short back then).

"It looks like it's going to rain," she said.

He looked at her attire and said, "Oh, I dunno. I'd like to see it clear up." The show closed.

In a segment from *Uncle Tom's Cabin*, he played an angel who had come from heaven to speak with Uncle Tom. The wires that suspended him crossed, and he faced backward at his cue. Instead of the correct line he said, "Uh, see ya later, Tom. I'm going back to heaven." Fired.

He yakked throughout the entire breakfast and paused to render his seagulls' comedy routine, Gertrude and Heathcliffe, seen many times on television in my youth. He admired funny folks and loved to paint them. He walked among the familiar, for he had worked the Hagenbeck-Wallace Circus, as had his father.

He ate and talked at once, which made him burp. "Oh, excuse me. How about that, a polite pig." He continued, "You're special because you make people laugh. Keep a log; write things down from day to day. I have enough to fill forty volumes."

Red Skelton took our pictures with a Polaroid camera for his scrapbook.

Then he spoke to me one-on-one and said, "Blacks are either good or bad, no in between. You'll have to be twice as good as everybody else, Danise. The folks out there'll judge you twice as hard."

No news to me. At the end of our breakfast, Tim Holst presented an official Ringling certificate to honor that gray-suited man who walked full of life.

His visit carried us through the run in Birmingham, and we headed toward tomorrow's town. From time to time the train required water intake for sinks, donnikers, showers or what have you. When necessary we stopped along the way. The clear blue of the cloudless sky beckoned me to observe the process one day when the train halted on tracks in a field behind drab houses. I proceeded to the vestibule where someone had opened the door and lifted the steel platform, which uncovered the steps.

Townies had appeared from the environs to get a load of the curious world of Barnum and Bailey, if only for a moment. I climbed down to join them.

"Hey, Danise!" Tina had positioned herself in the other entryway that remained half-closed. She waved from the door above a throng of locals mesmerized by her size.

I smiled then turned when our trainmaster, Charlie Smith, called out to the crew. They had connected hoses from our tanks near the underneath storage boxes—called possum bellies—to municipal hydrants for the hour-long procedure. I blended with the crowd. Gunther's men unloaded the animals and refreshed them with cool streams of relief and provided exercise. When the elephants lumbered from their moveable quarters for a break in the cushy meadow, Tina's audience skedaddled to ooh and aah.

Some water stops took place at night, and if the run covered several days, performers jumped off to explore any nearby town. Down the road, we paused at 9:00 p.m. for an assumed stop outside Spartanburg, South Carolina. The railroad cars rested on high ground and would stay put for one hour, so we heard. Tina and I joined others for a chance to get off and slid down the muddy slope to the bus station below. While we milled about, I sauntered into the restroom. The stall trapped me when the lock broke. Tina came for a look-see.

"Tina?"

"Yes?"

"I'm stuck."

For a couple of minutes, she tugged the door and I pushed with no luck. The only solution—squeeze under and crawl out. We returned to a vacant waiting room, experienced a rush of adrenaline, and bolted to the window.

No nostalgia existed of a happier America beyond the sight of a lighted, circus train going down the tracks in the middle of the night—except when you're supposed to be on board.

"It's moving!" We darted outside and scrambled up the hill, but lost footing due to the slippery earth.

For every one of my steps, Tina required two. She ran as fast as her short legs could go—not good enough.

"When you get there, tell it to stop!" she said from a distance.

Without the heart to leave her, I slid back down. We dragged ourselves up the incline as the coaches halted, then ran to the nearest vestibule. When I hoisted her up, she flopped over the locked, lower half while I remained on the ground in hopes that our home wouldn't move. The platform lay too high to heave myself up and over. She managed to unlock the door. Ten minutes after we boarded—scared, but safe and sound—the train pulled away and pushed on until morning.

The trek north through snow into Virginia continued my journey of self-awareness. The silent white stuff plummeted the temperature. The pipes on the train froze, which resulted in no water until it thawed. We moved onward over icy tracks and into a derailment. Performers tumbled from beds; coaches broke free due to faulty alignment or a switch man who did his job too soon. There were no injuries, just frazzled nerves. The show must go on.

One day, Peggy approached. "I noticed you left the train early yesterday, Danise. Where'd ya go?"

"I visited Underground Railroad—"

Someone strolled up and interrupted my answer. The young Caucasian man stood tall with green eyes and sandy-blond hair.

"Danise, do you know Billy Payne?" Peggy asked. "He's our sax player."

"I'm the one who gave you a ride to the building in winter quarters after you bought cold medicine or something," he said.

Memory served me well but only produced a smile.

"Danise visits historical places, Billy."

"Tomorrow, I'm going to see a war site here in Norfolk," I said.

"Can I go?" he asked.

I hesitated. My American education had taught me to expect a negative response at the sight of us together in a city south of the Mason-Dixon line. Life had steeled me against the false reality of "all men are created equal." A moment elapsed. The only way to catch my breath in the drowning pool of racism? Ignore the bums.

"I guess so. I'm leaving at 6:00 a.m., before our first show."

"OK, I'll meet you outside the Pie Car."

At the crack of dawn, we sat next to each other on the local bus and heard no comments from the other riders. When we arrived at the battleground, we looked through the window. Headstones of Confederate soldiers stretched into the distance. We exited, and I trampled underfoot the rebels and their dogma buried in the sod, perhaps tilled by the descendants of the Mandinka, one of the largest ethnic groups of the country Gambia in West Africa. Many of their sons and daughters had been stolen and shipped into bondage in the land of the free.

What manner of man strolled beside me? What secrets ruled the heart of William Anthony Payne? I wanted to know.

"How did you join up?"

"At twenty-one I first toured with The Russ Carlyle Orchestra. Years later when we played New York City, Keith Greene—you know, our music conductor—called my roommate. He needed a trumpet and saxophone player. My buddy didn't want to go, but I wanted a new gig. Keith said come on, so I rode Amtrak to their next town, auditioned, and got the job. I intended to play only for the two-week run."

"Why did you stay?

"The steady money in my hand versus starvation did it. That was 1977, two years ago."

I asked him his opinion of slavery, and he responded with a loathing for that sin. We talked of music and circus, then headed back to the arena. He escorted me to the girl alley, then smiled and left. My face flushed. And Bill Payne entered my life and stole my heart.

He had told me that his maternal great-grandparents had emigrated from Ireland, the country with the wagons of Travellers. His father's side hailed from Germany. The common thread that bound us together, a compassion for the nomadic lot.

In the cosmopolitan profession of circus, attraction showed no bounds. For a change, color carried no weight. Mixed couples walked hand in hand. *The Greatest Show on Earth* introduced my spirit to a rainbow world, yet the female in greasepaint received the cold shoulder from some of her fellows.

Protocol expected the fairer sex to ooze physical attractiveness, an impossibility with huge shoes; wigs; outlandish clothes; faces covered in red, white, and blue makeup; and big noses. How to catch male eyes? What a moronic topic of conversation in the girls' alley! The scantily-clad-low-cut-big-breasted-tight-form-fitting-fish-net-legged-high-heel-wearing-seductive showgirl, a constant reminder of my low status on a totem pole.

One day the dancers in Web outfits of black satin dresses that flowed over red-and-green petticoats paraded by a working man named Dummy. He held a camera and said in his nasal-pitched, gravelly voice, "Pretty picture." I noticed the line-up and jumped in. He threw a fit and flailed his arms. "No! No! Only pretty giiirls!"

My self-esteem fizzled a bit as I clumped-clumped away in my black-and-white oversized oxfords. My eyes opened to a glitch that existed in the mystical, magical, wonderful world of sawdust and glitter: the so-called place of a woman in a niche long held by the man. A role in Spec, for example, required me to push a heavy, metal soldier down the track with the men clowns. No problem. Every show, however, the performance director waited until he was beside mine to say, "All right, funny *men* (his emphasis). Let's go!"

When his subtle distinction subsided, another tiptoed into view. On the blue curtain that enclosed the women's dressing space, the masking tape read "Girl Clowns." The light-colored, narrow strip on the men's boasted "Clown Alley." No one excluded us from our greasepaint duties, however. We pulled our share. But the public had difficulty with distinction and spoke unaware of any faux pas to me with the occasional, "Excuse me, sir. May we take your picture?"

The presence of Peggy, Ruthie, Kathy, Tina, and me in the world of circus—dominated by men—bore witness to a plea for recognition, respect, and credibility. In 1979 the necessity remained for my gender to gain acknowledgement in this different segment of society.

I was a daughter of a military family. Second-class citizenship for girls prevailed as an unquestioned norm. My mind reeled to think that the fact reigned among those born under a wandering star. My career had only begun.

On March 27 the lights faded to black on the Ringling Bros. and Barnum & Bailey Circus train. We stopped for twenty minutes in the Holland Tunnel under the Hudson River for clearance into New York City. I prayed against a leak while plastered against the window. As a snake from the bowels of the earth greets the morning, we emerged into light and slithered to Twelfth Avenue and Thirty-Third Street. The locomotives came to rest on seldom used tracks in a deserted section of the city near the water. A wall barricaded Manhattan from us and our only neighbor—a lone, small diner surrounded by trash and dirt.

The next day I climbed the stairs in an opening of the fortification and hiked through the labyrinth of concrete canyons to a two-block-long post office. I paused out of harm's way on the edifice's massive steps. Yellow taxicabs flowed past as a river of churned butter. People scurried to and fro like ants. Across the living avenue, my destination: Madison Square Garden, our home until June 3.

The name stemmed from a park near the original building located at Twenty-Sixth Street. Four facilities bore the designation through time at three different locations, which included one leased by P. T. Barnum for the premiere of Jumbo. The structure we played opened in 1968 above Pennsylvania Station with its subways and railroad trains.

After my respite at Uncle Sam's mail service, I joined the herd of folks at the corner. The light changed, and we headed across as cows from a stall. At The Garden, a ramp circled upward inside the round facility past several levels. The circus performed on the fifth.

I trudged the ascent with my bagged oversized oxfords in hand until the familiar pungent odor of elephant signaled the summit. "Next time, I'll take the elevator," I said to myself.

After a pat on Jenny's trunk and a thanks to God that our alley stood close by, I flopped down to catch my breath, arranged my things, then stepped through the proscenium. Approximately eighteen thousand seats encircled the floor for thirty-six thousand eyes that would watch us for ten weeks. The stands stretched to the heavens.

In Baltimore we had performed a dress rehearsal for improvement tweaks in anticipation of opening in the Big Apple—the actual kickoff of the season. All was well, and that night the "brass"—Irvin and Kenneth Feld, their families, and city dignitaries—sat in a reserved area ready for the lights to grow dark. Before that, however, Frosty called the clowns together.

When we entered the men's alley, he cast his eyes downward and frowned. "OK, guys. Sorry to break this bad news to you at this time, but it seems we lost one." He paused. "Emmett Kelly, Sr. died today."

My heart sank at the loss of Mr. Kelly. As tramp clown Weary Willie, he brushed into history when he swept up the circle of spotlight on the floor with a broom. Later we sent flowers to his widow. No tradition existed to render a minute of silence. Instead, one gave a moment of laughter. For when those in greasepaint performed, a quiet audience meant failure.

We honored the notable man with the grubby face, then took our places under dimmed houselights for Opening. Kit blew the whistle, and the run that dug at the depths of stamina began. The ten weeks consisted of two or three shows a day, Monday through Friday, plus six-packs that involved three performances on Saturday and Sunday. No days off.

Labor strain. Exhaustion took over and aerial artists fell from on high. I developed mononucleosis. A cast discussion took place to formulate our grievances about the workload. AGVA union representatives would present our case to management. Many of the performers feared the meeting would jeopardize jobs and refused to attend. As a result, nothing came of it. But the marathon of twenty days straight with no downtime never repeated for the remainder of my time with Ringling.

The city offered diversion from overextension that stretched the limits of physicality. Billy and I jostled in the subway and threw in every Broadway musical time allowed: *Ain't Misbehavin'*, *A Chorus Line*, and *Eubie!* We escaped reality at our home on wheels—our sanctuary—and barbequed in the backyard where circus kids played. That is, until one found a perfectly preserved human hand lost to time. The mystery of its owner's whereabouts remained unsolved.

Ah, our silver slug! Snuggled on board, we slumbered away any cares. In my twilight dreams of blessed sleep, I danced on stage at the Shubert Theater with other gypsies. As we slept sneaky townies expressed creative, visual skills on the shell of our mile-long cocoon. Armed security, what's that? No problem. Before the last ta-dah in the ring, the coaches had received a fresh coat of silver paint to cover the graffiti.

By the conclusion of ten weeks, we longed for Philadelphia—a.k.a. Philly—the gateway for our trip west. At the final bow, Kit approached the microphone and raised his sparkled top hat. He spoke to the crowd, yet expressed my hopes: "May all your days be circus days."

After Finale, we ran off and packed our stuff. I bolted to the sidelines to observe. Gunther had changed into jeans, a shirt, and a baseball cap. He called the shots and crew members took tethers in hand. He led the elephants down that circled ramp into the night. His workers followed with horses, camels, llamas, and me close behind. After our parade lumbered to the train, we nestled in and waited.

I peered from the vestibule at Charlie, our trainmaster, who had completed his walk-through and returned to the engines. Once ready, the usual jolt began our journey, and we took our leave from Manhattan. The train snaked back through the Holland Tunnel and headed toward the city on the Delaware River.

CHAPTER TEN

HOBO LIFE AND CELLULOID

After Philly we battened down the hatches for a three-day journey toward the setting sun. We Wilsons had covered many miles in the air force and had seen a lot of the country's scenery. But this train trip to Los Angeles would gorge my appetite on deserts painted in hues of a pale rainbow. The rhythm of the wheels on our way to the pallets of pastel resembled the monotonous cadence of a relentless drummer, which resulted in a perfect time to catch up on sleep.

On the second day out, the locomotives pitched and rolled and prevented shut-eye. What a perfect time to bond, to lift the wool from my eyes on this circus thing and see what lie beneath. I peered through the window. "Maybe I'll visit the Jacobs family." My bumpy stroll down the corridor strengthened my sea legs and ended at their door. Lou's daughter, Dolly, answered. She presented an aerial act in the show and was close to my age. The master clown wasn't there. So after her mother, Jean, said hello, Dolly and I chatted awhile. What an insight that struck a familiar chord!

Although she had joined Ringling in her teens, she belonged to the domain of circus kids, who grew up with tigers for neighbors and bears for confidants. A teacher toured and taught the ABCs between acts. Each circus season brought different companions into Dolly's sphere. Having to leave behind friends was all too familiar. I attended nine schools by twelfth grade. New military orders every four years separated me from my buddies as we disappeared into a mist for parts unknown.

She introduced her pet bird. "They live fifty years." The feathered pal cocked its head as if to say something. She tried to coax a word from it, but it didn't make a peep. Dolly and I talked of girl things and train travel, and a new friendship formed. Whenever my stay at Ringling ends, Dolly and family would remain a part of me. When my visit concluded, she and her mother offered a welcome back to their home on wheels. Then Mrs. Jacobs smiled and said, "Lou's in the vestibule." I left, walked the narrow hallway, and peeked through the window.

Mr. Jacobs sat on the train's red step stool alone in the section that linked the coaches, his dogs Buffy and Knucklehead at his side. He absorbed the landscape that rushed by. The clunk of the door averted his eyes from the blur of scenery. He nodded at me. No words needed. The wind would only swoosh them away. I stood across the vestibule and glanced in his direction from time to time.

An incident that took place earlier popped into my head. We didn't start on time that day; the show held for five minutes. Everyone waited in costume to go on.

Lou exited his dressing room and asked, "What's da holdup?"

The performance director, Tim, said, "I don't know but there's dead air out there, and the audience is getting restless."

No hesitation existed on Mr. Jacobs's part. Years in sawdust called forth the wizard of the bewitching realm of greasepaint to the ring. With a hesitant gait, he set off to get his dog Knucklehead. Age may have caused his slow movement behind the scenes, but the curtain served as a time portal. A spring returned to his steps and transported him back to youth when he strode into the arena. What an honor to share the train's window on the world with America's king clown.

The young shall always need the old, the ones who have experienced the tomorrows of adolescence. The wings of the man with the funny face sheltered students and First of Mays. He imparted the tricks of the trade. When needed his encouragement nudged us on. The important function of the man under the cone head was immeasurable. For words of clown wisdom, Lou Jacobs. For guidance in the art, Lou Jacobs. For historical evidence, Lou Jacobs. For an army of one against the odds, Lou Jacobs.

My extended family grew. From that moment on, I called him Papa Lou like the rest of the clowns. Circus people ate together, lived together, traveled together, and became friends for life or thorns in sides. As a result, my little hobo world stretched.

# # #

We reached the Golden State, played San Diego, and headed to our premiere in Inglewood, California. Well-known actors of celluloid flocked to the notable, American icon known as Big Bertha or The Big One—just a few of the names used to dub the Ringling show. So many attended that we labeled the opening, Star Night. Actually, the evening benefited Project HOPE (Health Opportunities for People Everywhere), which provided medical training and humanitarian assistance around the globe.

Management's plan would coordinate the expected hubbub. When we arrived at the building, the girls took seats in the guy's alley.

"OK, gang," Frosty said, "there's lots of things to do, see. First of all, after we're finished here, go and mingle with the crowd in the VIP tent set outside in the parking lot. Answer questions, smile, but don't drink. Before you leave, though, we'll designate a big shot for each of you to escort into the arena during Opening. Hottay!"

"They'll ride an elephant or walk and wave for a parade around the track," Tim added.

I received a placard with the name of my connection to Hollywoodland in bold letters: Willie Aames—from the then-current television production *Eight is Enough*. After everyone obtained their assignments, Tina and I ran from their dressing area to ours. I set the sign beside my trunk, grabbed my camera, and we shot up the ramp toward the white canvas that glistened in the sun. We passed a fleet of limousines and stepped through the flap in full clown gear.

The who's who of the movie industry adorned the interior as place settings of silver on a table covered with fine linen. Henry "the Fonz" Winkler of *Happy Days* ambled past. The handsome Cesar Romero stood with LeVar Burton, Kunta Kinte in the miniseries *Roots*. He hailed from Sacramento, which broke the ice.

I had once wanted to be a part of their community, and my mind created a lunatic scene of pretense. Around me strolled beautiful blonds and dashing men. My black-and-white oversized oxfords carried me on a promenade. They clumped among bejeweled high heels worth one thousand dollars and obliterated my fantasy.

"Hello, what's your name?" someone asked from behind. "I like your character. It's cute."

I turned and faced legendary actor Jimmy Stewart—the man who spoke to an invisible rabbit in the feature *Harvey.* He who stood before me animated my painted smile, which revealed my pearly whites. Of all the souls there, Mr. Stewart was a real star. His works, from *Rear Window* to *Mr. Smith Goes to Washington*, had entertained my imagination. His portrayal of Buttons, the clown in the film *The Greatest Show on Earth*, sparked a conversation. I lived the real McCoy and had seen Hollywood's version of the circus, but I didn't want to tell James Stewart his motion picture was a bunch of malarkey.

"You know, we did have a wreck, sort of. (Cecil B. DeMille's handiwork depicted a horrific derailment with animals that ran helter-skelter.) Some of the cars jumped the tracks on our way to Norfolk," I touted.

"Oh, my!"

"Yeah, but no tigers escaped and ran amok or anything like that."

My time with the slender man of the silver screen ended when other clowns bolted over. A photo opportunity conserved the moment. I then sauntered off, found my celebrity, and enlightened him on what to do. An unknown person took a snapshot when he gave me a polite hug. Five months later it appeared in *Rona Barrett's Hollywood*, a gossip magazine. The article asked, "Who's this clown trying to make *Eight Is Enough*'s heartthrob, Willie Aames, look 'foolish'?"

At showtime we led cinematography's own from their gathering into the jurisdiction of the big top. We stood in line next to them and waited through announcements. The lights dimmed, and the spectacle began. Actors, clowns, and showgirls stepped out at the whistle and received applause that exploded like fireworks. High society clung to halters on elephants' backs. Others led giraffes and camels. The rich and famous squealed with delight at the recognition from fans of sawdust. Pride for my line of work swelled my heart. I no longer wanted to join the ranks of the kings and queens of the camera. To see them sufficed. The autographed placard served as a souvenir of my once-upon-a-time dream.

The extraordinary day ended and life transitioned to normal, save for one thing: someone booed Lou. A few days after the gala Star Night, I peeked through the curtain after my portion of come-in, and my attention veered toward a large group at the front track, ring one. The seats around them stood empty. Meanwhile, Lou passed with his faithful Chihuahua to present his Hunting Dog routine. The act progressed well until he "shot" Knuck (Knucklehead).

When his partner rolled down dead, that crowd gave him raspberries. "What was that?" Frosty asked while in full run to join me.

Stunned, I said, "The bunch over there's booing Lou!"

Frosty uttered expletives about PETA and left.

Papa Lou continued until the end of his number. He burst through the curtain, turned to me, and said, "Can't win 'em all."

I ran to the alley to prepare for Opening and told Peggy and Ruthie what had happened. They opened my eyes to the fact that not everyone loved the circus. Extremists, such as People for the Ethical Treatment of Animals (PETA), aimed to stop labor with God's wildlife by any means necessary: bomb threats and protests that involved sharing wrong information with people, for example. As a matter of fact, I remembered several of them had chained themselves to props during one performance with hopes to stop the show. How they accomplished that without detection baffled me. The lack of distinction between right and wrong in the minds of PETA, who was a thorn in the side, astounded my sense of morality.

Preconceived notion of circus abuse caused pandemonium. From my vantage point no mistreatment existed. Respect between man and creature stood mutual on *The Greatest Show on Earth*. Gunther showed consideration for his charges and still stood at risk.

Later when I asked him about the subject, he muttered something in German, then said, "Only a fool vould beat his animal performers, vich creates fear. Ya, ya, I got bit several times, though. They are vild. Trained not tamed."

I harbored their words and continued on, sure that more encounters lay ahead.

When our run in southern California ended, we bound for Oakland to play the same building where my audition had taken place. My spirit burst with pride for the chance to show off this strange, new world to my kin who would attend. That day would belong to me.

CHAPTER ELEVEN

THREADS IN A FABRIC

Tour seasons for Ringling covered more than twenty thousand miles in a two-year period. As a result, troupers who drove jumped at a chance to rest on the train, and those on board earned an opportunity to escape its confines. With that in mind, Billy asked if I wanted to take to the road for the journey north. At that great idea, he spoke to the show's drummer. "Hey, Bobby [Batchelor], need us to drive your Volvo?" Glad to get a break, he handed over the keys.

The next morning, Billy and I threw needed supplies—candy, gum, and more candy—into the car and took off. We headed to the Pacific Coast Highway, which outlined the ocean. The warm, summer breezes and previous three-show days had a lethargic effect. I put my feet on the dashboard and glanced at the hill to my right. Unbeknownst to us, we paralleled the silver slug. Billy honked and I waved, then a tunnel swallowed our mile-long home. We cut over at Santa Cruz to San Jose, and came to rest where my tomorrows began.

As before, we set up and began the run. After I joined *The Greatest Show on Earth*, the die had indeed been cast. My heart belonged to clowning. At the second of three shows on Sunday the entire congregation of the United Methodist Church of Rancho Cordova turned up. I shot outside to greet them, took pictures, and noticed a small group that approached from the left.

With Dad in the lead, my family and longtime friends, Mr. and Mrs. Blair, arrived for the third performance. With a thank you and goodbye to the church, I ran in their direction, grinned with every tooth visible, and hugged them with the strength of self-assuredness that had taken root at the first ooh and aah of opening night in winter quarters. Goodbye timid air force brat. When they followed me down the ramp, their eyes darted this way and that, but there was no time to sightsee. That would happen later.

The best vantage point of my work neared the curtain on the left side of the entrance. So we crossed the track and found their ticketed seats. It was a good location because any action that acknowledged the audience would take place toward their front-track side of the arena. I presented Mom a dozen, long-stem, red roses then left to prepare. We had previously played before eighteen thousand people in the Garden, but a bad case of the jitters settled in my stomach. Would my folks grant a seal of approval?

The performance progressed, and every gag and bit worked well. Once again I donned Garry's outfit and alley-ooped atop my pachyderm. We bolted around the hippodrome floor and halted in front of my relatives. After my topsy-turvy stance for her heave-ho-with-head-to-the-floor maneuver, I glanced at their expressions of horror and thrill. Later I sneaked into the bleachers midway through the show and kneeled where my older sister sat by the aisle.

"Vanita, the next number's called Spec. Kids from the audience join performers." I asked if her daughter and friend could walk in the parade.

"OK!" she answered.

I pointed to the opening in the stands near the track. "I'll meet them there when the lights come up."

When Kit sang about a ride on a teddy bear train, we bounded out and followed floats, horses, elephants, and showgirls. The line of artistes and young invitees stopped and greeted the crowd.

As I waved and watched my sister, I thought, "Thank you for paying my way to Clown College." Of course, I also paid back the cash.

After Finale the scheme to butter them up began with a visit to the women's alley. "This is Ruth Chaddock, Kathy Herb, and Peggy Williams." I hoped to eradicate any negativity toward my vocation because the three women epitomized dedication to a career in greasepaint.

"You remember Tina from Clown College," I said. She wasn't the first little person my parents came across. At the graduation performance, two men shorter than her passed by in a heated conversation flavored with curse words.

They viewed our cloistered section, and we exited. I introduced them to Frosty and, especially, to Papa Lou. Their backstage tour took place at the right time to witness activity behind the scenes: move-out night. Full exposure to sawdust greeted their eyes. They followed close behind in the midst of the show's hurry to get out of town.

"Whew! It stinks," my father commented when we neared the menagerie.

"Oh, that's the elephants, but I don't smell them anymore. I'm used to it."

"Whew! How can you get used to that?"

On past tiger cages, horses, half-naked showgirls, and scroungy working men.

I pointed to the entrance. "That's the back door. If you stand against the wall, you'll get a bird's-eye view of things."

My mother eyeballed the situation. "Is this all right?"

"Yeah. We have permission to be here."

As I said that, the elephants stormed past, led by Gunther. My family jumped back and plastered themselves in place. The herd of wrinkled flesh moved as a huge mass of gray and headed up the ramp for the train.

"I think we'll wait outside," Dad said.

"No, wait a minute. Let's go into the arena to watch them tear down the rigging."

They followed and stopped short.

"Mother cow! It's busy," he said.

"Yeah, there're three hundred people with the show, more or less, and a lot of them are working men. Civilians used to call them roustabouts. Each has an assignment. That's Sal over there pulling on the rope to lower the overhead support network. The green mat under our feet makes the hard surface easier to walk on—for animals and us. It also covers electrical cables that run across."

100

Pieces of apparatus that fell on the floor sounded like hollow metal to concrete. The crew wheeled tilted elephant tubs. In haste they pushed them as one propels a tire—hand over hand. The backstage area erupted in controlled chaos.

"Show props are loaded into those large, wooden boxes," I explained, "and taken to the appropriate wagons." Clowns pushed heavy containers near the ramp for transport. "They'll line all of the trunks up and move them out, too. There goes mine."

My father's interest peaked. "I thought you said the working men did that."

"Some of the clowns help for extra pay. That's called 'cherry pie.'"

"How long does it take for all of this to come down?"

"Believe it or not, in five or six hours it'll be on the train."

"Well, Danise, this is interesting," Mom said, "and different than anything our family has done."

During the tour they met Billy and showed no prejudice due to their accepting outlook and love of God. He did receive, however, a once-over. The visit also included the ins and outs of rail travel. On the way to car number forty-four, I introduced them to Charlie Smith, our trainmaster. He scurried about as the overseer of an operation that rivaled military deployment. He took the time, however, to explain how his team loaded wagons onto flatcars. We stood next to the tracks beside him.

"This is quite an operation," Dad said. He turned toward a worker on a flat (short for flatcar) who blew a whistle. "What are those for?"

"Well, we don't have radios," Charlie said, "so we use the sound-signal system. There's a man in front of the wagon, but he can't be seen. Now, see the guy on the Clark, the red machine that looks like a small tractor? He's pushing a unit with that but can't see what's ahead. So that he'll know when to stop and go, the man in front of the wagon uses whistles: One to go and two to stop. When it's time to back off the flats, he blows three."

"Well, I'll be," said Dad. "Sort of like flying by the instrument panel in bad weather."

The din of the motors that exhaled fumes, the chug-chug of the Clarks, and the precision of the hubbub would impress any Tuskegee Airman.

We bade Charlie goodbye and headed toward my coach, hoisted ourselves up the high steps, and entered. My family couldn't believe the size of my quarters. They crammed inside the little room and listened to my description of get-up-and-go. As I reached to show how a nail secured the cabinets for the run, a roach ran across my mother's lap—then another, and another. She sprang to her feet. The free-range pests infested our moveable home. My feeble attempt to make light of the situation didn't work.

"One crawled into a clown's ear while he slept. He woke and coaxed it out with a flashlight."

Mom reached for the door. "Well, I guess it's time to go!"

They never visited the train again. After the story of the *cucara-chas*, we deserted the room and noticed Tina, who was packing. Unbeknownst to me, she would leave due to problems and not return for a while.

Everyone in the family came for a look. My brother, Robert, arrived by himself and didn't care about the creepy-crawlies. He wanted to join up right then and there at a glimpse of the showgirls. My career choice thrilled my siblings. Mom's fears with regards to sleazy circus people subsided after she witnessed the intensity of our work ethic. Dad saw greasepaint and glitter, not as a stroll from logic, but instead as a trueness to myself. They accepted my life as a clown. All systems go.

They returned home, and we inched our way toward the arena called the Cow Palace in San Francisco. After we arrived at the building, the cast walked the corridors and found our dressing areas. I noticed that both clown alleys sat in an unrestricted space, which meant the public would pass our curtains on the way to their seats. Showtime proved it so, but what an interesting crowd!

Because an organization that promoted gay pride had bought seating for the entire house, some of the performers took offense and removed their kids from the presentation to shield their innocence. Nonetheless, when "doors!" sounded, the procession of spectators began. From time to time, I stuck out my head from behind the curtain for a glimpse. Drag queens, pretty enough to be showgirls, and their dates paraded by. I received a few winks in my boy-like Opening costume and ducked back into our girl-clown sanctuary.

They proved the most enthusiastic viewers that season, especially for Spec. The lights dimmed, and Kathy entered the arena donned in a full-length, multicolored, spangly skirt and an azure sequined top with puffy sleeves. On her back waved little sapphire wings, and her head supported a crown. She walked down the track and stepped onto a small platform. When the spotlight found its mark, she shimmered in the beam. A crew member pushed a button, which lifted Kathy into the air. As she rose she circled her star-shaped wand, and a loud cheer bounced off the walls. The crowd went nuts for the Blue Fairy.

# # #

Portland, Oregon; Seattle, Washington; Salt Lake City, Utah; and Denver, Colorado—the air force full speed ahead couldn't touch circus spunk. Two towns remained on the tour of my introductory year with *The Greatest Show on Earth*. The train sped toward the first with flame in its belly.

"Wake up! Wake up!"

The command yanked me from sleep, and I glanced outside. In the pale moonlight, the trees formed eerie silhouettes like goblins in the night.

Someone thumped on my wall. "Fire! Fire!"

The sound of heavy footsteps filled the hallway. When I hit the floor in my footed pajamas made from flannel and slid open the door, rolls of dense smoke tumbled in.

"What happened?" I thought.

Dancers flew past with rollers in their hair. We scrambled to rescue ourselves from within a coach that had rooms with windows made of forever-shut glass. We stumbled and coughed toward an uninhabited car at one end of our compartments. It was locked. Then we bolted the opposite way to the Pie Car. It was also secured shut. Trapped. We panicked despite no flames.

"Does anybody know Morse code?" Jacqui asked.

"I do."

"Little Bit! Give Danise a flashlight for SOS over the vestibule!"

Dot-dot-dot, dash-dash-dash, dot-dot-dot. But the engineer couldn't see the small beam. The dancers and I sprinted back to the empty cabin. Women fumbled in the thick air for a hammer or other blunt object and banged at the knob of the locked door.

"OK, there's a hole," one of the women said. "Whose arm's small enough to fit through that?"

The undesirable scene of dead showgirls and one clown the next morning prompted Jacqui to grab mine and shove it through. I twisted my hand until I could reach the inside of the door to turn the handle. After the others opened the door with my arm still in place, full of scratches from the wood, I pulled free. We piled into the vacant car, and right away familiarity bred contempt. Curse words spewed from mouths.

Adjacent to our 3' x 6' x 9' roomettes traveled a full-length residence with kitchen, living, and sleeping areas. Word had already spread that the former inhabitants, who ran the Pie Car but misappropriated funds, got the boot. At that occurrence their arrangement remained unoccupied.

We passed through and gawked at the berth's splendor—which included a private donniker—then beat on the next cabin. The technical consultant, Tuffy Genders, answered with a nonchalant, "Yeah, yeah."

Soon, the engines stopped to let another train pass, and the head porter arrived with help. Our trainmaster investigated and discovered that the generator had caused the ruckus. It had blown and fumed up a storm, which sent the pollution our way. He consoled us, but no one wanted to sleep amid smoke. We vacated our little inferno and skedaddled to rooms that belonged to the day's love of our lives.

Technicians fixed the problem, and we continued to Chicago and the International Amphitheatre. The day we arrived, I leaned from the vestibule as the train slowed. Veteran clowns had mentioned that slaughterhouses in full operation stood close by, because our venue had once served as a large meat distribution center. That explained the putrid odor that hung in the air.

The run ended feet from the back door of the building. Since we rested next to it, I waited until after setup, then grabbed the plastic bag that held my clown shoes and headed in. The inside configuration mimicked San Francisco and would allow the spectators free range. Nevertheless, members of our world would cloister behind flimsy, azure fabric draped from poles.

On opening day, dubbed Daley Day in honor of former Mayor Richard J. Daley, I strolled in and out of the crowd near the alley. Folks wandered everywhere. Around the corner, the midway barkers called out. "Breakfast here! Get your circus breakfast here!"—popcorn served Ringling Bros. and Barnum & Bailey style. Townies munched on the puffy, white treat and gazed at trapeze artists in bathrobes and clogs and at clowns without wigs.

I returned to the alley to prepare for Opening. Clothed only in a bra and panties, I glanced from my trunk at a couple who exploded with glee from my side of the blue curtain. "Look honey. This is where they change!"

"Hey, what are you doing in here? This is our dressing room!"

"We wanted to watch the clowns dress," the husband said.

"I bet you did. Get outta here!"

They departed a bit miffed.

I put on my Opening costume, then ran and peeked from the stands. A gentleman rose to the speakers' platform and tapped the microphone. After the audience quieted down, he introduced the dignitaries and members of the mayor's family who sat behind him. What a spectacle! The shorter-than-usual opening show served as a political rally with circus numbers interspersed among speeches.

The next day a group of young African Americans ran in my direction. A little girl goggled and said, "A black clown! I never saw one before." Then they surrounded me. Until then conversation with the public had been sparse. The first time I met a black cowboy, my reaction had mirrored the children's response. He had said more than one-third of the cowboys of the Wild West were African American, and the number remained strong. That fact had amazed me. So, I opened my protected bubble and let the kids in.

"There're three of us in the show."

"Ooh, you're a girl? I thought you were a boy!"

Once again, mistaken identity arose.

"Yeah, girls can be clowns, too. Are you having fun?"

"How'd you get your job?"

The explanation of Clown College and travel on a train around the country cast a spell. They stared in wide-eyed wonder with mouths agape.

"I'm gonna be a clown when I grow up!"

At that moment words emerged to the song in my heart. The "why" of clown became self-evident: inspire ebony dreams of *Yes, I can!*

"You can be whatever you want to be."

After they chattered and shot up the risers to find their seats, I remembered my childhood—one with no role models. The good guys always wore white hats and had white skin. With the emergence of the slaves' kindred into the circus ring, a catchy chance to prove the Establishment wrong existed with the black members of the world of little people, tigers, and wardrobe trunks.

I turned to leave, but a crew member called out. "Danise, you have guests." With him stood my father's cousin and my ninety-three-year-old great aunt. Cousin Sally had driven Aunt Roxie from Gary, Indiana, to witness her first circus. Dressed to the nines in a hat of green lace and a pink coat that swallowed her frame, the woman with an assertive manner looked at me and laughed her head off. The black purse on her arm, the program in one hand, and cotton candy in the other decorated her Sunday-go-to-meeting clothes as ornaments on a Christmas tree.

I conducted a tour behind the scenes, which included permission to pet an elephant's nose. Aunt Roxie squealed with delight, hesitated, and reached to touch the trunk that extended toward her. My visitors reveled in their stroll through my fields. When we approached the stands Sally led the way. Then my great aunt climbed the steps—not weak but sure-footed—and proved the words true: children of all ages.

The busy week climaxed when Billy said, "Danise, I'd like you to meet my family."

I was caught off guard by the whole thing, and wondered, "What would they think of me? Big feet, curly wig, and polka dot clothes—all encased a package tinted brown." Billy had sent a photograph of "Baby D," my persona's name, as a pre-introduction.

I agreed to meet his relatives, and the inevitable day had arrived. As we stood face-to-face, his mother, with her stately Irish features and beaming eyes, said, "Nice to meet you, Danise. We received Billy's picture, and I was shocked. You have blue hair!"

She did not mention my race, but instead opened her arms and engulfed me in welcome. His sisters smiled. We led them on a walkabout that wound near llamas in pens and horses in stalls. All was well, for there was no prejudice. The sun set. The day ended.

By then Billy and I had grown attached to each other. We both embraced the gypsy in our souls. The road of musician for him and air force for me led to a fusion into the largest clan on the planet.

Circus brought people together as threads woven in a fabric. The tapestry of our trail displayed the colors of life, and troupers bonded no matter how you buttered your bread. As a military brat, I had suffered the where-do-I-fit-in syndrome. The misfits born to make one smile had accepted me as a sculptured puzzle piece. How logical!

We Travellers stemmed from the same cloth, and when a rip developed the seams unglued. That is why at the end of the Chicago run, contract day wrenched the ties that bind. The orphan process began in the Windy City and ended in the next town—Nassau, on Long Island, New York—our last stop. At the drop of a hat, a sister arrived or a brother departed. Who would return for the year to come? Why did performers drop off the roster and others remain? No rationale was ever given. To quote a member of the Bulgarian teeterboard: "Mr. Feld say go."

At the conclusion of Clown College, unbeknownst to us, the ride in the car signaled acceptance to the show. Students who stayed at the Villas received no welcome aboard. The same existed on the road; if called to the room, you signed on for another season.

Duane Thorpe, a.k.a. Uncle Soapy, had been a Ringling clown long before Irvin Feld acquired the enterprise. He put his heart and soul into his performance. He understood, however, that young graduates replaced older Joeys. Never mind experience. I stood with a heavy heart next to him as he wrung his hands and voiced, "Hope I make the cut."

One's life's song may be innate, but one's privilege to sing lies in another's hands in our case. Contract day was the worse time to be on *The Greatest Show on Earth*.

By the end of Nassau, only Kathy Herb and I would come back to wear the paint in the women's alley. Many men clowns would not. Uncle Soapy, however, did cut the mustard. Three survived from our Clown College class of 1978: Bucky, Vogie, and me. Tina was long gone. After the holidays, we would walk through the red steel doors no longer First of Mays.

We packed our trunks for the last time that year. I said a final goodbye to Ruth Chaddock, my circus sister, and repeated the same to Peggy Williams, who had warned in winter quarters, "Save your energy, Danise. It's going to be a long season."

I stepped outside the blue curtain. Many artistes took their leave and stowed their paraphernalia in silence. Ringling's human collection that held the key to a world of magic treaded with heavy footsteps. What a travesty of justice to have your mission yanked from under you! Billy drove me to the airport, and I flew home for Christmas to rest for the storm that brewed. See ya down the road.

## CHAPTER TWELVE

END OF THE LINE

I bounded up the steep steps of coach number forty-four and entered the lifeless shaft. "Where is everybody?"

One of the showgirls exited her cabin at the end of the corridor.

"Hey, Judy, how was your Christmas?" I asked.

"Actually, I stayed and killed the roaches."

"How in the world did you do that?"

"With boric acid in the halls, the kitchen, the donnikers, and everyone's room. The head porter had a master key to all the locks. Hope you don't mind."

So much for security, but at least the need to bury myself in the sleeping bag no longer existed. No more pests would stroll across my face in the night. What a relief! I opened my door. "Hello, good ole hole-in-the-wall." The small compartment had become the container of my dreams that fit snug in the cubbyholes. I put away my stuff and jumped from the vestibule to saunter to the building.

"Hi, Danise."

"Tina!"

It had been awhile. She had left the show several times last season and lost her job. Disappointment in my friend had surfaced. Life unveiled color discrimination, but Tina had opened my eyes to a society also ignorant of size. Offers of employment lay out of her reach, as did the cabinets in her quarters on the train, countertops at fast-food joints, and the knobs in the large, communal showers, which prompted my help. Our fight against the powers that be had drawn us together.

"Are you going to the building? What's that?" Tina asked.

"Yeah, I'm gonna walk. Oh, this is for my new gag. It's a punching bag. I'm gonna see if I can get it in the show."

My little sister persevered with me during Clown College. We had been through so much at each other's side. But when she up and left, I convinced myself that her absence spared me from nanny duty.

Words faded into an awkward moment of silence. We both knew that those in charge would not allow her into the building without a job. Had she returned to reclaim her ground?

"I just wanna make it. I wanna prove I can do something," she had said the first day of school. But her personal conflicts overpowered ambition. She stared at the logo on the side of the coach. The corners of her mouth turned upward, but her gaze cast downward. Her countenance said it all. We hugged and walked in different directions. I never saw Tina Stotts again.

Down the gravel road, across the little bridge, stood the arena. I ran through the steel doors and into the building that buzzed with new-season activity. Billy waved from the bandstand, then greeted me with a kiss. Hellos from returnees carried my footsteps to girl clown alley where I sat by my trunk and fiddled in it until the curtain opened. In came another little person. "Hi," she said. "I'm Janna Townsend." Her face lit up and words flavored with a southern twang tumbled from her mouth. "I'm as happy as a pig in mud ta be here." When Tim called the troupe to the ring curb for introductions, we walked together and sat down.

I smiled at a broader band of the rainbow because the Felds had hired more than ten African American showgirls, which swelled the number of blacks. In fact fresh talent shone everywhere. The personification of Uncle Soapy's fears stood before me as well: bright-eyed, bushy-tailed, nervous, replacement Joeys from my alma mater of laughter.

I glanced at Janna, who fidgeted. "Tim's gonna introduce each group. We circle the ring and shake hands. That's how we get to know everyone." She followed behind me for the presentations, which served to receive us home. "Hi, Danise!" sprang from tight lips of the true-blue circus of last year who never spoke to me. They had wanted First of Mays to cut the mustard before accepting us, or so the rumor.

We would travel to different towns, which were not on last season's tour, and present the same program. Over the next few days, we brushed up production numbers, and the bosses filled vacancies of those not rehired. I coveted a great spot for a clown: inside a gypsy caravan. In the past the role belonged to Ruthie.

With one year under my belt and a love of greasepaint life, I approached Tim Holst, the performance director.

"Tim, how about me as the gypsy in the wagon?"

"I don't know, Danise. It's a solo, ya know. Menage opens with it in the light . . ."

"I used to watch Ruthie last year, and I know what to do midway down the track. No need to coach."

He spoke to the management team, who weighed the odds behind closed doors, and later that week they granted the request. In time Don Foote and Mel Cabral resized the twenty-five pound, multi-layered, pink costume to my measurements—which included the enlarged bodice of Nerf balls and a head cover that dangled faux, gold coins. And my feet poised ready to dance in clown footwear.

The first day of the dry run, I clumped-clumped in the passageway toward the vehicle of wandering souls that beckoned and stopped one foot away. It resembled those on the roadside long ago in Ireland—same shape, different shade. Topped with a curved, blue roof, the rose-colored carriage bowed out from the base. Flower boxes hung outside the painted windows.

I climbed the steps in the back and opened the door to a musty odor of discarded props and dirty horse blankets. A crew member shut me in. We waited. When an upbeat melody drifted from the band, the two ponies lunged forward. The gentle sway of the cabin mocked the interior of a ship at sea, and the attached lantern hit the sides in tempo. I judged our location according to the music, and midway down the track my sonata began.

I stuck my oversized oxford out the door first, then my face. We proceeded around the circumference of the arena floor and came to rest in the center ring. My exit from the caravan signaled the entrance for the elephants who bolted down the hippodrome track. Three stormed into ring two as I pirouetted to the ring curb.

Ever dance with a pachyderm?
The floor doth shake and your heart doth quake.

I improvised a tarantella. A twirl here and there of my skirt accompanied the rhythm of my tambourine. I belonged to the gypsy life and disappeared into the moment. My soul surrendered to elation. In other words—ah, the life of Riley!

#

Before the 1980 season started, the Felds switched Frosty to the Blue Unit. He worked Venice, however, to help the new boss clowns—Chucko, from the Fruit Vendor gag, and Kenzo—get on their feet. One morning I dragged my punching-bag equipment from the alley to practice. Fellow clowns buzzed past with their props, and showgirls sashayed toward the Pie Car, Jr. While I set down my stuff, Chucko and Kenzo approached. "Hey," Chucko said. His ever-present smile underscored mischievous eyes. His mannerisms mimicked Frosty's—his hero—so he stood with feet apart and put his hands in his pockets.

"We took out your gag."

"Yesterday, it was in. How come?"

"Yeah, well—it's not good enough. It's gonna be a replacement, see."

As a matter of fact, after they nipped here and there, only the production numbers remained. The ability to measure up permeated this daughter of a Tuskegee Airman. So I marched off in search of Papa Lou. He gave his heart to my development.

"Well, let's see your bit again," he said. We painted a face onto the inanimate bag on the pole to represent a ghost and covered it with a sheet. "Yank dat off and fight!"

With one punch it sprang to life and danced with Lou, who dodged and ducked. "Do it like me, and you'll be all right, see;

otherwise, it's shpaghetti (his pronunciation of the pasta)." His advice always inspired. Practice filled any downtime.

No reason surfaced to my knowledge why, but on opening night my gag returned to come-in. I sprinted into the arena, set my props outside ring three, turned around, and faced empty tracks—save for me. At the far end in ring one, the alley presented the loud Boxing gag. Behind me the crew set cat wagons with tigers that roared. The audience streamed in and paid no never mind to my efforts. But my gag was in.

Time in winter quarters drew to a close, and I joined Janna on move-out night. We packed our trunks and rode the bus to the train. "Wanna see my home?" she asked. "I can reach things."

She didn't inherit Tina's room but received a different one. Curiosity drove me to accept, and we climbed the steps to her car and trudged down the corridor. She opened the door and everything stood short. Maybe the Felds took Tina's struggles into consideration and thus scaled down the new quarters. Her cabinets hung at my waist; the bed reached mid-calf. Janna Townsend did not replace Tina Stotts.

Late into the night the train lunged, and we started the forty-nine city Rodeo Route—so called due to the two- and three-day stands similar to a cowboy circuit. Public relations followed every bend in the tracks. In Atlanta, Georgia, showgirls Cynthia and Leslie and clowns Skeeter, Garry, and I crossed the street from the building to Craddock Elementary School.

The principal greeted with a cheery "Hello, follow me." He led us to the cafeteria. When we stepped inside, pandemonium broke— giggles, cheers, and clapping. African American children, who sat in chairs placed in neat rows, lost their cool. We stood in a line on the stage, and hands flew up.

"Ooh! How did you become a clown?"

"How do you eat?"

Questions rained like never before, and we opened their eyes to another world of possibilities.

"You live on a train?"

"You dance in the air?"

Garry produced illusions to the eye through the marvels of magic. I juggled, and the dancers explained pirouettes from on high. The name of the facility where I had worked and learned of Clown College came to mind. "What child never made a trip to Fairytale Town where imaginations flew?"

Skeeter tied everything together. He had ridden with the basketball-playing King Charles Troupe of unicyclists—the first black contingent to grace Ringling's rings. We sat on the sidelines while he picked up his wheel, placed it underneath him, and paused. He looked at the students and took in a breath of air through his large, red nose that covered a third of his face. It collapsed and expanded, and the children exploded with laughter.

"I need a volunteer," he said. A sea of ebony arms rose, and an eager boy shot to the stage. "You're not afraid of heights, are you?"

"Nope. I'm not scared of anything!"

"OK, climb onto my shoulders and hold on."

They rode in circles with the child up top, who grinned and displayed every chopper. Afterward the boy shinnied down, took a bow, and returned to his seat. And the Clown College alumnus zipped once more. When he did so, his spirit transferred into his unicycle, which quickened the circle of rubber beneath. In full spin the definition between his legs and wheel blurred. Symbiosis. While the pro jumped rope on the cycle, I glanced at the children in the lunch hall and rebuked the naysayers of history. The revealed wonders of the life of deep-brown circus performers captivated the kids and proved *no* barriers surrounded African American youth.

Our program ended. To have belted the official song of the National Association for the Advancement of Colored People (NAACP), which had become the Negro National Anthem, would have been appropriate. Its words rang with victory over defeat and resounded hope instead of despair. For our performance at the school lifted each student's heart.

The 1980 hop-skip-and-a-jump stands continued with Savannah, Georgia, and Asheville and Fayetteville, North Carolina. Once again we passed through the cradle of the Civil War. I paced myself due to the itinerary, but I grew tired easier and caught colds often. I even had one for more than a month.

We chugged toward our next town—Raleigh, North Carolina—where Opening shouted a rainy, cold, and miserable welcome. A cure for the sniffles would have to wait. As the bus approached the building, everyone sat silent at the sight of plastic draped from the roof. "This is going to be rough," Billy said. We sloshed into the dark arena and learned the sheets conducted rainwater away, which would prevent it from dumping onto our heads. The show progressed without flaw around God's tears that fell.

During Clown College, Lou told us that in the era of the big top, circus personnel had bathed out of a bucket. Nowadays, the lifestyle had progressed to indoor plumbing. In Raleigh, the privilege involved a descent into darkness. Janna and I gathered our stuff after each performance and walked to an opening in the floor. A wooden, rickety staircase, lit by a single light bulb hung on a cord from the ceiling, led to the basement with the showers. We peered into the abyss and proceeded down the few steps. Our bare footfall echoed in the large, communal bath cells as we scoped it out for intruders. When I turned on the water, the nozzle rained liquid ice onto our skin. We soaped, rinsed, and dried in record time. The spooky enclosure and the freezing spray burned Raleigh, North Carolina, into my memory.

In subsequent weeks the abundance of newspaper and television interviews developed a skill needed in years to come. Everyone did his or her share. Garry White earned a nomination to Who's Who in Black America.

I exited the bus one Friday morning, and Tim Holst handed me a sheet of white paper. "Danise, here's your PR [public relations] promotion notice for the week." I took and read it on the way to the alley.

Ringling Bros. and Barnum & Bailey Circus Press Representatives
Publicity appointment from Ann-Marie
To Danise Wilson
   This will confirm your appointment with Fannie & Mr. Brooks of Ebony magazine.

Date: Friday, April 4, 1980
Time: 1:30
Place: DC Armory
Comments: This will be an interview and photo session for Ebony magazine.

I bolted on a wisp of air to a phone and squealed the news to my family. *Ebony* magazine! The prestigious journal boasted international readership with topics of interest to the black community. Its articles proved the African diaspora left footprints in time. *Ebony* helped shape my youth with pictures and historical accounts that reflected me, while television presented beauty and purpose in a package of blond hair and blue eyes. The first show wafted by. Afterward I waited by my trunk.

Soon Tim escorted two individuals to the girl clowns and called my name. After introductions he left, and the three of us held small talk. E. Fannie Granton looked here and there and asked, "What would be a good location for the interview, Danise?"

I thought a moment, then they followed me out of the alley.

On tented shows, working men threw what townies knew as sawdust inside the ring for cover. It was actually tanbark—shredded bark of trees after the extraction of tannin. Its use forever connected it to the world of the circus. I looked around. A perfect symbol of the circus circuit—a.k.a. tanbark trail—rested near the wall. We walked toward it.

"How about here?"

She smiled and sat on the elephant tub.

"The title of the feature will be 'Clowning Around for a Living.' Readers will want to know how you became a clown."

Questions flew. "How do you describe your lifestyle?" "What do you do for fun?" "Does your schedule allow leisure?" For two hours she logged answers onto a notepad. Afterward, I served as tour guide in the empty arena and pointed to this and that. At showtime my makeup removed with ease with baby oil, only to be reapplied for photos by Mr. Brooks. "Walk into the arena, Danise, and we'll take pictures of what happens next."

I peeked through the curtain at the public on the floor and grimaced at what would take place. Not one usher anywhere; nonetheless, my big feet led the way. Children of every hue rushed for a touch. After twenty minutes, rolls of film preserved the moment. Backstage, Garry and Skeeter joined us for a picture in front of the prop for the Firehouse gag.

By the end of the two-day interview, the writer had collected enough information to fill a small book. Thanks to the eye of the camera, the black community would see into the world of greasepaint and sequins. "You'll have to wait on the article, however. We're not sure when it'll appear. That's up to the editor." They stayed and watched the show, then said their goodbyes.

I coasted through move-out night, and after teardown we left Washington, D.C. Miles trudged by in the wake of anticipation. Each month after the *Ebony* interview, I ran to stores and turned pages of the magazine from cover to cover in hopes of the story. Not yet. Not yet.

After work one day in Jackson, Mississippi, the ritual repeated with a brisk walk to a local shop. I entered and found the periodicals lined on shelves. My quest stood out, thanks to the partial, bold, white letters EBO encased in a red rectangle. A full-face, cover photograph of the model Beverly Johnson hid the remainder of the title. I thumbed through the July 1980 issue and partway revealed, "Clowning Around for a Living: Danise Wilson Joins 'Greatest Show on Earth' as Black Woman Clown." What a sight! Me in living color.

The piece showcased pictures of come-in, walkarounds, Garry and Skeeter, and me on the ring curb during Menage. I grabbed ten editions, shot to the register, paid, and dashed to the building. Alexander Graham Bell's invention carried my words to my family: "It's here!"

The Johnson Publication shone, save for some erroneous information. I never acted or sang at Universal Studios as stated, and I never lived in Paris or Germany. But that didn't matter. The integrity of an *Ebony* feature eradicated the wounds of childhood and put me on the map.

Billy planned a celebration dinner in our next town, New Orleans. We pulled into the Big Easy and performers vacated the train to explore. We headed to The French Quarter with its narrow streets and old buildings that captivated my vivid imagination. Ghosts of pirates and voodoo princesses brushed past as we ate the powdered sugar beignets that morning at Café du Monde. At dusk, Billy, friends, and I headed to the notable Commanders Palace restaurant where the black waiters honored us with a tour. That gesture of welcome opened the doors to the home of the syncopated beat of Dixieland jazz music.

The following day, Billy and I stepped into the Superdome that would house us for the run. We stopped short and gawked. How the size overwhelmed! It dwarfed all previous structures, including Madison Square Garden. Information revealed the inverted bowl covered thirteen acres and stood 273-feet tall. Since the edifice sat approximately seventy-two thousand people compared to The Garden's eighteen thousand, the circus would perform only on one segment of the massive surface.

On our walk to find the band room and girls' alley, we stopped and observed on the sidelines as the crew enclosed rings one, two, and three with bleachers. Such placement sectioned off the leftover floor. They also hung a black curtain to shield the performers from townie eyes. Afterward Billy headed for the musicians, and I trekked to the summit of the Superdome's stands and peered at elephants below that resembled a row of raisins that swayed in tempo.

My spirit soared thanks to the boost in self-worth from *Ebony*, and the towns that followed brushed by as an idle fancy. In Glens Falls, New York, the building nestled in silence, surrounded by pine trees and sunshine. The show continued as usual until one day when the cry "clowns!" curdled the blood and shattered the stillness as a rock to glass. The band burst into a number I no longer remember and the song, reserved for such an occasion, packed a wallop.

Kathy, who rested with her three dogs, sprang from her chair. "Come on, Danise. Let's go! Something's happened on the floor. We have to distract attention from whatever it is. Grab a prop!"

Without hesitation she grasped Thysbe, her smallest canine, while the other two, Panda and Zeke, sat upright. Kathy shot toward the blue curtain and bolted into the hall. I jumped, snatched three juggling balls, and peeked out. Clowns ran helter-skelter toward the proscenium with me close behind.

The hubbub of voices disclosed that Pedro and Luis had fallen from the high wire.

We dashed because, in circus history, diversion from an emergency in the arena rested on funny peoples' shoulders. The crew had turned on the house lights, which revealed our turnaway show. We ran in and spaced ourselves up and down the track. We exploded cigars and juggled clubs and balls, for example, in order to render the scene less of a threat. The spectators, however, strained their necks to gawk at the two who had lost the battle of defiance with their tease of death.

Thank God the safety net hung in that town; elsewhere, it didn't. We learned that the strands of knotted cord had caught Luis. Pedro had bounced off and required the emergency team. As they rushed him away, the announcer said, "Ladies and gentlemen, Pedro Carrillo is on his way to the Glens Falls' hospital and will be leaving with the rest of the circus this evening. His partner Luis Posso is unhurt. Thank you."

Pedro remained after we left, however. The company marked time, and several towns down the road, breathed a sigh of relief when the Carrillo Brothers tickled the sky with their toes once more. I spoke with Pedro after he came home. "When you fall, you have to go back up," he said, "or fear will take over." If that happened, one would never walk on air again. "It's my life, so I'll go up." And he did.

Another bump in the road hit mid-season. A few clowns skedaddled. Even Janna left. I was sorry to see Lenny Wolen go. "I'm going on tour with Carol Channing in a show called *Sugar Babies.*"

He had advised me during the New York City run to sign up with Screen Actors Guild (SAG). "Have your circus contract with you. Since AGVA's your parent union, you'll get in for half price. You never know when you'll need 'em for film work—better protection and more pay."

I followed his advice and joined the association of professionals for three hundred dollars.

The show didn't skip a beat despite those who left, some without notification—called "pull a creep"—others who forewarned. No matter. If needed, students who had passed through the hallowed halls of the funniest university on earth would arrive to fill in the blanks. The deans had taught that "clowns are pegs to hang the circus on," a phrase attributed to P. T. Barnum himself. Thanks to Clown College and practical application, we who knew how to time a pants-drop carried on.

I had become the first in my family with such a career, and I loved the vocation. The end of my second year neared, and Clown Car presented a chance to demonstrate development and to justify a renewed contract. A switch from the rope used to pull my horse from the vehicle to a riding crop proved more logical for a jockey, in my estimation. I didn't ask to make the simple swap, however. Mistake.

The day of my ingenuity arrived. We piled into the car and zoomed around the track at the usual breakneck speed, then into the ring. The door opened and out bounded clown number one. In turn I crawled out without the tether, trotted the circumference, and hit my fanny with the flexible whip. I approached the Datsun and motioned for my faux stallion to exit.

Kenzo, one of the two boss clowns, sauntered over. "What a ya doin', Danise?"

"Pretty neat, huh? I thought of this myself!"

"You're not supposed to change the choreography. Where's the rope?"

So much for initiative. Protocol also prohibited idle conversation in the ring. So, I took off.

"Who do you think you are? I'm your boss clown—Hey! Come back here."

Too late. A gallop carried me away with my scruffy, two-person equine on a chase of the absurd with Kenzo in close pursuit. After

Clown Car ended, the two bosses called a meeting with Tim Holst and me.

"What were you thinking, Danise?" Tim asked. "You didn't consider the flow of things. You're a lazy clown. How can I trust you in the ring or what you say in interviews?"

"What?"

I reminded him that I volunteered as a unicyclist, begged for the gypsy role, and worked hard on gags. "I'm gung-ho and talk up about the show for the media, remember *Ebony*?"

How did a riding crop produce such a tongue-lashing? The unbelievable accusations flew as rocks from a slingshot. When it came right down to it, no matter my defense, serious trouble would follow. Had they trapped me as a rabbit in a snare? Mr. Holst requested a written explanation within forty-eight hours. My inner self always buckled when face-to-face with those in control. Tim's barrage sucked the wind from my sails, and I floated lifeless on a sea of tears.

"Try to be calm, Danise. You're OK," Billy said.

Two days elapsed, and Tim acted like nothing happened. In fact he ceased acknowledgement of my existence. The invisibility that I desired as a child caught up with the adult me. And I walked as if made of cellophane.

One month of towns later, we pulled in to Champaign, Illinois. Close by in Rantoul, the performing bug had bitten me at the age of seven. After the riding crop debacle, a visit to the familiar ground of Chanute Air Force Base would have spelled relief, but time flew by.

City after city, life showed its wit at the art of constriction. In Indianapolis the dam broke again, but not with me that time. The lights shone full and bright, and the cast bounced onto the track during Menage one evening only to witness one of Gunther's crew receive a beating next to ring three. He hit back. "My tooth!" rang out from the assailant, which made another man mad. Person number three grabbed an elephant guide (called "bull hook" by townies) and took off after the first guy. It required four men to pull them apart. Meanwhile, the entire troupe styled to the King of the Gypsies, Gunther Gebel-Williams, yet strained our necks to watch the fight.

Tempers boiled and blew the top off the pot of fun and fantasy. The steam exploded when contracts took place. Tim carried out his end-of-the-year mission as escort for those to return, and his footsteps approached the girls' alley. He called out, "Kathy Herb and Bernie (the First of May girl clown), come with me."

I waited as they took the walk. The clock ticked. My turn to sweat. By the end of the day, the Felds had not called "Danise," which resulted in a perfect execution of the tablecloth pull.

Our mentors taught the sight gag in Clown College. Plates and cups stood erect on a cover over a table. A passerby yanked it away. As with the cloth, the Felds jerked the ground from under me.

My corner of the sky had folded. "This is what I was going to do for the rest of my life." My stomach rumbled. My breath shortened. My knees trembled. One question needed an answer: Why had my time with Ringling ended?

In a fog I exited the alley, turned, and trudged toward the meeting room to pull rhyme or reason from the nonsensical. With each step, sobs of sadness transformed into a salty manifestation of defiance and fear. That which required all my power lurked ahead: confrontation with authority. In the blink of an eye, my destination lay before me, surreal. Knock, knock. Someone opened the door after a moment or two.

"I would like to speak to Mr. Feld." The door closed, then reopened. I had wanted to talk with the father, but the son came instead. "What happened? Why wasn't I hired back?"

"I don't know, Danise." Exasperation veiled his face.

He could cite no reason for the cut, and at that point the quest to remain with *The Greatest Show on Earth* grew into a lesson in futility. The younger Feld stood aloof with crossed arms. I grasped his hand.

No one mentioned in Clown College what to do when your universe implodes, when your contract is not renewed. A cornucopia of thoughts about my dream of passion swirled within my head. The following words to the man whom I, in error, believed controlled my future summed it up: "Thanks for my two years, for there was nothing more I wanted to be than a clown with Ringling Bros. and

Barnum & Bailey Circus." I turned and left and wanted to spew the day from my gut.

Self-assurance rose after the *Ebony* feature a few months earlier. Who knew ink from pens—or lack of it—could also dry the bones?

My walk in the corridor led to the blue curtain. I peeked past it at Billy, who sat at the empty bandstand. He approached, and we stood face-to-face but said nothing. An unspecified person had told him the news. It was move-out night, and the overhead rigging rained about us. The crew flew past, wheeling elephant tubs up and out into the night. We walked into the hall where clowns performed cherry pie and pushed trunks into wagons. We observed the goings-on, then locked eyes. "I'm gonna stay on the show, Danise, for a bit," he said.

I loved the world of sawdust. But the lifestyle crashed as a payload from a B-52 bomber. What to do? Two towns remained in the season to find a solution: Cleveland, Ohio, and Nashville, Tennessee—the end of the line.

There stood Garry White, a vagabond of a higher class!

The Chandler family of Great Glemham, England.

Uncle Fred of Great Glemham proved the king of the Hula-Hoop.

Fairytale Town where imaginations flew.

An escapee from the world of cartoons: our Clown College bus.

For words of clown wisdom, Papa Lou Jacobs.

Pie-throwing class. Yech! Shaving cream!

Bobby Kay encouraged us in makeup class. "Shut up and put that shit on!"

With the help of the handlers, alley-oop in elephant riding class.

Girl clown alley of 1979: Peggy, Ruthie, Kathy, Tina, and me.

Gunther Gebel-Williams walked larger than life.

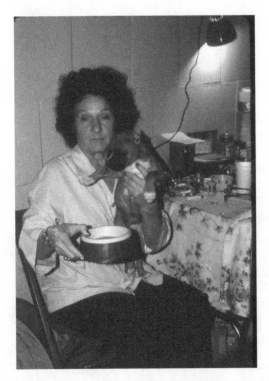

A tired wardrobe mistress Ellen ben-Said, a.k.a. Miss Ellen, a.k.a. Mama.

Fruit Vendor gag. "Hey, where's my cabbage?"

First of Mays of The Greatest Show on Earth, Red Unit 1979.

We do-si-doed on one wheel. I'm third from the left.

Painting the train.

With his silver chalice, our chaplain blessed each car for a safe journey.

Danny Kaye and friend.

Horses taking a break during a water stop.

I met a big-hearted, happy soul in Red Skelton.

The man in the white baseball-style hat was Charlie Smith our trainmaster.

Of all the souls there, Jimmy Stewart was a real star.

I fondly called our circus train the silver slug.

That's Sal over there lowering the rigging.

Uncle Soapy, a.k.a. Duane Thorpe.

Elephants alley-oop to long mount during Menage.

Billy and The L.A. Circus band.

With Bob Zraick, hilarity rose to a higher plain on The L.A. Circus.

Gerry Cottle, the modern-day P.T. Barnum.

Our mobile, billboard truck let folks know who we were.

The door to one of six school shows a day for Gerry Cottle's Circus.

"Ladies and gentlemen, the Queen!" Alias Elizabeth Richard.

Cal, Margo, me, Zeke, Garry, Ron, and Ivan of UniverSoul Big Top Circus.

Aurora's stage name was Nayakata. She was pure poetry of pretzel.

UniverSoul Big Top Circus clowns of 1994.

Sawdust and glitter took a back seat to Rosa Parks.

In our backyard, lobsters had soul.

"Don't they have motorized stake pounders now?" George Coronas Circus.

One-third of our home on the circus train 2002.

Me and Sad Sack, the Wonder Dog of Ringling Bros.
and Barnum & Bailey Circus.

CHAPTER THIRTEEN

THERE'S LIFE AFTER RINGLING

My spirit slumped because of my belief that apart from sawdust and elephants, there was no life. I returned home with my fine-tuned funny bone and dealt with the post-traumatic shock of a collapsed world. The protective shell of childhood resurfaced and trapped me indoors, safe from questions about Ringling. Three months passed before I sought and found work: tax return sorter with the Internal Revenue Service in a warehouse from midnight until 4:00 a.m.

The daylight hours lingered, and the tube eased my mind. The phone rang one afternoon and broke the din of televised words in a fake domain. I answered it, and his voice carried through. "Hi, sweetie. It's me. I'm coming to Sacramento." The year that was did not sever our love.

Our tomorrow began when Reverend Hirschfeld, the pastor who favored Fred Flinstone, spoke. "Do you, William Anthony Payne, take this woman to be your wife?"

"I do."

"Do you, Danise Lenora Wilson, take this man to be your husband?"

"I do.

"Where you go I will go, and where you stay I will stay. Your people will be my people," we both quoted from the Book of Ruth.

On July 18, 1981, in the tiny church in Rancho Cordova, Billy and I became one. Afterward we packed our orange Datsun 510 and pointed it toward New York City for come what may.

We arrived on the East Coast and drove onto the Verrazano-Narrows Bridge. To the left of Billy through the window stood Lady Liberty in the distance. Beyond her the tall concrete edifices of Manhattan took advantage of my lack of experience with the grandiose. We crossed into Brooklyn and toward the Fort Greene section of the city where the top floor of a seamless row of homes, called brownstones, served as our residence. We possessed a bed, a card table, and two chairs—gifts from my aunt Margaret—and lived with mice, a hole in the middle of the floor, and the ability to peer through the bottomless fireplace into the apartment below.

Billy secured employment at the Thirty-Fourth Street branch of Macy's department store with me at the Brooklyn facility. Those jobs paid the bills, but it would take something bigger and better than *The Greatest Show on Earth* to rescue me from rejection.

One day a still, small voice illuminated an idea. With nothing to lose, I donned my one and only suit, boarded the subway, which propelled me into Manhattan, and marched to the United Nations. A guard set me in the right direction. "The recruiting division's across the street in that high-rise building." I thanked him then headed to the other side of First Avenue.

Inside the nondescript structure, the receptionist with stiff hair pointed the way to my request: the guided tours unit. "The hiring process is in full swing at the moment," she said. Good timing. After I stepped through the appropriate door, a woman clothed in a paisley dress granted an on-the-spot interview. She discussed basic generalities and asked why I could serve the Secretariat, which administered the policies and programs of the institution.

"Mrs. Payne, you have answered well, and you are enthusiastic about working for the United Nations. There will be two more question-and-answer sessions, and the requirements to carry on are a bachelor of arts in any subject and the ability to speak two languages. Are you able to meet those prerequisites?"

How about that. My trip through college had not taken place for sheer formality. Plus, relief set in that the juggling on the quad didn't put the skids on graduation.

"Yes. I have a bachelor of arts in French, special studies in consecutive and simultaneous interpretation."

"Good. We will need your high school and university diplomas, the latter with your degree. If you pass the interrogations, there will be an extensive background check. Are you willing to continue?"

"Yes, ma'am, and I have my certificates and can send for copies of the transcripts."

"Very well then. The remainder of the meetings will be conducted in French. I'm going to schedule one for today."

It had been five years since the romantic language rolled from my tongue, and my mind flipped like a good teeterboard act.

"Oh, I actually have another appointment in an hour," I lied.

"OK, let's see." She searched the engagement book and found a time slot. "There is an opening next week. Will that period be suitable?"

"Yes, that will be fine."

I left thankful. But I returned home, found my college books—beginner and advanced—combed from cover to cover, and read out loud. Learn-to-speak-French tapes from the library drew five years of repressed memory to the surface and unveiled the vocabulary within. After repetitions with the recorded instructor day and night, I stood ready to strengthen my weak knees.

The other cross-examinations took place in the impressive facility of the world organization, which bordered the East River. I arrived early on the scheduled day dressed in the same suit, descended the stairs to the basement of a building called the General Assembly, and sat in one of the four chairs in the hallway by a room to await my turn. A door opened, and the interviewee before me exited and shook her head.

"Oh, my God," she said. "Are you next?"

"Yes, why?"

"Get ready because he begins in English but switches to French mid-sentence, and it threw me off."

"Thanks for the warning."

After she continued down the corridor in tears, a Caucasian man with cropped, sandy-blond hair peeked out and called my name. As

I entered and sat down he said, "Hello. I'm Kevin Kennedy, training and briefing officer."

He wore a dark business suit and took his seat in the gray, barren space and reviewed my application.

"Tell me about your job as a guide at Universal Studios, Mrs. Payne."

"We conducted three-hour tours for people from all over the globe and explained the process of moviemaking, which included camerawork illusions and sound effects."

His gaze centered on my face; then, out of the blue it happened. He didn't blink or hesitate. In French he asked, "Could you explain the difference between the policies of President Francois Mitterand of France and those of President Ronald Reagan?" I remained silent for a moment and tried to formulate an answer, but a lot of nothing swam through my mind. The only logical response: "*Non.*"

He smiled and said, "If you had guessed, your process would have ended. Because of your honesty the final dialogue will take place immediately in the adjacent office."

Mr. Takashi Endo from Japan, chief supervisor, and Mme Eliane Freeman from France, chief of the guided tours unit, greeted me as I entered and handed over my forms and resume. Mme Freeman looked at my paperwork and said, "*Ah! Vous parlez francais!*" Pause. "*Vous etes clown?*"

For a half hour, life as a circus clown took center stage. Answers flowed with ease due to the crash course. On my birthday in 1982, I received a formal letter of appointment as a tour guide in the Public Information Services of the United Nations. After that extensive background check, in mid-March a request arrived "to report to the Information Desk in the Visitors' Entrance to the General Assembly Lobby" to begin my "tour of duty" with the Secretariat. Far removed from greasepaint. One year and a half had elapsed since Big Bertha, and with that appointment I *knew* life existed after Ringling.

I stood with twenty-three guides from eleven countries hired that year. We represented twenty-eight nationalities with me, once again, as the only African American. In the three-week training period, we learned the entire history of the institution: its beginnings, structure, protocol, and functions of the various organs and agencies. Each day Mr. Kennedy briefed on world situations.

I arrived in the morning, headed to the locker room, and donned a deep-blue uniform and heels. The arm band signified my victory over assassination of spirit: Nations Unies/United Nations. My tours in French and English led the public of many nationalities through four chambers within the building and dealt with volatile situations. The state of affairs that concerned me the most existed in Namibia in the southwestern region of Africa. Under the stranglehold of South Africa, its independence stood crucial due to the system of apartheid, the strict racial segregation against nonwhites—especially blacks.

The stench in God's nostrils, called racism, held its ground on the continent of my forefathers. Caucasian visitors from that region spoke with violence in favor of that evil system. I found it difficult to remain neutral throughout the tours, which resulted in a battle of wits.

Namibia won its authorized independence from South Africa on March 21, 1990.

Thanks to the mobility of military life, I had developed an interest in the world. A glimpse into the mosaic called humanity continued during my employment. I learned through the other guides how symbiotic we are as a species. After work we experienced each other's cultures. Those from China led us to Chinatown for authentic meals. We dined with the Israelis on dumplings called matzo balls that floated in broth and learned the meaning of *shalom*. Fellow employees from Japan, Sierra Leone, and Egypt accompanied me to soul food restaurants and ate collard greens and chitterlings dubbed "chitlins." The fellowship among guides demonstrated humans could get along, but the daily briefings gave insight into the destruction of self that invaded man's time. One can't compare the United Nations with *The Greatest Show on Earth*. They occupied opposite ends of a pole. Each reflected, however, features of the human race: the United Nations, the art of hate; the circus, the aptitude to laugh.

#

The job presented a great opportunity, but New York City exploded with entertainment arts. Oh, to perform! Thankful Lenny Wolen had advised membership in SAG, I pounded the pavements of Broadway on my time off to pursue film and theater.

One of those days, I strolled up to a sidewalk vendor who sold a variety of periodicals that lined his three-sided stand and asked, "You got anything that tells about auditions?" He grumbled and pointed to a newspaper. The title *Back Stage* gave away what lay inside. I opened it and glanced at the notifications of the when and where of who casted what. Satisfied, I paid and would buy up-to-date issues as needed.

Weeks later a notice caught my eye: "Needed for casting director Sylvia Fay—Screen Actors Guild background performers (also called 'extras')." The morning of the call, I dressed in casual attire and sneakers. With my 8" x 10" headshot and a list of my show experiences on a sheet of paper taped to the back, I headed out the door. The D train sped me into the city, and a transfer to the number one train deposited me at my destination.

A crowd of hopefuls stretched down the street, around a building, and inched forward as cows toward a barn. The cattle call required half a day to reach the door. We entered single file. The directors sat behind rows of tables that displayed placards with their names. "Drop your pictures and resumes into the containers," they said. No audition required.

My homework had uncovered that Ms. Fay had casted such projects as *Taxi Driver* with Robert De Niro. I made a beeline for her, held my information over the box, and shook her hand. "Hi, Ms. Fay. My name is Danise Wilson-Payne. I was a clown with Ringling Bros. and Barnum & Bailey Circus. I can juggle, and ride a unicycle and an elephant, and I would like to work for you." When I dropped my picture and resume into her carton, her shocked expression said it all. Chutzpah had returned.

The phone rang late one night. A man spoke.

"Hi, Danise Wilson-Payne?"

"Yes."

"I'm from Sylvia Fay casting. We want to use you on something you might enjoy. Do you have any clothing that looks shoddy to portray a destitute person?"

"Yes, I do."

"I thought you might as a clown. Background performers need to bring their own costumes. The production's a made-for-television movie about a bag lady named Florabelle. They'll need you for two weeks and will shoot in the different boroughs. It's called *Stone Pillow*. By the way, it stars Lucille Ball. Want the gig?"

"Yes!"

Even without the clothes I would have lied then gone to a thrift store for a shopping spree. What a return to my original dream!

The United Nations granted vacation days, so I stuffed ragged pants and baggy sweaters from circus life into my suitcase and hoofed it to the subway. I looked out of place dressed in a knit cap and scarf, holey gloves, second-rate shoes, and a long brown coat on that warm, spring day. My getup suited the part, for no one sat beside me on the crowded car. Steep steps carried me from a busy New York street to the High School of Performing Arts in mid-Manhattan, which served as our rendezvous point.

I stepped through a portal, and the beloved world of the movies waited within. Large, bright, round lights framed the inside of the door, and I goggled as a First of May. Men stood on the sidelines and held microphones—called booms—on long poles. I stood next to a huge fan that rested out of the way. One of the crew scurried over. "This's called a Ritter. It cools the set between takes. Are you a background performer?"

"Yes."

"OK, go in there." He pointed to a room.

The extras, dressed like lost souls, clustered and awaited instructions. Our actions would animate the background of a scene—business similar to walkarounds at Ringling. The assistant director, AD for short, entered and issued vouchers which stated call time, meals, hours worked, and such. We filled out the form and held onto it. Afterward he didn't divulge scene particulars but instead summoned names.

"Danise Wilson-Payne come with us."

They led us into the front hall for inspections and ensured our look fit their need. Then we sat to mimic the homeless at a shelter.

"Stay put and look dejected."

"Places!" Someone turned off the Ritters and the bright lights on. Then, footsteps from the side stairs that led to the level below attracted my attention. A shadow appeared first. In silence a woman dressed as the quintessential vagrant with unkempt hair under her hat emerged. In an instant, I recognized Lucille Ball. The queen of shtick stopped in front of me for a *tête-à-tête* with the director. I burst into a toothy grin but kept a lid on the thrill, then melted into the nonessential. The man in charge took over. "Action!"

The drama centered on a social worker, played by Daphne Zuniga, assigned to learn about humanity's members who slept on the streets, hence the title *Stone Pillow*. She pretended to be a drifter, befriended Florabelle, took up her plight, and found accommodations for her.

As a consummate professional, the notable Ms. Ball proved worthy to watch. Disagreement with the director caused no hesitation on her part. At one point the blocking became mishmash in her estimation, and she insisted on changes. After a discussion, the boss man complied.

The magic continued. Outside we toted bags filled with paper that simulated possessions and wore bulky apparel to depict the cold of winter. One day's shoot, however, took place during a heat wave, and the star almost succumbed to the temperature. Crew members rescued her near a doorway.

At the end of the first week, the extras sat sequestered in a classroom when the AD entered with a list. "OK, thanks for the work everybody. You're released. Don't forget to turn in your vouchers completed and signed. The following people are to return. If unable, let me know."

He called ten names, plus mine. I glanced around and those who appeared to have climbed from the fringes of society remained.

And thus began a silent association with Lucille Ball. The morning of continuation, she poked her head into our holding room. "Good morning, my motley crew." Save for those words, however, no interaction took place between star and extra. We clamped our mouths shut, but we sat grateful for the privilege.

After Ms. Ball left, one of the background performers who had worked on shoots before leaned into me and said, "Look at the grub. I'm gonna grab some food."

I glanced at the side table and joined her. We helped ourselves to pastries, orange juice, and coffee. And in the late afternoon, we dined on barbecue or sandwiches with the company. The rare "thanks" from the *Stone Pillow* team included a restaurant one day.

They had provided a motor home for the "motley crew" to ensure on-time arrival for filming in the different boroughs. But the schedule couldn't accommodate a ride through busy streets to the blessed meal. We walked in costume. Business men on the crowded sidewalks gave wide berth, and women held onto their purses against us—a cloud of hobos. The diner received forewarning, and, dressed in tatters, we supped like royalty.

Later in the week the assistant said, "The next neighborhood will look like World War II hit, but we have permits for the location. The crew's already there, and Ms. Ball will show up after you, extras." We gathered our gear, boarded our $100,000 mode of transportation, and took a trip into squalor. We maneuvered the concrete canyons and dodged potholes. Trips' end—a contrast between the haves and have-nots in a boarded-up section of Brooklyn strewn with junk cars.

We filed from the vehicle onto broken asphalt. The other ten climbed the uneven stairs to wait inside a tenement that would double as a homeless shelter. I stopped on the walkway to gaze upward, curious of what would follow because above me, people leaned from every window up and down the street. We eleven, unknown bums received no recognition at our exit. But the residents had heard about the appearance of the distinguished comedienne. Bed sheets blew overhead in the breeze to attract attention to the "We love Lucy" signs that adorned the glass panes of the dilapidated buildings.

Soon the long, black limousine approached and came to rest three feet from me. A hush filled the air. The door opened and out stepped Lucille Ball. She glanced at the people and removed her knit cap. Ah, the red hair! The roar of the neighbors carried down the street like a tidal wave, and they shook the white folds of fabric. The actress raised her hands, circled 360 degrees, acknowledged her fans, and entered the building.

The director captured our contribution to the story throughout the Big Apple for another seven days; then we turned in our vouchers. Showbiz had not slammed the door. I earned my bread and butter from several shoots in New York City and discovered that I did not inhabit an isolated island. For every star seen on camera, thousands waited in the wings; at each call, hundreds vied for a chance to be an extra.

I had convinced myself at Ringling's Star Night in Los Angeles that my dream no longer included movies, but this ride on the celluloid path changed my mind. The film lifted my performer spirit and opened my eyes. The golden platter of movie-star life vanquished the previous woes of the tanbark trail, and a bounce returned to my step.

I returned to the United Nations after *Stone Pillow*, auditioned for plays on the side, and added an off-Broadway production of *Bye Bye Birdie* to my belt. The city brimmed with performing arts, especially music—perfect for my husband. He found work in the orchestra pit for *Gypsy* and national tour of *Sugar Babies*, for example. William Anthony Payne sprang to life.

However, an innate urge to move every four years—an odd holdover from a childhood in the military—clenched me in its grips.

I used the excuse of stress from the hustle and bustle of life to urge Billy to leave the metropolis and its vibes. That plea severed him from his dream and has plagued me until this day. We loaded our orange Datsun 510. The bridge in front of us connected one to the pulse of the city. We drove in the opposite direction, and the heartbeat grew dimmer. A chance to stay at the United Nations until retirement, also lost. But the drive to go pulled. Of fools and clowns. Hello, setting sun.

#

Southern California presented a variety of jobs to keep our heads above water. In time Billy's talent allowed him to tour with such shows as *The Debbie Reynolds' Show* and *4 Girls 4,* which starred Kaye Ballard, Kay Starr, Helen O'Connell, and Margaret Whiting.

A fifteen-minute drive for me led to the door of the prominent Central Casting, which supplied extras for TV and film. Inside, a room filled with tables and people busy on calls. After my registration, the pulse of moviedom beat in my arteries once more with the work. But something didn't sync. I wanted to clown. A goal surfaced to study funny women and perfect the art. As a result, the Museum of Television & Radio (renamed The Paley Center for Media) stepped in as my latest school of pie-in-the-face.

The first week of my reawakening, I drove forty minutes from our apartment in North Hollywood to downtown Los Angeles and checked in with the attendant. He assigned a viewing location, then directed me to a log of tapes where yesteryear's artistes waited on rolls of transparency for a chance to dance with the spotlight again. I chose my video teachers and sat in a chamber of cubicles and flipped a switch. Vaudevillians performed before my eyes, and Bert Williams sang "Nobody" for me. I moved on and clicked a button to the great black comedienne Jackie "Moms" Mabley. Her genius, self-apparent, but she worked stand-up comedy. Tapes of African American women professionals in the art of physical slapstick proved difficult to find. Thus, color faded to a meaningless status.

I leaned back in the chair. "Stone Pillow and Lucille Ball." I shot to the aide, made my request, and returned to my place. With my face to the screen, television archives revealed the shtick of one of the best of my gender in the *I Love Lucy* program. Girlhood memories came to light of an actress named Imogene Coca. Her rubber face and mile-a-minute facial expressions had impressed me as a child on the series *It's About Time.* With another touch of the start knob, excerpts from *Your Show of Shows* solidified my resolve to use my moveable mug, thanks to a window on the world of Coca and Sid Caesar.

I observed, laughed, and absorbed my chosen mentors—all masters. I took a break each day and ended every afternoon with *The Carol Burnett Show* and the queen of physical timing. Each of the three performers impacted my development, and my brain served as a sponge.

During the weeks at the Museum, I discovered Fanny Brice. She had bolted to stardom with *The Ziegfeld Follies* in the early 1900s and had created a little girl image named Baby Snooks. An audio interview made its way through static to my headset and disclosed her desire to retire her bratty four-year-old alter ego to "keep from looking silly." Her words, an inspiration to age my persona. Lessons learned from the four recorded tutors satisfied my endeavors.

After Ringling, my suitcase contained "Baby D" on the right and empty space on the left. A new me would fill the gap. She would ride in harmony with Danise and allow unmistakable identification as a female. Time to become the potter to clay and sculpt a character.

African American women have asked, "Why don't you have a black style? Leave no doubt about your identity in the audience's mind." Indeed.

At Ringling, a white gentleman had shaken my hand and slipped a written letter into my palm: "I've been following the show to watch you perform. It's good to see a black, lady clown." In parenthesis the note continued, "At least I think you're black . . ."

I mulled over both cases but remembered history's pages with Zip Coon and blackface minstrels. Clowns depicted life in a charade of overblown qualities. Behind the masquerade my race needed no more stereotypes.

To begin, I walked to the thrift store up the street from our apartment. As on my search for a trunk as a First of May, the insides of this one served as a huge catchall. The employee glanced from her book, then ignored me. I fingered the clothes on the racks, found a lady's tailcoat tuxedo, an ankle-length dress three sizes too large, and handed over money to the bored salesgirl. At home I completed the look and donned a red hat, round glasses, and rolled-down-gloves. With my hair pressed and curled slightly under, I stepped into my oversized oxfords, and "Baby D" aged into a woman.

Each of the two personalities varied in mannerisms: The first—shy and meek, a shadow of my former self. The latter—mischievous and resourceful, the emergence of attitude. What a difference!

"Baby D" shall always remain close, like the soul to one's body. She has been the "me" behind the mask. If needed, she would return with ease as donning bedroom slippers.

For Billy to exercise his chops on clarinet and for me to grease the joints from lessons of Burnett, Coca, Ball, and Brice, we put ourselves in motion on the road in Los Angeles and played senior citizen centers. The two of us entertained at Jewish homes for the elderly, for example, in front of survivors of the Holocaust and veterans of vaudeville. The once-upon-a-time specialists of variety sat arched in a permanent state of bent in wheelchairs. Their eyes, dulled with time, brightened at our antics. After the shows, they showered us with pointers on useful shtick. We performed at French festivals in Santa Barbara, California, then passed the hat.

Months later an opportunity surfaced. At a get-together Dick Monday, a former Ringling clown, approached us and said, "I'm involved in a production with a woman named Wini McKay. We're going to call it The L.A. Circus. It's a nonprofit with a grant from the City of Los Angeles Cultural Affairs Department." He paused, then asked, "Would you be one of the clowns, Danise? Billy, think you can get a band together?"

We didn't hesitate, but answered yes to both questions. The first day of rehearsal, we drove to a park in Burbank and maneuvered the car into a space at the curb. We exited and found the community's recreation center where kids played basketball on the inside court. "Here we are," Dick called out from the stage. Billy and I climbed the steps, and after Dick closed the curtains our tenure at The L.A. Circus began.

Early one morning noise from the living room drew me from sleep before the sun appeared. The clock read 2:00 a.m., so I rose and sauntered in. Billy hunched over the table and arranged sheet music that covered the wood with a symphony of notes. The creation of his opus would repeat until showtime. Meanwhile Dick shaped the alley.

I had worked with other funny men and women before, but when introduced to Bob Zraick, hilarity rose to a higher plain. He was older with years of clowning under his belt. His movements and expressions, pure Chaplin-Keaton-Marx Brothers-esque. We practiced several gags and one musical number. The arrangement included Billy on saxophone, Dick on musical saw, me on accordion, and Bob on violin that exploded—or not—at the end of the piece. When it didn't blow up on cue, Bob rocked from toe to heel and looked at the sky.

Ringling Bros. and Barnum & Bailey had begun my trip into the art of ha-ha-ha. The fast-paced L.A. Circus took me one step beyond into the gift of improvisation. We clowns experimented and twisted old-time slapstick into an avant-garde clown form. I had no idea how Dick devised the unique creations that stepped from the norm into the surreal. But he, as the character Bob Largehead who sported an itty-bitty toupee perched on top his oversized, fake cranium, woke from a nap and encountered live furniture. Zraick was a picture in a frame, and I, the grandfather clock.

Showtime! When we made our debut, the crowd filtered past the ticket takers and into the bleachers. The round, yellow-and-red canvas wall—called a sidewall—enclosed us under open skies. No big top. With his late-night opus completed, Billy took his place before the band. In a scarlet, old-style circus jacket with gold curls of cord on the front, he raised the baton.

At the downbeat, the multiethnic town of celluloid dreams bounced with brisk klezmer music from the Jewish experience. My husband doubled on clarinet and saxophone. Latin songs embellished our juggler, a winner of the Golden Clown Award—the circus version of the Academy Awards. The tunes of jazz swirled around Pa-Mela Hernandez who climbed the web and enticed the blue of the sky to envelop her ebony skin. Our small troupe with one elephant and one dog packed a wallop with traditional circus melodies as well for the audience who filled the stands. The show barnstormed throughout the City of Angels and played its various districts. We performed at parks, malls, or hospital lots only on scheduled dates, not all year long.

Thanks to this well-received intimate outdoor exhibition equipped with one inflatable circus ring, my new persona blossomed due to freedom to clown. We lived L.A. Circus for three years until one day in October 1992 when the phone rang.

CHAPTER FOURTEEN

CONTROVERSY

I stood in the kitchen and held a bowl over soapy water. Dirty dishes would have to wait, though, because when the phone rang in the living room I walked over and picked up the receiver. "Hello, Danise. This is Tim Holst. It's been a long time, but I want to ask you something."

In fact it had been twelve years since words passed between me and anyone in upper management at Ringling. They had booted me out the door the last time we spoke. What did the performance director want?

"We received a call from a man named Gerry Cottle, who owns a circus in England. He inquired about you for his Christmas production." He cut to the chase. "Well, Danise, how would you like to star in a British presentation? Billy will be in the band."

All the sour grapes that remained from *The Greatest Show on Earth* a decade ago turned to sweet nectar in a blink of an eye. Billy and I had always wanted to work overseas. With that trip we would experience the difference, if any, between the two worlds of sawdust: European and American. And I would have a chance to visit my one-room schoolhouse, to rekindle past friendships, and to reacquaint my speech with long-forgotten expressions. My spirit soared, and I said, "Sure!"

"He has a one-ring show. It starts in December, but you'll have to be there before that. He'll give you the particulars. The next step is a conversation with Gerry Cottle." He spoke more and ended with,

"OK, I'll give him your number, so expect to be contacted shortly. Thanks, Danise. Take care."

I hung up and flew into the bedroom where my husband sorted clothes.

"Billy! That was Tim Holst. We're going to England to be on a one-ring show!"

"What?"

"Yeah, you're gonna be in the band."

I explained what Tim had told me. He sprung from the side of the bed as if jolted by one hundred volts of electricity, and with hands clenched above his head said, "This is it!" Without further discussion, we agreed to step through the magical door. If nothing else, it would be interesting.

The next day the man in Great Britain telephoned.

"Hello, is this Danise Payne?"

"Yes, it is."

"I'm Gerry Cottle, and I'm glad you'll be with us."

"Thank you. I'm looking forward to this."

"The circus will perform in the town of Wembley, which is in the northwest part of outer London. Don't worry about the cold; we're not under the big top. We play exhibition halls. You probably don't know much regarding England, but Wembley is in the borough of Brent. But never mind . . ."

He spoke of himself, his production, and pertinent information, then continued.

"You're going to do school presentations, television promotions, and such before rehearsals. To begin, do you have a clown name?"

I chose my original self to go on the journey. Children would relate to her with ease.

"Yes, 'Baby D.'"

"We'll need photos of yourself as 'Baby D' and any publicity material, Danise. Federal Express it and we'll reimburse your costs."

"OK, I can send all of it in a day or two."

"You'll be well taken care of, and England will sweep you off your feet!"

I told my parents the news, which resulted in elation on their end. While there, a visit to Great Glemham and families from my past would be on tap.

I researched and discovered Gerry Cottle set his career in motion at the age of fifteen when he joined Roberts Brothers Circus. He absorbed information and acquired management skills, which allowed him to launch Cottle and Austen's Circus with his business partner, Brian Austen, in post-World War II England. The tough life of the road resulted in a fight for survival.

Born to be a showman, he mastered the tricks of the trade. He knew how to remain one step ahead of the game by using gimmicks to catch the eye of the media that would ensure success. When other well-known British circuses, such as the Bertram Mills' and Billy Smart's productions, closed their doors, Cottle became synonymous with the genre. He rose to the top as one of the most influential impresarios in Great Britain and toured two big tops. In subsequent years, he added funfairs with amusement rides and midway sideshows.

The ball rolled, and Billy and I submitted applications for passports and a work permit. Conversations with Gerry took place during that time, and we set a day for a private meeting. My head reeled due to preparations for the trip; nevertheless, I flew from Los Angeles to Sarasota, Florida, to meet him.

Unsure what that circus man looked like, the next morning I approached the tables by the hotel's pool. An attractive, middle-age man with thick, black hair rose and extended his hand. "Hi, I'm Gerry Cottle." He made a logical guess as to my identity; I was the only black person around not in a maid's uniform. A broad smile behind his dark mustache calmed my jitters. Introductions to his entourage of reporters ensued, and we spoke throughout breakfast.

A few hours after the following daybreak, we zoomed to Ringling's winter quarters in a taxicab for a meeting with Tim Holst. Gerry sat beside the driver, and a troublesome journalist sat adjacent to me. He had a false sense of reality, thanks to United States' television that depicted African Americans in substandard conditions who packed guns and ransacked everything in sight.

"What's it like growing up in the ghetto?" he asked.

"How should I know? I grew up on air force bases."

I turned my back and glanced out the window. Soon the road called Tamiami Trail came into view and led to the building with the blue roof. My steps into the arena at winter quarters rivaled the fun of fourteen years earlier in 1978. I bounded through those red steel doors into the welcome of the familiar. Clown College stood in full swing.

Inside, a surprised Bobby Batchelor, the drummer with the Red Unit from yesteryear, and Ruth Chaddock, long ago dubbed my sawdust sister, offered hugs in the still cold and damp facility. Irvin Feld had passed away in 1984. But instinct turned my gaze upward toward the ominous window at the top of the stairs. The son, Kenneth, inherited the office. Nonetheless, memories flooded like a tidal wave. We met Tim. I smiled while our group climbed the same steps I dreaded in school, then followed him into a smaller room to talk generalities. Afterward Gerry and the newspaper man waited in the hall.

"Danise, I'd like you to speak with a group of boys joining up with Ringling for the new season," Tim said. "They're a young, black, acrobatic troupe from Chicago." To be exact, they hailed from a rough housing development known as Cabrini-Green. Soon The Chicago Kidz [sic] opened the door and sauntered in. They sported braids and wore shorts hung below the waist that revealed underwear. "Kidz, this is Danise. She was a clown with us twelve years ago, and she's going to speak with you awhile. We'll meet you downstairs afterward, Danise." Tim closed the door and left.

Young and inexperienced to circus, the troupe smiled and took seats that faced me. Their mannerisms proved a life full of years of difficulty within the inner city. What to say? I grew up in a private little world within compounds sequestered from neighborhood violence. My youth shared no similarities with theirs save for one thing: an ebony hue. We held idle chitchat, and they listened to my experiences of Ringling.

"Did you have problems because you were black?" one asked.

"My chances to perform dwindled before the end of rehearsals my second season. I believed at the time it stemmed from being black *and* female. Most of my troubles came in towns. A cop drew his gun on me once between shows in Jacksonville, Florida."

Their eyes widened and another blurted, "That better not happen to me!"

The smallest Kid piped up. "We've been told to keep our noses clean and do our jobs. What do they think we are?"

I paused. "Martin Luther King, Jr. said the world should look at our character, but people still label our race as troublemakers who are up to no good. They're wrong." I echoed Red Skelton in Birmingham. "Because of prejudice it's necessary, unfortunately, to be two times as good as the rest because you are going to be judged twice as hard." My memory of the children who surrounded me in Chicago prompted, "You'll be role models for the African American kids in the stands, who'll watch you because you're black."

The polite, young men absorbed my words about circus life and the trip to England. How nice it would have been for the Kidz to travel through a color-blind world. My time with them ended with hugs and "see ya down the road."

I rejoined the group from England for a short tour of the grounds. They preferred a longer one, however. The brevity might have been to ensure no disruption of classes or to save Ringling's tricks of the trade from Gerry's eyes.

What a rough few days in Sarasota! The blur began after that initial breakfast by the pool and lasted until a half hour before the return flight to Los Angeles. Interviews and pictures and food and wine swallowed time—a shadow of things to come.

I returned home, and the next day's dialogue catapulted the stakes higher. "I'm going to get this thing started," Gerry said over the phone, "with a bit of a raucous by explaining to the press why I need you over here. Only the clowns know it's a setup. I wanted to forewarn you. It'll cause a lot of publicity, but mum's the word."

I would soon learn of the creative mind of Gerry Cottle. Within the week, we received a newspaper dated November 19, 1992. The British journal, *The Daily Telegraph*, quoted Gerry, "British clowns are hopeless. They're not funny, and they're not original." He described them as "stroppy, untalented, trade unionist and prima donnas, who don't help the team." The title of the article declared, "Cottle Brings on the Frowns." His solution? Bring in an American. The controversy began.

A few days later the mailman delivered another package that boasted three stamps: one of Queen Elizabeth, one of Carrickfergus Castle, and the other of Windsor Castle—*par avion*. I opened it and removed the paperwork. An artist's drawing in brilliant colors of a lion, zebra, tiger, elephant, flying trapeze artists, and a clown who held the words "Gerry Cottle's Circus" leapt from the top of the cover letter. My contract had arrived, and we read and signed the documents.

Meanwhile England's press had a field day with Gerry's statement that referred to unfunny Joeys, and a whirlwind of publicity took off. First, the British Broadcasting Corporation (BBC) phoned from eleven thousand miles away and asked my thoughts on the brewing storm. The business manager for the show, Malcolm Cannon, had forewarned me about that call. I played the innocent bystander.

More periodicals arrived. Under my picture in *The Daily Mail* the article stated, "This is the face which has British circus clowns preparing to down their baggy trousers in protest at an American invasion . . ." Additional newspapers, radio stations, and television channels jumped on the bandwagon and propelled Great Britain's media machine into hyperdrive.

The November 20 issue of the *Daily Mirror* tumbled the pomp and circumstantial world of Parliament into one of high jinks and absurdity. Page thirteen boasted six pictures of the Cabinet, which included the prime minister. Each sported superimposed clown faces and noses for the feature headlined "Who says this country hasn't got any clowns?" The war of words grew downright vicious when the account gave names such as Jo-Jo, Mr. Whippy, and Bozo to its members and continued, "Roll up! Roll up, folks. It's the greatest show of clowns on earth—the *Cabinet*."

Martin "Zippo" Burton, secretary of Clowns International quipped, "Mr. Cottle has been, and always will be, his own best publicist."

I chattered through interviews with a long string of dailies and for broadcast programs. The press nabbed Billy as well—all before we left the United States. On our side of the pond, the American media got wind of the ruckus and conducted a chat in our apartment for NBC's *Today* show. The frenzy snowballed after a segment on the television program *Entertainment Tonight*. By the time we flew to England, the controversy stood in full swing. Gerry Cottle, the genius.

The brouhaha set my world on fire, and my corner of the sky reopened with a vengeance.

With passports and work permits secured, on November 23, 1992, Billy and I flew from LAX on Virgin Atlantic Airlines toward Heathrow Airport in London. When we descended into clouds saturated with rain, an attendant called out over the intercom, "Will passenger Danise Payne please make herself known to the stewards before disembarking?"

"Why?" I thought and raised my hand.

"Danise, would you be so kind and remain seated until all have exited?" the steward asked. After the plane landed, travelers retrieved overhead luggage and glanced in my direction while they inched down the aisle. Billy and I moved toward the door, but a gentleman prevented our escape. "So, you're 'Baby D'? I am the chief of security of Heathrow Airport. It's bloody awful out there; the press is everywhere. There are clowns outside protesting your arrival, and we're here to see you safely through all this."

The senior officer, his assistant, and eight uniformed bobbies—London policemen—circled the wagons around Billy and me. With radios in hand and no nonsense, they led us to customs to reunite with our baggage. We met Malcolm Cannon, Gerry's right-hand man, who escorted Billy on but left me surrounded by the cavalry. We waited. The chief faced me and asked, "Are you ready?"

I thought, "For what?" but said, "Yes."

"Right then. Here we go."

We walked, and my eyes darted to the right. The expressions of the tourists, who scurried to and fro, read, "Who is that?" or "What did she do?" Our entourage proceeded down a narrow passageway, turned the corner into the ticket area, and ran into a mob of mass hysteria. Paparazzi were everywhere. They yelled and waved to catch my attention. Later in the day, Mr. Cottle mentioned that an unsuspecting, black woman with heavy makeup and blond wig set foot in the lobby before I had entered. She screamed and ran in the opposite direction when rushed by news representatives. "Are you the clown? Are you the clown?"

"Danise, look this way!"—"Danise, over here!"—"Look in my camera!"—"Danise, Danise!" More than twenty television crews, plus photographers and correspondents from around the globe, pushed in. The force backed me into the wall, stunned. In that crowd stood one of the photojournalists I had met in Florida, and out of that horde stepped the modern-day P.T. Barnum—Gerry Cottle.

He grinned from ear to ear and put his arm around me to pose. He turned me this way and that. The cameras flashed an eternity, but in the nick of time he said, "Enough!" We hurried down a hall with tight security—no press allowed—and joined my husband and Malcolm in a small room. "Billy, you wouldn't believe what happened to me out there!" A blessed chair caught my collapse.

Gerry had hired the Mark Borkowski public relations firm that represented specialty celebrities and entertainment clients, such as Michael Jackson and Led Zeppelin rock group, for example. With the agency's help, my arrival had been "bigger than that of pop singer Madonna," so said the airport's press officer.

After my recovery, Gerry led Billy and me outside to the rear of the airport. A line of photographers stood by an empty car. They snapped pictures; then the three of us climbed in, and Gerry inched us down a side road toward the city in the hallowed solitude of our enclosed chariot. Peace flew out the window as soon as we drove around the bend. Reporters lay in wait, and automobiles appeared from nowhere.

Our host glanced at the rearview mirror. "Look at that!" He pressed on the gas, and we zoomed through narrow streets and concealed alleys of London as a rocket out of control. I slid across the front seat, Billy the rear. The pursuers careened behind every step of the way. The man responsible for the brouhaha beamed like a Cheshire cat, quite pleased.

We screeched to a halt at a hotel for the first conference. I glanced through the windows, and clowns adorned in fabric of bright crimson, avocado, and lemon checkers blocked the way. They chanted in unison and waved signs: "Over Paid, Over Rated, and Over Here"—an echo of the complaint about American GIs in Britain during World War II. Other placards read, "Yank go Home." "I can't understand all the fuss," Gerry Cottle said. He exited the vehicle, and a pie hit him in the face.

Someone whisked Billy and me inside to a top floor suite for my metamorphosis. To our surprise, two people had gained access. "Hi, I'm Valerie Grove of *The Times,* and this is my photographer. I'm going to ask you a few things." I hesitated, then placed my suitcase on the bed and withdrew the pieces of the patchwork known as "Baby D." A vanity boxed up my face against the tide of her questions. While I put on my one-piece, flowered jumpsuit with puffy sleeves and giant baby hat and slipped into my oversized oxfords, she hit with a fact unknown to me.

"The real obstacle is British unease. How do you think you'll fit in a society that is uncomfortable with women clowns?"

A million thoughts jammed my head. As a matter of fact, my gender caused acknowledgment problems in the United States. Spectators believed that I cross-dressed and called me "sir." At Ringling, production costumes didn't help. Kids had remarked, "You're not a real clown." A wall to scale existed due to the rarity of black females in the business.

For advice in the battle for approval, I had already contacted an authority on the issue: Annie Fratellini. Her grandfather and his two brothers shone as kings of the sawdust in the early 1900s. Born into the notable family of France, Annie received training early in life and became a noteworthy circus clown in their country.

"It will always be a battle, Danise," she had written. "Don't back down. Once they see you're serious, they'll have no choice. Your determination will open the door." Later Billy and I met Ms. Fratellini in Paris and spoke in person. From all her gracious advice, a simple response came to mind for Valerie Grove's inquiry on acceptance: "Anything they can do, I can do."

Ms. Grove proved quite the professional interviewer with difficult questions, a pleasant challenge. "What makes you laugh?" remained unanswered because I couldn't pinpoint the "what."

With my character completed, we exited the suite, met Mr. Cottle, and followed him to a large conference room. He stepped inside first, then Billy, Ms. Grove, and her photographer. I entered behind them and glanced around. Thirty reporters, each with a microphone, had crowded in and were rearing to go. Others waited with their mechanical boxes to transmit television broadcasts. They stood among cables that covered the floor like a nest of intertwined snakes at rest. Gerry motioned for me to sit in the lone chair behind a long table at the door. Then the bombardment began with an explosion of quiet thunder and miniature lightning—the sounds and flashes of the cameras. "Welcome to England! What do you think of the hubbub?"

Question after question plum tuckered me out. What a reception for my return to—unbeknownst to those present—the land where my dreams had formed!

When finished we zipped to another hotel for one night, where I collapsed on the bed. Billy turned on the boob tube for the six o'clock news: "'Baby D' has arrived in London!" said the newsman.

The next day Gerry drove Billy and me to the Farm, his residence in the country, which doubled as the circus's winter quarters. His family extended a greeting and served tea and crumpets, familiar fare from my childhood. Afterward we walked the grounds past a row of small trailer homes.

"Those caravans are for the performers," he said. "We'll move them to Wembley." I grimaced at their lack of size, but Gerry's words caused my thoughts to perish. "You two will stay in a flat across from the exhibition hall."

We entered a barn. "I'd like you to meet someone." An older man approached, extended his hand, and spoke with an incomprehensible accent. His name, Sonny Fossett. Indeed. The Fossett family stretched back generations. Not born into the famous circus clan, Sonny took their title due to association and developed into a well-known clown. My heart leapt at his introduction.

After his indecipherable words, Billy and I followed our host for a stroll in an immense field and chatted. But mid-sentence Gerry dashed in the other direction, then Billy. They didn't bother to tell me why. "What's going on?" I thought as I spun my head around in time to see an angry bull elephant charging our way. We had invaded his territory. I bolted and caught them both, and we shot across the meadow into the house.

"Is that elephant out there all the time?" I asked.

"Oh yes. It's his field. Right," the boss man said, "I'm hungry. Let's go eat."

# # #

Thanks to the show, the York House Hotel in Weybridge, Surrey, suited as our respite for the next few nights. The hiding place, nestled in a quiet part of outer London, sat opposite a small field used for the game of cricket. Proprietors greeted with a smile and showed us to our room up an enclosed staircase. We set our suitcases down and looked through the window. Lanes meandered past buildings of white plaster and brown, wooden beams—picturesque, like Great Glemham. We sauntered outside to enjoy some much-needed solitude after the whirlwind of the first days in the country.

Unaware Gerry Cottle had concocted the controversy, our hosts wanted to convey "the average Brit held no malice." America's Thanksgiving Day occurred the next day. To express support, the staff prepared a welcome meal. Billy and I dressed for supper that evening, descended the narrow stairway, and entered the small dining room.

The walls displayed mementos of home: baseball gloves, bats, and pictures of ball players. We joined Malcolm Cannon and a few others at a table covered with a white linen cloth set with place settings of china. On each plate, a traditional British cracker—complimentary paper rolls about the size of a hand. "Do pull the ends, Danise and Bill, to reveal what's inside." Miniature prizes rained onto the porcelain.

With that cue, our hosts began their declaration of acceptance with blueberry muffins and vegetable soup, buffalo chicken winglets, and prawn cocktail. Immediately, the clank of sterling silver to delicate ceramic filled the room.

Then they buzzed around and served the main course of traditional turkey and trimmings that we washed down with a glass of wine. To finish the statement, a dessert choice of Alabama, chocolate fudge cake or deep-dish, American apple pie functioned as the exclamation point of approval. We Yanks greatly appreciated their hospitality, and I shall always remember their warmth.

At the end of the breather in Weybridge, Malcolm drove us to our flat in Wembley. School shows, personal appearances, and interviews blurred the weeks before circus rehearsals. Thus the one-bedroom apartment covered in wall-to-wall carpeting with a kitchen and separate living room became a sanctuary.

One noteworthy act of publicity took place on live radio at the nerve center of the BBC in downtown London. No costume or makeup required. The night before Billy and I checked into the Saint Georges Hotel, which resided across the street from the station in an exclusive area of the capital. Once again our stay was complimentary.

Bright and early at 8:00 a.m., I passed through sliding doors, cleared tight security, and received a visitor pass that read, "Welcome to BBC Radio. Expiry Date-02 Dec 1992." A guide escorted me through the stark, gray labyrinth of the headquarters to wait with the other interviewees in a small room. A wall of glass separated us from the broadcasting space.

A door opened and out walked the moderator, and said, "Good morning to you all. I'm Lucy Cacanas, hostess of *Midweek*. This will be an interesting session."

The program centered on current affairs and world situations. She introduced everyone on the panel. Although I didn't know of them, through the power of the media they beamed when she presented "Baby D." We shook hands, followed her into the studio, and sat in assigned seats around a table—each position equipped with a microphone. I have long forgotten their names, but what a lineup!

"Good morning to everyone listening. Today we have a group from different walks of life. I'll begin with the young lady on my left . . ."

Guest number one had won the Laurence Olivier Award (England's version of the Tony Awards) for best actress in a play. She discussed theater in the country. The next sat tall and distinguished. He spoke of the Russian revolution and his future DNA test to prove himself a descendant of the czar. Each speaker's story developed more passion. And the gentleman to my right? His battle for the eradication of the hatred of Jews and his success as a Nazi hunter rendered him a mighty man of valor. "What was I doing there?" I thought.

"Danise, what do you think about the fight to end anti-Semitism? Do you think it's possible?" Ms. Cacanas asked.

With Ringling I learned the art of clowning, the United Nations, diplomacy. During the BBC interview, however, I swung among tall pines in hopes to grasp a branch. Trying to fit in with these notables reminded me of a phrase from my past: to be a clown is to be a poet, an artist, a politician, and an orangutan. A response that stemmed from my experiences with hate tumbled from my spirit: "You can amend the laws in every book, but until you transform man's heart nothing will change."

After that extraordinary afternoon, we returned to our flat in Wembley and prepared for the next phase of publicity: school visits.

CHAPTER FIFTEEN

SNIPPETS OF SAWDUST

I would present a single-handed show of sixty minutes that decreased to a half hour due to the incredible number of six a day. On our way to the schools, we rode through villages in a small, mobile, billboard truck that boasted, Gerry Cottle's Circus. Thanks to the controversy, the public offered the red carpet even when my face bore no makeup: "Good morning, Baby D."

Though I had once lived there, British names conjured up visions of knights and ladies. Hay Lane School in Grove Park, Kingsbury and Shaftesbury in Harrow, Middlesex—from one to another we traveled—Billy; our driver, Guy; and me in full getup. The dark, gray buildings of brick or stone stood down narrow lanes. With each step closer, lunches of tangy rhubarb smothered in sweet cream drifted from memories of my primary education. The air also carried the aroma of shepherd's pie. Such a long time ago!

One day we approached a school and noticed uniformed students who were enjoying games on the blacktop. After Guy parked the truck on the side of the fenced-in playground, we exited, retrieved my props, and walked through the gate. "Ooh, it's Baby D!" they cried and dissipated yesteryear. The kids shot toward us and reached and tugged at my clothes. Billy held my mini-unicycle out of harm's way. Both he and Guy tried to keep them at bay, but more than one hundred screaming, young people engulfed me as the open sea had claimed the Titanic.

Panic wreaked havoc on my composure. I gulped air in short breaths and dug my fingernails into my husband's biceps. He and Guy did their best to help—my knights in shining armor.

I moved toward a door where a female face peered through the window. Her words permeated the glass pane. "Oh my, oh my! It's Baby D!" She bolted to the rescue, grabbed hold of my arm, and yanked me inside. After Billy and Guy tumbled in, she slammed the door shut and left the mob outside. "I'm the headmistress. I'm ever so sorry about the children. They are very excited to have you here." I excused myself and headed off to find the loo—the restroom—in order to hide the tears that crested behind the lids.

Afterward in a lounge, a sip of tea with grateful teachers calmed my nerves; then they escorted the three of us to an assembly hall where I set my props. When the sound of footsteps approached the entryway, I turned and the entire student body filed in with hushed enthusiasm and nestled on the floor. I spoke of Clown College and displayed skills aided by volunteers. The application of makeup with a demonstration on one of their own revealed a clash of cultures.

British vocabulary had slipped my mind since childhood. I described the first two styles—whiteface and auguste—with eye contact to the kids. American idioms flowed for the third explanation. "A bum is an example of a character." At that point, their mouths hung open. "Several famous clown bums worked in America . . ." Their eyes widened. I didn't understand their reaction and glanced behind me to see what Billy and Guy had done to cause the shocked expressions. Nothing. My words continued, on and on. "In America, Otto Griebling was a famous clown bum." They sat aghast.

After that portion of the show, I walked toward the back wall to my bodyguards, picked up my unicycle, and Guy whispered, "Danise, the word bum means buttocks!"

In spite of verbal blunders, the path down memory lane returned me to the familiar. I had been the sole child of color on the floor for assembly events. At yet one more school in another section of London, the patter of little feet filled the chamber. Eyes beamed from freckled faces framed by curly, blond locks. They rested in orderly rows. One differed. A lone, black girl whispered my name, "Baby D. Baby D."

I sauntered over and bent down. "Yes?"

She looked up, smiled, and touched my spirit. "I'm brown, too."

After weeks of presentations, the final one occurred in a village dotted with homes of smoky mortar. At my last ta-dah, the head-mistress approached. "Thank you, Baby D. We're ever so delighted to have you here. The students have prepared a special thank you." She set a stool in the middle of the floor for me then called out to the kids. "All right children, take your places."

Girls in pleated, plaid dresses and boys in gray pants and white shirts with short ties stood. Rosy cheeks glowed. The matron stepped to the piano, nodded in their direction, and played an introduction from the film *Oliver!* When she raised her arm to conduct, high-pitched voices caressed me in acceptance with the song "Consider Yourself."

I had come full circle. A British accent no longer carried my words. But the land that had embraced my family in the past covered me with its wings. The melody cemented Great Britain and me.

At each location kids focused on every syllable and cheered in appreciation. They volunteered hugs and wanted autographs, which caused my fingers to cramp. Open arms bade a welcome in school after school. When I made my way through the corridors to the teachers' lounge before each show, the clump-clump of my oversized oxfords alerted the young people to the presence of "Baby D." Heads poked from classrooms with shouts of glee. In spite of mob-scenes, to stroll those halls had been a blessing from God and filled my heart with joy.

Daily plugs also took place. As a result, utter exhaustion became my companion. To avoid an overload of personal appearances to promote the show, Billy and I toured the city during any time off and stayed out until sunrise, which compounded the weariness.

One morning we headed to a station, paid the fare, and boarded the bus for a trip to Great Glemham. Visions twirled in my mind while we bounced on the road. Would memories match reality? At our destination, thanks to a phone number from my mother, yesterday's friends walked with us. Our cottage still guarded the street corner. Onward to my one-room schoolhouse that—to my discovery—now served as storage. We passed the lunch hall, the vicar's house, and the church of stone. My recollections had harbored it all, and I strolled with happy feet. The Chandlers no longer lived there, however. Mr.

Chandler and Uncle Fred, the man with the Hula-Hoop, had since passed away. "Mrs. Chandler lives in another community," the friends said. "We have her phone number." With my fingers to the dial, that journey back through life beckoned as well.

The train swayed on the way and stopped under the white sign that identified her new town. We wandered the narrow streets and found her flat. Anticipation swelled at the name on the eye-level placard: Rose Chandler. Knock, knock! A moment passed, then a wisp of a woman I shall always remember opened the door.

Time had taken hold of both of us. Age spots framed her smile, and her curly hair had thinned. I stood taller than her now, but she held my face in her hands and said, "Oh lovely! My Danise." Billy and I spent the day with her family, and fatigue slipped away. Yesterday had stolen its way into today, and the past had become my forever filled with a memory of friends in a quaint village across the sea. The visit calmed my spirit.

We returned to Wembley, and the sun rose on tomorrow. We left our flat, which lay across the street from the exhibition hall, entered the building, and followed the sounds to the circus ring where a few people milled about. The bandstand rested on risers above the performers' entrance, and Billy disappeared through the curtain to meet his fellow musicians. I remained alone.

Gerry Cottle approached with a smile. "Right, Danise, let's get you set up. You're going to share the dressing room with two of the stars." He led me to a side room, opened the door, and turned to me when one of the women drew near. "This is Mary Chipperfield."

She owned the distinction as one of Europe's premiere animal handlers. With grace, the equestrienne would present horses that worked with no tethers or riders, a.k.a. liberty horses. They would raise their hooves and float on air around the ring in a dance to waltz music. She also took care of a liger—an odd animal that is part tiger and part lion with a large head and a somewhat striped body. The other woman worked in a Russian acrobatic duo.

I shook their hands then glanced around. I didn't receive any indication of what to prepare for gags before we left the United States; therefore, my mini-unicycle, clubs, balls, a lota bowl—a container ever-full of water when turned over—and my accordion came along. These would create a miniature land of toys in my selected area. When finished, we returned to the ring. Gerry nodded, then departed.

As two younger men strolled over, my excitement grew, for I longed to work side by side with Europeans. What would their reaction be to me, the first female of my race in greasepaint on a par with the England-born? How would the fall-down-slapstick-pie-in-your-face comedy of the United States fit in? Would professional etiquette be possible due to British concern over women clowns in general? Time would tell.

The one with dark hair spoke. "Hi, I'm Beau." He pointed to his companion. "This is Dingle. We're the other clowns."

And we began.

"We're going to provide several displays and one ten-minute pantomime," Dingle said.

In the United States mimes presented the silent art with the illusion of objects, but an explanation clarified the contrast of semantics. They described it as a traditional skit with spoken lines. The theatrical format in the ring blended theater with circus. This combined style would put itself forward later in our season during a visit to another show in Great Britain.

Ours involved a ghost, played by the ringmaster, and three people who slept, played by us clowns. Two days of practice involved the men who reacted from the sack to noisy gadgets. They ran across the four-poster bed and hid under the covers. I would stand to the side, because how would it look to the audience with two guys in bed with a girl? Across the way, at a tap on my shoulder, I circled in slow motion with the intruder from the nether world. Our emcee, in the guise of the phantom—thanks to a sheet—revealed himself in the end.

When we moved to the incomparable, timeless Clown Car, I thought to sail through; however, their version threw a curve. The small open automobile had a breakaway rear seat.

"We drive around the ring. When I pull this lever the back falls, and you topple onto the ground, Danise," Beau said.

My tumble would provide the laughs.

"Is this safe?" I asked.

"Sure. We've done it a thousand times. Here, we'll demonstrate. Dingle, sit back there and I'll steer."

The jalopy started with a soft explosion, and they puttered in a circle. How easy when Dingle slowly rolled onto the floor! Going against that still, small voice, I sat. With a loud *thunk*, the rear seat broke away and jettisoned me with a thud. First, a flop followed by a backward roll; then I landed on the side of my neck and remained flat in the prone position. Buster Keaton would have been proud.

"Are you all right?" they asked in unison.

My unintentional pratfall packed a wallop and caused my head to spin. I bit my tongue in the process, which triggered a lisp. "Yeth. I'm fine, but I don't want to do that again."

My neck hurt for several days after. Needless to say, I did nothing during their version of Clown Car. One night, months after we returned to California, unbearable pain jolted me from sleep. Billy rushed me to the hospital, and the doctor diagnosed a herniated disk that had resulted from trauma to the vertebrae.

By the time the show started, the ensemble had set the pieces of the Cottle circus.

Jeremy Beadle, the ghost in the pantomime, served as ringmaster. What a vivacious human being! With dark hair, mustache, goatee, and mischievous eyes, Jeremy possessed a bundle of energy and a quick smile. His love of a good joke rendered him the perfect host of the telecasts *Beadle's About* and *You've Been Framed*. The hidden-camera productions—extreme versions of the American program *Candid Camera* that starred Allen Funt—televised such high jinks as the removal of roofs in the absence of homeowners.

"Those broadcasts made me bloody infamous," he said, which made him a natural choice for emcee.

To add fuel to the controversy, circus employees had stuck little blue stickers with Jeremy's likeness on light posts, phone booths, and anywhere else they could find all over London. The labels read, "Beadle Backs British Clowns." (This happened before my arrival.)

The presentation stemmed from the good old days of fantasy, and Jeremy carried the public into the world of make-believe. From day one—dressed in sable slacks with a scarlet sash around his middle, a white shirt and ruby bow tie, and topped off with a red tuxedo jacket—Mr. Beadle raised his hand that held a black top hat. And the show began.

"Ladies and gentlemen. Welcome to Gerry Cottle's Circus!" On with horses, a mule that rendered riders airborne, a knife-throwing act, and clowns. The audience inhaled the excitement, but they missed the drama of backstage.

One day I sat with feet propped up next to my table and fiddled with a costume. The door burst open, and the Russian woman stormed in and muttered something in her language. She threw herself into a chair and looked at her elbow. I glanced at Mary, who leaned in and whispered to me, "Her husband dips her too low during the spins. She must have brushed the coconut-hair ring mat again. That answers the bruises on her arms."

To escape her flavorful, Russian words, I exited the dressing area and took the chance to wander. I followed the call of the midway sideshows to the magic presentation at the rear of the stands. The public strolled among games; snacked on cotton candy, called candy floss; and bit into sweet Baby D Dummies, lollipop pacifiers. Children lingered in front of a small, portable theater and grimaced at the *whack! whack!* of the traditional Punch-and-Judy puppet performance. Popcorn vendors treated me to a complimentary bag of their sugary, salted snack, and I moseyed on.

Through another door, the inside setup with amusement rides enlivened the building. The walls snared the screams of delight and fear that hailed from the house of horrors and lightning-fast roller coasters, propelling the sounds throughout the funfair. Oh, the allure! One thousand-plus miles separated me from my country; but one glance at the ring and a whiff of the menagerie, and I was home.

The normal day at the circus involved us all. Mary Chipperfield absorbed the "oohs," but a gentle giant named the Mighty Miklos captivated the crowd. With a large but not overweight frame, he towered over my five-foot, four-inch stature. A brown goatee complemented his short, auburn hair. His small, round eyes rested center of his face.

After I became accustomed to the order of acts, I hid behind the bleachers during one show. Jeremy faced the audience and said, "Feast your eyes on the curtain!" The spotlight danced from him to the crimson fabric that draped open. Dressed in a spotted Tarzan outfit, the Mighty Miklos entered as a Roman gladiator. He stood motionless with arms bowed and fists clenched, the cue for his wife to hand him an iron bar. He grimaced and bent the rod while his biceps of steel bulged. Several crew members puffed as they carried huge chains into the ring. They wrapped them around the colossal man, then attached them to a mid-size Chevy pickup. "Who would dare tempt the Mighty Miklos?" Jeremy asked the audience.

Ten people rushed to fill the truck bed. *Boom! Boom! Da-boom!* The drums sounded. The Hungarian Hercules inched forward step by step until the vehicle moved. Then he lay on the ground for his finale. While Billy and the band played, "Jesus Christ Superstar," a prop man drove the loaded Chevy across his chest.

One day Billy asked the muscleman, "How did you start your act?"

"I electrician until I discover I make money as strongman. I start out wid Volkswagen Bug and getting bigger and bigger cars until I ended wid truck."

In 2008 Billy and I saw the Ringling show in Las Vegas, Nevada. When the lights dimmed partway through the performance, the drums banged, "*Boom! Boom! Da-boom!*" The curtain opened, and Miklos stomped into view.

My wish to witness traditional European, musical clowns—who sported a different look and played a formal role as opposed to the American standard—came true one day when Gerry treated Billy and me to another circus. We boarded our mobile billboard truck and headed into the city on the Thames to a tent illuminated in the night near a pub.

At the outset, the proper clown entered. His gloveless hands caressed a trumpet. Uniformed in the color white, he wore a spangly coat dress that reached below the knees. Ruffles jutted from the ends of the long sleeves, and his boots (not oversized) stretched up to the base of his frock. His head sported a cone-shaped hat. White greasepaint covered his face, neck front, and one ear. Red veiled the other, as well as the lips and tip of his nose. An extended, black brow arched over his right eye.

Two characters—one a little person, dressed in checkered outfits and shoes with spats—followed the first clown. They, too, toted a trumpet and a tuba. Banter between musical notes pitted the duo in plaid against the dignified man in white. After several minutes with differences resolved, they formed a line across the ring, played a classical song, and bowed. Such performances strengthened my determination to incorporate the accordion and concertina into my work.

An invite to their closing night party, which took place in the pub, ensued. We entered and stepped into the side room. Although everyone wore street clothes, I recognized one of the checkered men, who stood by himself, and wanted to say thanks for an enjoyable presentation. My husband meandered in a different direction. My approach to shake hands with a fellow clown resulted in the shock of my life.

His face turned to stone, and his finger poked my chest. "You are not needed over here," he said. "You don't understand the one-ring show. All you know is Ringling, and that's not real clowning."

The man under the makeup had never walked in my shoes. He jabbed and jabbed unaware that I left the single ring of The L.A. Circus to venture abroad or that I had once lived there. And I took offense at his reference to *The Greatest Show on Earth*. "The only reason you're over here is because Gerry wanted to go after the colored audience."

Prejudice. Few "coloreds" came, however, even though we played to turnaway houses. He badgered and prodded. "You're not funnier than British clowns and besides, you're a Yank. You don't comprehend our sense of humor, so how could you be funnier?"

He plastered me against the wall speechless. In the blink of an eye, the old nemesis of intimidation resurfaced. I retreated to eight years of age and again suffered the horrible weapons of the game of dodge ball. The shell of my childhood at Eastlawn Elementary School emerged from its burial place and engulfed me as if to say,

"So, there you are!" Weakness. Fear. Introvert. But I forbade the haunt of yesteryear's enemies. "Not this time."

The barrage took place for an endless minute. I stood defenseless. The ruse of Gerry's "unfunny, British clowns" had hit a bitter note in him. Everyone, including Billy, continued conversations oblivious to my situation. Someone finally came to my rescue and pulled away the man who had made us laugh.

I had always wanted to witness a European circus, to speak with peers. That incident left no sour taste in my mouth. My early years, spent surrounded by Great Britain's warmth, proved a different sentiment, as did the receptions of the townies and school kids.

Circus had been my Tin Pan Alley, my bedfellow, the creator of dreams at twilight. "How do you think you'll fit in a society that's uncomfortable with women clowns?" the interviewer had asked. The man with the funny face confirmed his unease. Or was it my colored blood?

# # #

Gerry Cottle's Circus continued with turnaway shows. Miklos pulled the Chevy truck filled with people. Baby D circled with Jeremy the ghost, and the petite Russian sported new welts. At our Finale, the entire cast formed a line across the ring. A crew member unrolled a scarlet carpet before us, then skedaddled out of sight. Jeremy Beadle held the microphone up, paused, and said, "Ladies and gentlemen— the Queen!"

When a woman approached from behind the audience and stepped through an opening in the barrier onto the ruby runner, the stunned crowd mumbled, "Is that really the Queen?" Elizabeth Richard earned her bread and butter as an impersonator and resembled the monarch to a T. At the sight of the lady of faux-royal blood, the spectators hesitated, then stood one by one. For authenticity, I moved forward to present Her Majesty with a dozen red roses—every single night. She received the bouquet, we bowed and curtsied, and the astonished audience clapped.

Fond impressions of that season filled my soul as the first black, female circus clown on the continent that bore chimney sweeps and Oliver Twist. Questions found answers: How would I be received? Remembrances of Great Glemham, fictional or real?

The Clown College trip through the rabbit's hole had taken me a long way. My memories began in England and some had stayed there. The teddy bear that sat on a shelf in my hole-in-the-wall on Ringling's train bridged the past. My grandmother had given me the stuffed animal after we Wilsons arrived back stateside years ago. The tag in his seam read, "Teddy Kuddles," but I called him Sooty. The origins of the odd name evaporated during my adolescence and left a life-long mystery.

One day in our flat in Wembley, the television solved the riddle. A voiceover spoke of "an updated version of an old program about a puppet bear named Sooty." He mentioned the years of the original broadcast, which coincided with my family's tour of duty in England. I caught my breath and listened as if a lost friend had returned. The question of the moniker hounded me until that day. The bear is worn now but became the tie that bound me to my beginnings.

Only one door remained shut. British sense of humor differed from American. The musical clown had been right on that point. Folks on both sides of the Atlantic enjoyed slapstick, but the key to open blessed laughter lingered out of my reach within my past. Indeed we spoke the same language, but when the Mayflower crossed the sea, communication severed.

There were different approaches that created guffaws. The British clowns relied on the spoken word technique. I depended on body language. One method did not stand better than the other. They were both separate branches of the same tree. Nonetheless, for the first time a descendant of African slaves held her own in the country where the man Philip Astley in the 1700s earned the title "Father of the Modern Circus." Ah, comedy. Albeit, theirs proved a bit raunchy with farts and smoke from the bum.

Ever grateful to have gone, I never would have had the chance to visit the Chandlers or my one-room schoolhouse if not for this opportunity. We never would have met that creative circus boss man,

Gerry Cottle, or run from that bull elephant. "Running and fighting is good for survival. I've done plenty of both," Gerry would say. It was his show. I loved it.

Guy drove us to the Farm for goodbyes to the Cottle team, and we headed to Heathrow Airport. Fame disappeared in a flash. Unlike our arrival, only anonymity chased us through the streets, not press. Baby D had arrived, but the season was over. We returned to Los Angeles with a scrapbook full of school children's drawings of their day with the American clown. Our work in a European circus, accomplished. Now what?

CHAPTER SIXTEEN

AMERICA IN
BLACK AND WHITE

I n minstrel shows they smeared on greasepaint or burnt cork. Silent
film stars wore woolly wigs and rolled their eyes. The mammies
and uncles of their imaginations sprang from the depth of an
ignorant heart. What would pull a race's dignity free from the muck
and mire of the lowest echelon of entertainment?

"Danise, did you know there's going to be an all-black circus?
Pa-Mela and I are going to do a double trap act. It's called Universal
Big Top Circus."

In 1994 a new day had dawned.

My friend Mari Kohl-Lewis divulged the details about the newcomer sure to set spirits on fire. She said the owner lived in Atlanta,
and his name was Cedric Walker. "Here's his number."

A chance to perform with such a production after fifteen years
of "headin' down the road" proved too hard to pass up.

I had to be included and contacted him to introduce myself. He
answered, "Bernice!"

Ah, the bone of contention that had shadowed me from my first
day in the ring surfaced again. Even though I had performed on Big
Bertha's Red Unit, Bernice Collins—who had graduated from Clown
College the year before me—had already joined the Blue Unit. She
owned the distinction as the pioneer African American woman clown
at Ringling. I never claimed the honor, yet accusations hung over
my head from the get-go like a cloud.

I answered his question, "No. My name is Danise—"

He interrupted, "Denise, uh, Aubrey?"

No. Pa-Mela Hernandez (whom he had already hired) and Denise Aubrey blazed the trail for women of color on *The Greatest Show on Earth* with their aerial act called Satin.

"No. My name is Danise Payne, and I'm a clown."

Silence.

I spoke of my credits and Billy's capability. The next morning I sent a promotional packet, which included the *Ebony* magazine article for an extra boost. Days later he phoned from the Peach State, hired both of us, and the dialogue began.

"Billy will use his expertise as a music consultant," he said. "I have only one clown, however—Russell B. He's an older man with forty years of birthday party experience, but excited about the show. Think you can find more?"

That was an easy task. Garry White had introduced me to circus in Oakland, and he had shared the alley with Skeeter Reece at Ringling when I joined up. The style of each complemented the other. Garry's smooth movements flowed. Skeeter carried on in a highly animated way. They defined the essence of the art. Without hesitation, I gave them the new boss man's number. After consultations, four funny people completed the alley of Universal Big Top Circus.

Once again, Billy and I packed our stuff and hit the road bound for Georgia—this time for the initial season of eleven days that would test the waters. Tented shows required trailers, but only a few of Universal's artistes had worked under canvas. Thus we met the troupe at a Holiday Inn Express, our home for the run.

After Billy parked, we stepped through the automatic glass doors and followed the hubbub to the restaurant on the right. Someone called to us as we entered, and Pa-Mela, and Mari rushed over. In the café stood the King Charles Troupe of unicyclists, clowns Garry and Skeeter, and other performers. The American circus community counted few African Americans, and we figured the bulk had signed on.

After our long-time-no-see reunion, we headed to check-in and spoke to another interracial couple. "I'm Ron Pace, and this is my wife, Chris," the burly man said. "We're a cradle act under the name Sugar and Spice." They said that they had worked their number—which involved hair-raising, backward, hand-to-hand flips in the air—with other one-ring companies. Due to an extensive career, they lived in a rig in the backyard. After chitchat we received our room number, emptied the truck, then returned to the excitement.

Gray, drippy skies filled the next day. Billy and I dodged the sprinkles for the short distance to the Atlanta-Fulton County Stadium. Before us stood—like a mirage from a dream—the symbol of 201 years of a unique entertainment. It rested on the asphalt and beckoned in the rain. Guy ropes stretched from the height and sidepoles of that blue-and-red circus tent. These tied to steel stakes two feet in length, each spaced evenly around the perimeter that secured the strong, coarse cloth against blowdowns. We stopped short and cocked our heads to the side. "It's leaning," Billy said.

That was an understatement. Our first canvas home tilted. Good thing we didn't believe in omens. We learned later that the lessor of the sidewalls and top was a circus man named George Coronas. He and his crew had set it up. It was not their fault that the ground slanted. As the years progressed, we played rocky or asphalt lots at incredible inclines. For alleviation, Mr. Walker would position and level a solid ring on risers three feet off the ground. The blend between circus and theater mirrored the setup at Sacramento's Music Circus.

We approached the office trailer. Someone peered through the window, and their words, "Here comes that famous clown," filtered outside. Two people descended the stairs.

"Hi, Danise and Billy. I'm Cynthia Walker. Cedric's told me about you both."

"Nice to meet you too," I said. "This is quite something. I've wondered about a circus like this for years."

The man stepped forward. "I'm Cedric." With a slender frame, he appeared to be in his fifties. A modest smile trickled across his face, and he shook our hands with the casualness of someone used to the unknown. "Hi, you two. Welcome to Atlanta. Yeah, it's gonna be unlike any other show and definitely different than Ringling."

"We'll do anything we can," Billy said.

"Thanks, Bill. Not only will you help Tom with the music, but you'll also be one of the crew. Is that all right?"

"Sure."

A thin guy with short hair strolled by dressed in a T-shirt and beige jeans.

Mr. Walker called out, "Ted, meet Danise and Bill." He turned to us. "This is Ted McRae. He's gonna present elephants and lions."

The young man broke into an instant grin. How nice to meet one of the rare men of color in his field!

"How long have you worked with animals and where?" I asked.

"I haven't started yet," he said. "This is my first circus."

"What?"

"Yeah, Cedric's my cousin. He remembered my pet snake and asked if I'd go in the ring with the lions and elephants. Why not?"

Right then and there, the seasoned words of Gunther Gebel-Williams surfaced: "I got bit several times. They—the cats—are trained, not tamed." I couldn't believe Ted's foolish guts and fixed my eyes on his unmarked, radiant mug.

"So, you've never been in a cage?" Billy asked.

"No," answered Ted. "I'm a forklift driver. Excuse me—duty calls." He turned and walked away.

His audacity stunned us speechless.

Billy studied Mr. Walker and asked, "What prompted the idea to tackle this?"

"Well, ever hear of a man named Ephraim Williams?"

We had. In the 1880s the notable African American had ushered in a new era as a forerunner with his own circus.

"He inspired me," Mr. Walker explained. "I've worked on the creative side of shows: stage manager for the Commodores singing group, tour organizer for rap music artists, and co-producer of gospel plays, for example. Yeah, I've tried a lot of things, made a million here, and if it was lost, went for something else.

"My friend, who you'll meet later, was a disc jockey, and we partnered. His name is Cal Dupree, a.k.a. Casual Cal. We discussed this and that and decided that circus was the way. He's gonna be the ringmaster."

He spoke of how he had sought advice from other show folk on the logistics of his venture, but had been met with resistance. The bulk of his hands-on help stemmed from the world of rock music, he said, by way of Tom Marzullo. Mr. Marzullo had hired a Canadian crew that specialized in the desired computerized laser lights and rotating spots. (Later Ringling would adopt this cutting-edge innovation for the circus scene.)

I observed this latest circus man and considered: With little knowledge of the way of life, the lingo, or the different breed called circus people who possessed an unprecedented stamina, Mr. Walker and his friend emanated chutzpah. They wouldn't tread water alone, for the unique ship on the sea of sawdust promised to be a phenomenon with success in its wake. Mr. Walker had mentioned that sponsors leapt on board: La-Van Hawkins—owner of InnerCityFoods and franchisee of Checkers fast food restaurant, the Coca-Cola Company, the KFC Corporation, Burger King, and Dr Pepper, for example.

"I'm going to call it *Your Circus of Dreams,*" he said.

The show's maiden voyage would occur during that year, 1994, in Cedric Walker's hometown of Atlanta, Georgia.

"Well, Danise and Bill, I don't want to keep you too long, so go on into the tent and look around. We'll talk later."

Cold air greeted our entrance into the empty shell. Cables that covered the slope of the asphalt made each step difficult, but we familiarized ourselves with the surroundings. The tedious progress required to raise the proscenium mesmerized us until someone yelled, "Cats over here!" The sound of semis drew us into the backyard.

Due to the lack of African American animal handlers, the new boss man disregarded the bounds of race to pull from the tried-and-true. A blond woman hopped from a truck, and we recognized her. Kay Rosaire, a descendant of circus generations, rolled in with the king of beasts. She would transform Ted, who dared to portray Daniel in the lions' den. They hoisted portable enclosures of meshed metal, and a ruler with a shaggy mane and large canine teeth loped from the long vehicle.

The chug and fumes of diesel engines permeated the yard, with yet another noise joining the din. "Bucky [Steele], set your rig over there!" Bucky's entry meant one thing: elephants, which I loved. The gargantuan, gentle creatures were a true symbol of circus, so we lingered, our excitement heightened. Bucky would also teach the ropes of presentation to the forklift operator, and First of May, Ted McRae.

We stood to the side as one of the crew maneuvered the sizeable trucks—an art all its own. He placed himself in front of the new arrivals and pointed his index finger toward the drivers. A quick, small circle of the hand to the left or right directed them to turn the wheels accordingly. Within minutes, vehicles of any size were stuffed into tight spaces as pegs into holes.

Billy and I greeted Bucky, who then opened the King Kong-size doors on the side of the transport and entered. After a moment or two, the huge, mobile box swayed; a gray, wrinkled trunk emerged, then three jumbo-size bodies. Bucky led the massive stars to hay strewn on the ground. Then: a guttural rumble. A trumpet-like blast. Ah! Elephant contentment. What a welcome into the world of canvas and semis!

As days zoomed by, Billy set music with Tom Marzullo in the office trailer. Each act had come self-contained and only needed practice time in the tent. Clowns rehearsed wherever we dared—hotel rooms or in the parking lot. In due course, lighting and sound checks would take place under the big top.

How rough a beginning! Rain or shine. Snow or wind. True troupers, Billy and I would learn to powder on asphalt and track through the mud. We shared outside, unheated dressing accommodations. Someone, however, thought similar artists should change together—regardless of gender—which put me in a tough spot. My metamorphosis transpired in men's clown alley with the robust male acrobats. A glance here and there, and—whoa, baby, whoa! The winter weather stiffened fingers, and makeup was applied as if with arthritic hands.

No cookhouse existed, which resulted in a daily hunt for meals. KFC stood across the street, but we soon grew tired of the same thing. Garry and I combed the neighborhood until we found a small restaurant. Each day we returned with white plastic plates loaded with flavorful collard greens, almond yams, stewed oxtails, and buttery cornbread. After we answered the cast's inquiries of "Where did you get that?" the diner exploded with business. We managed fine in those early days because we possessed the spirit of Marco Polo.

The show pulled together thanks to the old hands of the trade. After a blur of preparation, the November 3 opening night charged in like a roaring lion. The troupe piled into the van and headed to the slanted big top with its turnaway house. That is to say, sold out.

"OK, y'all, gather around," Cal said.

Like circuses in buildings, the entranceway for performers under canvas was called the back door. We crammed inside and could have charged a lighthouse beacon with our excitement.

"All right everyone, this is the night we've waited for," Mr. Walker said. "I know you won't let me down. We've got something here . . ."

I looked around and smiled. Ethnic sneers of childhood had been dealt a death blow. Young ebony-hued men and women stood ready to turn a page of history.

He continued, "I know how to draw in people. All y'all gotta do is perform. OK, Cal, you wanna say something?"

"Yeah, a prayer."

We bowed heads, held hands, and Cal spoke the words. Afterward the houselights dimmed, and the spotlights came up. The extravaganza didn't begin with the traditional whistle; instead, the speakers blasted the upbeat tempo of a song lost to memory. A crew member yanked open the curtains. Look out, world. Here we come!

A little person named Zander Charles, a.k.a. Zeke, was Cal's sidekick. Dressed in a sable suit, hat, and sunglasses, he quick-stepped up the ramp and into the center of the ring. The crowd went nuts to see him boogie down in the spotlight. Casual Cal was flashily turned out in a yellow zoot suit. He burst through and strutted stride-style to join him.

"When I say, 'Big Top,' you say 'circus,'" he said.

"Big Top!"

"Circus!" the audience responded. The spectacle with soul dished up a different kind of show.

Universal Big Top Circus embodied the spirits of those who had survived the middle passage. The syncopated notes of jazz mated with the melancholy of the blues—both complemented by the funk of hip-hop. The sound: loud and to the point. The audience clapped to the beat, and the tent seemed to sway to the rhythm. The theme highlighted the culture of the African American and the history of our ancestors. And, yes, Ted McRae presented the elephants, but, dressed in a loincloth, he portrayed Hannibal. The King Charles Troupe zipped around the ring on unicycles and played a unique game of basketball.

The show also granted me my first solo. At home in our living room, I dreamed up a routine to "Hero" by Mariah Carey. The trumpet's lilt from the theme music of Federico Fellini's movie *La Strada* served as an introduction.

Cal announced me. "A graduate of Ringling's clown school, she was the first black, female clown at Ringling Bros. and Barnum & Bailey Circus's Red Unit and the first to *ever* perform in a circus in England. Ladies and gentlemen, Danise Payne."

I closed my eyes and gave glory to God. My heart raced and butterflies coursed through my belly. The darkness hid my placement of props in the center of the ring. Then a bright beam from overhead showered down at the start of the poignant tune. Dressed as a washerwoman, I took off my cleaning hat and donned a tailcoat tuxedo. The words to the song "Hero" summed up my life from past to present because it focused on the discovery of personal strength.

I tossed a ball into the air, then a second, and a third. I juggled the three balls with ease—under the arms, two in one hand with a circle of the other. "Go on girl!" the crowd responded. Hat manipulation followed: derby twirl to the right. A few flips of the bowler accompanied my pirouette. "That's right!" the viewers said. Near the end of the number, I paused.

I had never performed before a sold-out house of our race. Oh, how uplifted I was by the experience, especially after years as one of few ebony souls in a show amidst a sea of white. Like a mirror, Universal Big Top Circus reflected me. I was no longer the little girl who talked funny. The audience sprang from their seats at the end of the melody, and they erupted in "Hush now!"

The ties that bind caused emotional fireworks. With arms stretched to the sides and head tilted up, at that moment I could have been the ignited powder in a canister on the Fourth of July.

The show progressed with aerialists, acrobats, animals, and clowning. Casual Cal and Zeke led the troupe into the tent for Finale. We encircled the ring while the taped singers declared that from that day on, we would not be stopped. The spectators bolted to their feet, and Universal Big Top Circus made its debut.

Women in golden costumes, clowns with big shoes, and Ted in a leopard-skin loincloth exited the blue-and-red big top. "OK, y'all, go to the VIP tent." Toasts, speeches, and laughter followed.

Mr. Walker entered to a round of applause. He had hit black gold. "We did it. A lot of effort went into this, and I just want to thank you." He continued, and his words pumped us higher.

Circuses draw visitors from different walks of life. Ours was no exception. My brother attended as did Kenneth Feld from Ringling. We told Ricky (Mr. Walker's nickname) to expect him to visit to scope out this new kid on the block, a habit of circus owners.

That Saturday after the third performance, I was relaxing behind the scenes when someone said, "Hi, Mr. Feld." He stood to the side with his hands in his pockets, intrigued. Most of our cast had earned a paycheck from him in the past, so we greeted and surrounded him. His views of the enterprise didn't matter. Competition? No chance. *The Greatest Show on Earth* couldn't keep up.

Ricky called a meeting before the closing date of November 13. "Since we sold out, I've extended the run for another week." Good news. No one wanted to leave, and more work meant additional pay. After those extra seven days, we did close, and everyone scattered across the country to his or her home.

We held odd jobs during the year until the 1995 season called for a return to Georgia. Ambition and guaranteed money seemed to be dangling before us. But a bump in the road developed for Billy and me. Ricky didn't rehire him for some reason. We had been together on every show through the years. His lack of employment cut like a knife into the ribs. He took me into his arms. "Don't worry about it. It's only for three weeks. You gotta go." So, I headed to Atlanta by myself. Once there, I shared a hotel room with one of the dancers and her vivacious mother.

The returnees met new faces and improvements. My own dressing space stood among those that filled a tent in the backyard. A welcome sight. But we still had no heaters in the dead of winter. The first day it rained and pools of the cold drops tickled our feet. So we dragged in pallets for a makeshift floor. One morning the curtain to my little alley opened and there stood Ricky with a young woman in her thirties.

"Danise, you're gonna share your area. I want you to meet Nayakata, a contortionist from Spain." He sloshed away.

Nayakata and I looked at each other, smiled, then glanced around. My 3' x 6' x 9' hole-in-the-wall on Ringling's train was larger. The small enclosure fit my trunk—which sat on the raised, wooden slats—and me. Nayakata stood in the three-inch-deep water with nowhere to go.

"Hi, I'm Danise. I'm a clown."

"No English."

"Oh, *me llamo Danise y soy una payasita*." One semester of Spanish served me well.

"*Me llamo Aurora*." In English, "My name is Aurora." She worked under the name Nayakata.

Soon the flap flew open again. Her companion entered, crammed two portable platforms into the small cubicle, and left. He returned with a pair of chairs, sat, and grinned. The stilted conversation resumed but plunged. I misconstrued his name from Piko to Paso to Pato, to which they replied, "Aie, no! Pato is *quack, quack* [the word duck]!" Failure to communicate broke the ice.

A woman from Valencia, Spain, had adopted the young African named Aurora. Groomed from childhood, she had performed in Europe and was more than a contortionist. The first night she performed I hid under the stands and discovered the poetry of pretzel.

Nayakata lifted herself onto a round, elevated stand and eased backward, hands behind feet. The audience's "oohs" and "aahs" accompanied the graceful twist of head under arm. Paco set an odd, metal spike before her, and she rose with care to a perfect handstand on the balance apparatus, toes pointed to the cupola of the tent.

The onlookers combusted into applause, which egged her body on to form the letter *C*. She rested on forearms, and her feet reached for a top hat in front of her face and placed it on her hair. Easy like Sunday morning. Nayakata sipped water from a cup through a straw and puffed from a cigarette with the use of her foot. The white smoke caressed her ebony skin and drifted toward the top of the canvas. The audience bolted upward with a jolt of electricity in response to the first black contortionist we had ever seen.

The second stationary season proved the magnetism of Universal Big Top Circus once again. For the next year Ricky booked enough towns to fill a three-month test period on the road. This would ensure the possibility of a full run of ten months later on. To our relief he also rehired Billy, and we both held positions with the circus for many years to follow.

I returned to Los Angeles, but before we left Southern California, my mind retreated to Ringling. I thought about Papa Lou and his dog, Knucklehead, and about Cowboy Clown, Mike Keever and his mule sidekick. They both drew chuckles alongside their animal companions. I wanted to branch out and find a four-legged partner. A slow, long-eared basset hound would fit my scheme to squeeze laughter from a turnip. We purchased her from an American Kennel Club breeder and named her Sad Sack, the Wonder Dog.

My internal motor revved. I was eager to be a part of the black creativity that the rest of the country would soon witness.

CHAPTER SEVENTEEN

BONA FIDE CIRCUS LIFE

With his job secured, Billy and I left Los Angeles and headed to my parents' house in Rancho Cordova. We wanted to buy a rig, but Mom and Dad donated their personal truck and nineteen-foot, fifth-wheel camper. "We no longer need it for vacations."

We packed our belongings and battened down the hatches in preparation for the journey as my air force family had done in the past. Military get-up-and-go had come full circle. I hated goodbyes, yet converted into a life laden with "see ya down the road." Ever grateful for my parents' generosity, my husband and I transitioned from train to caravan, bona fide circus life.

Opening day for the third season closed in, and time arrived to leave. With eight-week-old Sad Sack in place, Billy pulled away. The side-view mirror framed my mother and father. Hand in hand they waved, a picture frozen to time. Tomorrow and the open road awaited.

We arrived in Detroit before anyone. The rocky lot at Chene Park greeted us with no water, no electrical hookups, no tent, no nothing. The wind blew its cold breath around us, and the sky enveloped us in a gray blanket of rain. Billy looked outside. "I have an idea." He exited the truck and plugged the trailer into a nearby light pole. "Power's on!" At those words, I remembered how Dad had created heat when he set an inverted clay flower pot over a lit stove burner and followed suit. Yet, we remained cold, wet, and miserable. Even the dog's teeth chattered.

The minute the circus made its debut in Detroit, news spread like wildfire; word of mouth served as the best advertisement. As a result, we sold out the entire run in the city of Motown, left them begging for more, and headed west to Billy's home, Chicago, Illinois. That was a good thing because a stone's throw away revealed black hair salons, unlike the Ringling circuits. I had long ago eliminated the permanent to straighten my hair and now preferred the hot comb's touch to natural tresses. A short stroll to the hairdresser washed the soot of travel away.

Chicago, also known as Chi-Town, gave us turnaway crowds as well. Onward, onward, and the momentum grew. The final stop for the trial tour returned Billy and me to the town of celluloid. We set up in Exposition Park near the University of Southern California and the Memorial Coliseum and Sports Arena. McDonald's Corporation joined as a sponsor, and on November 8, 1996, Bank of America presented our Opening.

No Ringling Star Night blitz took place, but the evening buzzed with Winnie Mandela from South Africa; singer, Anita Baker; actress, Kirstie Alley; and Aunt Ernestine and my family.

I had become full-fledged circus. Chimpanzees in funny little outfits lived next door. Lions and tigers secured neighborhood watch. Universal Big Top Circus topped *The Greatest Show on Earth* in some ways because I had a stake in its creation and success. We all did.

My kin arrived, and dressed in the formal attire of my latest persona, I ran from our fifth wheel to greet them. We sauntered behind the scenes and toured the difference between canvas and building, between absolute air force and catch-as-catch-can circus. "This is the backyard. Human and animal performers are here in designated spots like puzzle pieces," I said. We maneuvered the maze toward the menagerie and stopped to observe a lion shake his hairdo before he lay down. We carried on through the center aisle past different sizes of rigs. Portable, wooden clotheshorses displayed white tights and red leotards that dried in the sun's warmth. We turned right.

"That's the pump-out vehicle. Remember, Daddy, you told us to stop at truck stops on the road to empty the waste. While we're parked on the lots, the service comes to us for the trailers and portable, public donnikers—circus for toilets." My family held their noses, and we continued toward our mobile quarters, stepping over hoses that snaked to fireplugs for precious water. We sloshed through the liquid that stood in pools here and there. "Bad connections," I explained. Barbecue grills adorned the makeshift lanes and proved that circus folk loved charbroiled food. The backyard equaled a walled sanctuary where uninhibited artistes strolled free from outsiders' eyes.

My birth family witnessed a close-knit lifestyle that bonded me to my sawdust brothers and sisters. As we explored the grounds, my father came across as an old soldier who inspected the troops, minus his dress blues. Their presence meant the world to me. When they visited Ringling Bros. and Barnum & Bailey Circus, my spirit jumped with excitement. But when they sat in the front row of Universal Big Top Circus and watched me alone in the spotlight, my soul was released from its confines as a butterfly set free. My black-and-white, oversized oxfords lifted me like winged feet. To do a solo was my greatest show on earth.

A few days later, I ambled in the back when Pa-Mela's voice rang out. "Rosa Parks is here!" The entire troupe shot toward the rear gate, and I followed suit. "All right," Cal said, "don't suffocate her. Move back y'all. Give her some room." We parted like the Red Sea, and into our midst, arm in arm with Cal, stepped one of the heroes who had dislodged our feet from the ravages of hate.

She sported a dark blazer over a paisley dress, large glasses, and a blue turban that covered gray hair. With a balloon in one hand and a program in the other, Ms. Parks traversed our transient neighborhood. I then ran inside and hid under the stands. She entered the big top to instant recognition. When she sat in the front row, sawdust and glitter took a back seat. I dedicated "Hero" to her that night and at the end of the number reached out and embraced history. What an appropriate way to end the season.

We retreated home to prepare for the first ten-month tour. Nineteen ninety-seven dawned as a year of changes. Universal Pictures threatened to sue over the use of the name, which brought about a clever revision. We no longer answered to Universal Big Top Circus, but instead to UniverSoul Big Top Circus.

Ricky bought a bunkhouse and positioned it alongside the tent for the permanent crew of working men, who lived a difficult life out of suitcases. Their day began before sunrise and ended around midnight. Additional help to erect our newly purchased blue-and-yellow Canobbio big top stemmed from local men out of work. Therefore jobs stayed within the community. We welcomed the new add-ons. Huge, outside ducts that connected to massive generators piped in blessed heat when the sun limped across the sky; they blew in iced air when the same took revenge.

And so we hit the road and joined ranks with other circuses. We never competed because we blazed a new path. UniverSoul traveled into the inner city, populated by shades of midnight blue to able to pass for white—neighborhoods left off most tanbark trails.

We drove streets in need of repair and set up shop surrounded by worn houses. Liquor stores abounded. Likewise, churches. The route served as a banner that America still put forth an invisible line of a lesser degree of apartheid between her peoples. I hadn't understood the bussing away of African American kids near Connally Junior High. But why a food problem? I shopped for provisions only to have the odor of spoiled meat clog the air once inside a market. To circumvent that, a search for a mall led me across town where Macy's and Nordstrom enticed white greenbacks. Notable emporiums and good grub. And it was so.

Disparity between the races proved a hard pill to swallow. I had traveled my country's roads many times in the past, but the vagabond life of the canvas of soul reestablished the truth. America remained entrapped by color.

Yet experiences surfaced like never before. Military existence served a platter void of ethnic distinctions, but on our itinerary culture exploded at every turn. Sounds of rhythm and blues drifted from storefronts. Barrel-like barbecue grills, called smokers, lined the pavements. Life teamed with afro-centric manner of speech and style of walking. Salons with the smell of cooking hair and intricate braided dos to rival Queen Nefertiti's filled our route as on no other. When my feet treaded sable sidewalks, I encountered a familiarity that never bred contempt.

Your Circus of Dreams was on the move. We set up on asphalt and in deep mud. The latter required wood chips to support wheels that would sink and stick in sludge. We played the same towns as Ringling: Washington, D.C; Greensboro, North Carolina; Denver, Colorado, for example. *Always* to sold-out houses with people who came to see their own fly through the air with the greatest of ease. The poor sections of each city reminded me of the richness of black. My mind retreated to Chanute Air Force Base with relief that the Ajax did not remove my pigment.

#

One day Cynthia Walker knocked on our door, and said, "Your mother phoned, Danise. Call home."

Melancholy rose and lodged in my throat when my fingers dialed the number.

Daddy answered, "It seems they found something during an exam."

I closed my eyes and hoped against hope. "Was it cancer?" I asked.

He paused. His response crossed him into eternity: "Yes." The possibility of the unacceptable hit head-on.

Unbeknownst to me doctors had discovered that which wreaked havoc in my father's colon in 1996. *That* explained why we inherited their truck and trailer. When Billy and I flew to Sacramento, I trudged down the hall to the bedroom and peeked in. The sun's brightness shone through the window, yet darkness enveloped the shadow of my father's former self. The enemy caressed Dad with its grip. How could that be? He lay motionless.

After eight months of chemotherapy, he had opted for no more due to the nausea. As a result, the disease shot from his colon to his liver to his brain and entered his lungs. Seven different pills fused with his body four times a day. Two kinds of eye drops swirled around his cornea—all with hopes to push back the tide to come. Cough syrup laced with codeine eased the pain. Not really. Daddy began his journey.

I always hated separation, and the death of my father would be the ultimate loathing. In the days that followed, I sat at his bedside and held a conversation bound to nowhere, read short stories, and reflected on his words that had taught us his history.

"In 1939," he had said, "succumbing to pressure to include African Americans, the Civil Aeronautics Authority initiated the Civilian Pilot Training Program to see if our race possessed the capability to fly for the military—my dream."

What an insult to believe a people, based on their skin color, did not have the aptitude! He passed the cadet exam in Illinois and entered the United States Army Air Corps. Assigned to the Ninety-ninth Pursuit Squadron on April 2, 1941, Dad became an original Tuskegee Airman of World War II.

He attended the Link Trainer Instructor School at Chanute Field in Rantoul, Illinois, because he held a degree in aeronautical engineering. At the training grounds in Tuskegee, Alabama, my father taught the first class of black aviators to fly by instruments in case of inclement weather.

Our lives had been structured by the armed forces. I defied the military system that instilled fierce pride of sons, which overshadowed the second-class citizens called daughters. Females stood short of the notch on a measuring rod. The unfair yardstick had unleashed a silent rebellion in a corner of my soul. Perhaps that was the root of the shyness that shall always remain an unwanted companion.

Daddy had followed the rule of thumb. His verbal discipline kept order in check. However I no longer needed his elusive approval to substantiate my existence, and now it was too late. I stared, helpless. He motioned for me to come closer. With the side of my face next to his, I waited for a whisper of words. He kissed my cheek instead. The simple action resounded like a sonic boom.

"Daddy, are you afraid?"

"No. I know where I'm going."

On April 11, 1997, he soared away. Our family held the memorial service that Thursday. In recognition of a fallen warrior, the honor guard from McClellan Air Force Base presented a twenty-one-gun salute. My mother received an American flag, folded tight, stars positioned up over the blue background—a perfect triangle. After goodbyes at the cemetery, my mother kissed his plaque. Remembrances of childhood flooded my mind and living water found its way from between the lids.

We remained thankful Ricky allowed the leave, but the time to head back approached. Billy left earlier in order to prepare for move-out night. I needed to recoup and returned by Amtrak. After condolences from fellow performers, we pulled out of Philly and moved toward New York City.

A toll payment allowed us to cross the George Washington Bridge over the Hudson River for entrance into Manhattan from the west. The first site was a sanctuary called Randall's Island Park located in the East River. We made our way down to 125th Street, then straight through the borough. Kudos to my husband's skill behind the wheel. He drove with the dexterity of a mouse in a maze.

"We have to take that ramp on the right, Billy, to the Triborough Bridge. There's another fee."

"More dough? I forgot you can't get in or out of this town without forking over something," he said.

We edged up for payment number two. Directions indicated a maneuver to the left. We were on the right. Billy turned on the blinkers, but the swarm of cars zoomed past. With trailer in tow, we careened to the left, ignored the horns, and followed signs. We dished up loot for a third charge to inch onto Interstate 278. Access to Randalls-Ward Island—our destination—required a final chunk of change.

Our setup stood near a center for the mentally ill and criminally insane located on the isolated oasis surrounded by water. The locale didn't bother us. In fact, in the still of night after the show, the circus covered us with its wings and we slept in peace.

At the end of the sold-out run, the crew of UniverSoul Big Top Circus folded the canvas and packed the cupola. We returned to Manhattan and exposed our lives to its black Mecca.

Harlem's borders extended from 110th to 151st Street and west of Fifth Avenue. High-risers made of mortar and brick encased the nail-strewn, cramped lot laden with shards of glass. On this rested our blue-and-yellow Canobbio, which sat adjacent to an elevated section of the number one subway train. My first ride on that particular route revealed a stark occurrence. At 116th Street most of the white passengers scurried off like rats from a sinking ship. Too bad. A journey through the hemoglobin of American society began with the next stop of 125th Street.

Harlem. Out of the pages of her past flew memories of the Apollo Theater and Billie Holiday, Charlie Parker and jazz, the Savoy Ballroom and Ella Fitzgerald, street corners and Malcolm X. Also in that folio for posterity—the words of James Baldwin and Langston Hughes. The trip allowed the rider an experience into the very heart of soul.

With our turnaway shows, a new Renaissance, flavored with the roar of lions and the trumpets of elephants, filled the streets. The conductor of the number one train showed his approval each morning with a blast of the horn. While the cars streaked overhead, the attached American flag waved in the breeze.

CHAPTER EIGHTEEN

MUD SHOW

Donnikers and bouncing fleas
Pie-car food and strife
Country roads and sawdust dreams
But, chaos in circus life?
—D. Payne

With a run of one week completed, time neared for the mad dash to get out of town, and we said "see ya down the road" to Harlem. The explosive reception for UniverSoul propelled us onward. The show was new compared to Ringling, and changes took place. The black crew transitioned to Hispanics. Performers left for one reason or another, and thus, I said goodbye to Nayakata, Garry, and Skeeter.

I thought that the alley was lost until Ricky hired three distinct young men as replacements mid-year: Ronnie Mosley; the formal Kevyn Johnson, attired in tuxedo; and a talented kid named Jonathan Martin. My belief in fairytales continued as the new contingent of funny people started over in Chicago.

Several ideas bombed, but thanks to time and circumstance, we hit a zinger: boxer Mike Tyson bit off part of Evander Holyfield's ear during a professional bout a month before.

We ran with it for a soul version of the Boxing gag. Thin Jonathan would portray the pugilist in a constant state of movement; Dapper Dan Kevyn, the referee; and tall Ronnie, the opponent.

"I'll be your little old grandmother, Ronnie, and sit in the audience to cheer you on," I said.

We rehearsed behind Ricky's back to prevent a repeal. Then we would present the piece in the show without approval. We risked the boot, but aspiration prevailed.

Showtime. While our ringmaster stepped into the ring, I sneaked into the front, sat with the crowd, and spotted the boss man in the stands. Casual Cal began: "When I say Big Top! you say, Circus! Big Top!"

"Circus!" the crowd responded.

"Oh, y'all think you're good, huh? OK, we have some folks who wanna make you laugh. Here are the clowns of UniverSoul Big Top Circus!"

When the music—the theme from the movie *Rocky*—started, Jonathan burst from the curtain and flailed his arms as fast as a humming bird's wings. He crawled under the ropes and into position, then Ronnie stomped in to "Eye of the Tiger." Kevyn motioned, "Do not poke eyes," by pretending to jab Ronnie's. He demonstrated, "Do not stamp on feet," on Jonathan's shoes. After he clanged a small cymbal on a rope, the match kicked off.

Jonathan blurred in the ring, but Ronnie lugged. With all the changes in the show, we hoped the false-ear shtick would have the onlookers rolling in the aisles. On cue, Jonathan crawled under Ronnie's legs, jumped on him, and sunk his pearly whites into the brown-tinted, latex appendage on the side of Ronnie's head. He jerked toward the audience, bared his teeth, and flung the fake ear in their direction. The combustion of laughter almost blasted the cupola into orbit.

I bounded into the ring. "Foul! Foul!" An accidental double KO from my purse ended the gag. The spectators jumped to their feet, and we ran off. The ecstatic head honcho shot to the back of the tent and greeted, "Classic!"

One day, I wandered into the tent to watch Ted rehearse the lions. The house lights dimmed, and the spots came up in the enclosure. One after the other, the slow cats loped in and sat on perches like they had a thousand times before. One of the lions tilted his head backward, and his mane that flowed as a field of wheat validated royalty. He closed his eyes, opened his mouth, and impressive teeth framed a bored yawn.

Ted conducted the symphony of felines, but this practice was out of the ordinary. A cloud of smoke filtered in. The unfamiliar setting agitated the lions, and their eyes focused on the nervous Ted. Kay Rosaire, who stood outside the mesh-wired barrier, sprang to life. "Never switch a set routine with wild animals! That's dangerous!" She entered the pen and seized command of the whip. The woman of experience calmed her voice and ordered the confused beasts into their cages.

True troupers understood that any threat to safety—such as one step to the left of norm with untamed creatures—moved hilarity and high jinks into another realm. The unexpected incident with the big cats took me aback, and I exited the tent. I did not know that the next day would be bleak.

Pa-Mela Hernandez had been half of the duo called "Satin" at Ringling—the first African Americans to do aerial work on *The Greatest Show on Earth*. Her career on the edge enthralled audiences on many productions. She had learned different acts for Soul Circus since its inception in 1994, and she rejoined us mid-season after yet one more: a single-trapeze routine.

I sneaked under the bleachers her first day back and peered around the legs of the spectators to watch her performance. Her music began, and she soared like an albatross. Mid-flight she reached backward to execute a maneuver but instead said hello to thin air. It happened in the blink of an eye, her plummet to the ring floor. She lay sprawled in place as a rag doll thrown away. Screams, then hushed silence, deafened the ears in a surreal scene of broken glitter. I bolted to the back door and joined those who had crowded in. Someone summoned an ambulance, and a siren drove home the inconceivable. The paramedics rushed in and lifted her onto a gurney. Billy and I followed their blue-and-white vehicle in our truck to the hospital, where the doctors' prognosis stopped time. Pa-Mela's life transformed: she broke her hip in several places.

What a roller-coaster ride! Before we left town at the end of the 1997 season, George Coronas asked Billy, Ronnie, and me to tour with his production during the off-season. He had leased his tent to Ricky during Soul Circus's first years and still accompanied us. "It'll be a few fun dates in Illinois," George said. "I want Ronnie and you for my clowns, Danise. Bill, on sax in the band."

After our short season, his show would kick off. The ideal situation paired Billy and music with me in the ring. In addition, a fresh company and boss would allow us to unwind. So off to Illinois.

The three of us, plus a basset hound, made our way to East St. Louis, Illinois—shy of the Mississippi River to the west. We proceeded to our first stop, a large expanse of asphalt. Billy and I positioned our rig within the show's confines and connected water hoses and such—backyard business—while Ronnie helped another man erect the canvas. I studied them because they pounded the stakes with a heavy mallet, which was new to me. As the gandy dancers of days gone by, the two hammered in succession until the posts sunk halfway into the concrete—brutal, thankless work. Ronnie's shirtless skin sparkled with sweat in the heat. He wiped his brow and called out, "Don't they have motorized stake pounders now?"

In the early evening after setup, we rested in our lawn chairs at the door to our home on wheels. We faced a small meadow and every now and then surveyed our portable work place. In the distance the sound of a train drew near. By then, George's blue-and-red big top stood upright in full glory of any passersby. As the locomotives inched closer, the engineer blew the whistle. It snaked in front of us, and the emblazoned words "Ringling Bros. and Barnum & Bailey Circus, *The Greatest Show on Earth,*" came into view.

I sprang from the chair and waved. "Hey!"

Performers in the vestibules repeated the greeting, and a nameless soul among them asked, "What show are you?"

"George Coronas Circus. I used to be on The Red. What unit are you?"

The silver slug moved out of earshot and made the reply inaudible.

However the spirit of circus moved, it functioned as a magnet for the vagabond. A few years earlier, Billy and I had boarded a local bus in England for Canterbury on a day off from Gerry Cottle's show. Along the way, we spotted a blue-and-yellow Canobbio in a vast field. After a note of the location, we returned the following afternoon as homeward-bound birds. In spite of UniverSoul's troubles, circus was our life. When Ringling's train passed, the familiarity amongst the sawdust and the glitter warmed our hearts.

Never a turnaway crowd, empty stands faced the ring for our second stop. That didn't put a damper on things. We performed under the umbrella of the Shriners International organization, which sponsored different productions on tour. Their moniker replaced the name of the actual enterprise, so a banner on our fence proclaimed Ainad Temple Shrine Circus, Olney City Park Parade. Equipped with flowers that squirted and bulbous horns, their clowns joined our troupe to earn money to support hospitals where kids under eighteen received treatment regardless of their ability to pay.

And so we played Olney, Illinois, with its famous albino squirrels. Next stop: O'Fallon, Illinois, and the return of the title George Coronas Circus. Sometimes we entertained without a tent or sidewalls and on other occasions beneath the fireproof surrounding. It rained a lot. When it did, George cancelled the performances, and we headed to Du Quoin, Illinois. It poured there too. We retreated to Olney and more drizzle awaited. We traveled to and fro between the two towns and never opened in Du Quoin. No life competed with troupin' across the byways of America. No gas bill. No electric bill. No newspaper with the world's pitfalls. To the townie we lived on the fringes of society, but the gypsy knows everywhere yet nowhere. And we trekked on.

The wind blew equipment from the rear of our pickup during one of the repeat trips.

"What was that noise?" Billy asked.

"The barbecue grill top. Should we stop and get it?"

"Naw. We'll rescue it on the way back."

It was not there on the return, so we continued to Olney once again. That time we set up on the fairgrounds without the big top. A rigged curtain hid the performers from the audience that sat far away in the stands. We couldn't tell if they enjoyed themselves, but we did.

Only a few rigs took up space in the backyard on George's show due to our small troupe. Never mind. At each sunset, we sat around long tables and chowed down on charbroiled burgers. We never noticed how the air hung heavy with the pungent smell of pachyderm pee as it fused with the mouthwatering aroma of barbecued bovine.

Thanks to the downpours, our environs stood knee-deep in sludge. That was real circus—an authentic mud show. A mud show was a small show that traveled overland—not by train—and frequented muddy lots. The elephants loved it. They sloshed and flung the soggy dirt everywhere with their trunks. But the brown ooze wreaked havoc on clown shoes. For such adventures, I had purchased footwear that resembled Mary Janes with a bulbous toe section topped with a spotted bow. Constructed of a cheaper grade of leather, my mud-show shoes with rubber soles saved my precious oversized oxfords.

I felt completely at home. Somewhere out there, the great Wallendas walked the high wire. Barry Lubin, an instructor at Clown College, transformed into Grandma on the Big Apple Circus. The largest clan on earth comprised a considerable number of troupers, and Billy and I counted among them. So, let it rain.

Billy, Ronnie, and I ventured into downtown Olney for lunch one day. The narrow streets and old storefronts suctioned us into one of Norman Rockwell's paintings. We found a small diner and entered. Our invasion created the sudden sound of silence from the patrons who ate at square tables covered with red-checkered cloths. A waitress with a plastic smile and a teased, bouffant hairstyle approached and sat us. We had dined in soul food restaurants in Harlem and catfish joints in St. Louis. Oh, how the air chilled inside that establishment! Let it go. In a week, we would leave the cold ambience behind for warmer hearts.

Later, Ronnie and I ventured to the get-anything-you-want Walmart for supplies. A United Parcel Service (UPS) truck screeched to a halt, and an African American delivery man jumped out and sprinted toward the doors with a box. "A black guy!" I said. We bolted in his direction, happy to see someone of our hue. Ronnie spoke first, "Hi, Soul Brother!" The driver's manner changed from everyday boredom to shock, and he shot into the store. So ended our journey in a Norman Rockwell painting of a perfect world.

After our little jaunt along the paths of Illinois with that final stopover in Olney, the tour ended. We parted ways from Ronnie and George Coronas Circus and returned home to enjoy one month of rest and relaxation before the next season of UniverSoul.

After thousands of miles of travel, my parents' Ford bit the dust, and we bought a Dodge Dakota. In due time, we headed out with revitalized spirits and a song in our hearts.

We bounced into Atlanta. Billy parked our trailer behind the ever-present, chain-link fence and set tin containers under the little stabilizing legs. "Fill the cans with water," my father had said, "to keep ants from climbing up and in." Afterward Billy skedaddled to help with move-in. I placed a pallet in front of the door for an extra step, hooked Sad Sack outside, and wandered off to find the other clowns.

Spirits rose because Skeeter had come back, but exasperation set in when he left after an injury. Russell B had passed away, and Jonathan and Kevyn no longer worked on the show. Nonetheless, Ronnie and I plowed on town after town as soldiers who wore armor of willpower. When we landed in the Big Apple, the rib-tickling duo changed within the week.

I walked past the cookhouse (the name for Pie Car on tented shows) at lunchtime, and someone called out. "Hey, I want to be a clown. I'm funny. Let me work with you." I turned toward the man in a dirty apron who held a spatula that dripped with grease and smiled.

"Yeah, everybody thinks it's easy," I thought.

To my surprise the older guy knocked on our door one afternoon in full hobo getup. "My name is Robert Dunn, but since my head is bald, call me Onionhead." We spoke, and he told me of his pleas with Ricky, who gave in. At that point our two-member army of hilarity increased to three when the big-footed soul joined our ranks. Mr. Dunn's boisterous personality differed from mine and Ronnie's, and his good-natured, tramp clown character added a fresh dimension.

So another restart for the clowns. Despite trials and tribulations, UniverSoul allowed us the chance to perform innovative material.

In the past Garry, Skeeter, Russell B, and I had presented a soulful Barbecue gag at the insistence of the boss man, who had specified the song as well. The three of us revived it. At the cue, Onionhead entered the ring, set the props, and tended the grill. Ronnie sauntered in, then dozed on a chair. After he sat, my character, Big Mama, sashayed up the ramp two steps behind him then hovered over the food. My hip sway was easy due to my dress made of heavy-duty fabric that covered my big, fiberfill derriere. The reliable Nerf-ball-size-fifty bust balanced my torso. The breakaway getup held together at the seams thanks to Velcro and flew off when yanked from behind.

To the rear of the audience, our sound technician hit the button at our nod, and the taped melody blasted throughout the tent.

I placed my hands on my hips and lip-synced, "Tramp!"

"What'd you call me?" Onionhead mouthed.

"Tramp. You don't wear continental clothes or Stetson hats."

"Ooooooo, I'm a lover . . ."

We pulled shtick out of the air: a drop onto the ground due to a weak chair and a prolonged sneeze due to too much pepper, which blew off the dress. We did our best within the confines of the tune, but it hadn't worked with Skeeter and Garry, and it didn't with us either. Our efforts produced only two laughs: the collapsible seat and the flying garment. Ricky gave his own idea the ax. So, "Hero" one more time. Spirits dipped, and we moped among the sun's rays that played peekaboo with the trees of Prospect Park in Brooklyn. Ah, New York City.

One morning I opened the door of our trailer to soak in distant rhythmic beats of a lone bongo player. "Good morning," a man said. I turned in his direction and there stood a dignified, clean-shaven member of the Nation of Islam. Spaced here and there, his fellows rested in the military at-ease position. They would prove the content of their metal as guards of our world prior to the second performance on our first three-show Saturday.

I held a plate over soapy water when an unusual sight—for our neighborhood—caught my attention through the window. Thirty people—all who happened to be white—clung together and walked past the fence. They held signs that read, "Circuses are cruel to animals!"

"And so it begins for us," I thought.

They had never witnessed our presentation; we would have noticed. What prompted their protests? What proof? They passed the backyard where our trailers and animal cages sat and headed to the front.

"What's going on there?" someone from the troupe asked.

In the blink of an eye, memory of Los Angeles and raspberries toward Lou's Hunting gag at Ringling surfaced.

One of the high-wire walkers emerged from his rig. "Animal extremists are here!"

What would happen when a bunch of Caucasians challenged an African American production in a black neighborhood? "I've gotta watch this."

I bolted from our trailer to join the impending racial riot and shot around the tent to the midway. The public meandered when they approached. I peeked from behind the portable donnikers and observed the handsome men of the Nation spring into action. Dressed in immaculate, dark suits, they formed a line between UniverSoul and the nemesis of circus. On cue from an unseen signal, they eased forward as a wall set in motion by the touch of a button. With purpose in their steps and without expression, they continued to tread ahead in silence.

Before they knew it, the fair-skinned demonstrators stood across the street—pushed to the side as one brushes away water with a squeegee. The ebony-hued men in bow ties did an about-face and returned. They marched with a cadence to rival the dressing of the blues viewed on flight lines of any air force base. On the other side of that wide street, the People for the Ethical Treatment of Animals (PETA) sauntered away. Beautiful. May peace be upon you—*As-salaam alaikum*.

# # #

The season drew to a close, and time neared to secure work. It proved wise for each performer to approach Mr. Walker, or you might have found yourself at rehearsals with no gig. Sugar and Spice, the other interracial couple, had experienced that blow at the start of our second year. They had arrived in Atlanta for the 1995 season without knowledge that Ricky hadn't rehired them. Chris and Ron gathered their belongings and zoomed away from the circus of soul. Due to that incident, I needed to know and headed toward him.

"Hey, Ricky, I haven't heard anything of next year. What's up with the clowns?"

He cast his gaze downward. "Well, Danise, I'm not going to have any."

"What?"

"Yeah, I think I'm going to do something different."

He explained his idea, but the words faded away. After five seasons, my tenure ended with no forewarning. We didn't argue or seek an explanation. Anger fueled Billy and me. We threw stuff into the truck, hitched the trailer, and dashed off the lot—exasperated with *Your Circus of Dreams*.

Our route carried us north on Interstate 35 out of Dallas, Texas, and west on Interstate 40 through New Mexico. In Arizona, my husband and I passed our favorite, yet lonely, tourist stop: Jackrabbit. The sign beckoned, "Here It Is!" at the freeway turnoff, and a giant statue of the animal greeted visitors at the entrance to a lone curio shop. We also zoomed past the ruins of Two Guns, a western town lost to time. Onward with a right turn onto Highway 93, up a long stretch of road, over the Hoover Dam, and into a mass of neon surrounded by beautiful desert. Welcome to Las Vegas.

Billy and I secured odds and ends of work. After one year the man who had struck black gold called. "Danise, this is Ricky. Can you both return for the 2000 tour?"

He used clowns anyway and wanted me back on board with Billy to call the light cues again. Our scales of experience weighed the pros and cons: gluttons for punishment or repetitious, townie life. The lure of money proved more powerful, so we hitched our wagon to a falling star. At our trail's end, the recognizable Canobbio.

He had requested my solo as a presentation, and the season progressed. Toward the end, I cornered him about the year to come.

Encircled by his guardians, he said, "You're not coming back, Danise. I'm tired of 'Hero.' It was a fluke anyway."

A fluke! I didn't accept the implication of blind luck. The recipe at the onset of Clown College had evolved. The one-third cup of uncertainty had become self-assuredness. The one teaspoon of goofy shone as the ability to make laughter. Boldness overshadowed the pinch of introvert. Experience seasoned all the above. When baked, the golden brown "me" with oversized oxfords had surrendered every ounce of talent for Mr. Walker's success.

"I'm going to have Cuban clowns next year," he said. "They sent a tape of their work. Both Cal and I like them. Do me a favor. Can you watch it and tell me what you think?"

The true meaning of the phrase "familiarity breeds contempt" surfaced. Would I observe the video of those who would take my place? No. I stood face-to-face with a man who had scaled walls. But so had his performers. To be black in our field required girded loins. We, too, had enjoyed success.

My question to him: "Ricky, why can't you let folks know that they're not to return?"

With arms crossed while the Nation closed around him, he stated, "I am not responsible for your career."

The bomb doors of my mind opened and dropped thoughts such as "Maybe this clown thing wasn't a great idea." Notion not accepted. Everyone possessed a gift. I had found where my place lay in society. My heart belonged in the ring protected by a layer of sawdust.

The elation of opening night in 1994 came to mind for an instant. I opened my mouth to speak but hesitated. Words chosen with care would serve as a safety net over thin air, in case the need for his show arose in the future. Yet cautious phrases remained trapped. "Ricky, lose my number. Don't ever call me again because if you do I won't know your name."

By then life resembled a rodeo route—all over the map. We returned to Las Vegas, removed everything from storage, and moved into an apartment. Our nineteen-foot rig paid the price for constant abuse. It bit the dust. The sides bulged. The back wall rotted. The floor sunk when walked on. My knees weakened. My hands drooped.

To sever the tie that bound us to Soul Circus's tanbark trail, we donated our home on wheels to the Make-A-Wish organization in remembrance of my dad.

Ringling Bros. and Barnum & Bailey Clown College did not provide survival know-how with our greasepaint kits. Alas! We secured townie jobs, and a year dragged on—until a familiar man crossed our path.

CHAPTER NINETEEN

RECLAIMED GROUND

I gotta get back to get-up-n-go
A toot on the whistle and "On with the show!"
Dear Father in heaven, I pray to Your Grace
Let me return to pie-in-the-face . . .

—D. Payne

I stood at the bottom of the escalator that led to Madame Tussauds wax museum—my place of employment—and noticed the younger Feld immediately. His hair had thinned with no noticeable gray. I hadn't seen him in many years, and the lapse of time had created genuine enthusiasm.

"Hi, Mr. Feld!"

He stopped short, caught unawares, and after a moment asked, "How's life?"

He mentioned that he ate lunch in the adjacent casino and was on his way out. Our conversation continued with a little bit of this and that; then he shook my hand to leave but did an about-face and observed me with the passersby. After they departed, he approached and smiled.

"Danise, how would you and Bill like to come back on my show, Blue Unit this time?"

I gaped, then without any regard for my current job said, "Yeah, that'll be fun."

"I'll have Tim [Holst] give you a call." Then Kenneth Feld left.

That night I told my husband about the opportunity. The decision required no effort. Las Vegas offered a break from frustration and shenanigans, but monotony hit hard. We rose in the morning, bathed, worked, ate dinner, and slumped to bed. Day after day—same thing, same order. Townie life did not square equal to "see ya down the road." We thought nothing about packing up and moving out. It had become second nature. We pulled a creep from Sin City, threw caution to the wind, and headed to Tampa and a different winter quarters.

Florida proved its usual self that time of year: hot and muggy. We followed instructions to the unfamiliar site, parked, hooked my basset in the shade, and walked to the building. The setup lay behind a chain-link fence. We checked in with the uniformed guard, passed his shack, and stopped for a look. Stands lined the arena floor. At the far end, the elephant doors.

Billy, who would join the crew, said, "I'm going to the backyard to find out my assignment. Will you be all right?"

"Believe it or not, I'm nervous. I hope they don't expect more than I have to give." Indeed, our drive across the country had been laden with anxiety on my part due to a remnant of self-doubt that lingered still. "I'm not Annie Fratellini."

"You'll be fine, sweetie."

"Yeah, well, I'll search for the alley."

After a kiss we moseyed in opposite directions. "Hey, Danise!"

I turned toward the greeting that echoed through the air. Ruth Chaddock and Peggy Williams waved. They hung on with the company in new occupations after their clown contracts ended in the 1970s. The two came my way, and we spoke for a bit.

"The clowns expect you—the returnee." Ruthie pointed to the left. "The alley's down those stairs."

The three of us hugged, then they resumed work.

When I faced the steps and entered, activity stopped. A gentleman, large in stature, hovered over the others as a papa bird. He and a woman came forward and extended their hands. "Hi. I'm Greg DeSanto," he said, "and this is my wife, Karen. Welcome to the Blue

Unit." He called to the others. "Gang, this is Danise. She worked the Red Unit under Irvin Feld."

Greg had spoken to me before we left home and mentioned that they'd be there to coach in winter quarters. Kenneth Feld had closed Clown College in 1997 for an unknown reason and had hired them for their expertise as previous employees.

I surveyed the surroundings while the group gathered round. In addition to me and two other women, the contingent totaled twelve—fewer than the thirty-two in 1979. Among them a tall, African American guy with dreadlocks and a rubber face. "Hi. I'm Gregory Parks," he said. Next a thin, wiry kid with a big smile introduced himself as the boss clown. Their youth encroached as a lion upon a gazelle and expelled my Peter-Pan sense of age from its time warp.

Years had moved on, but not with me, and memories tugged at my heart. I glanced at the ever-present wagons emblazoned with *The Greatest Show on Earth*, and reality hit hard. Absent—Irvin Feld, Papa Lou, Uncle Soapy, and Gunther. All had died—passed from sawdust to tomorrow. Ringling concluded the 109th edition when I left at the end of 1980. This year, 2002, would usher in the 132nd edition. Twenty-one years of changes had taken place with me, most of them centered on boldness. Had the show altered?

After chitchat everyone carried on with work. I exited the alley to view this different winter quarters. Ah, the smells remained the same. The rancid stink of tiger pee mixed with the pungent odor of elephant. Home. After my self-guided tour, I hightailed it to bring back my gear to store in a heavy, blue, wooden chest that George Shellenberger had made in the 1970s for our paraphernalia. I would buy another wardrobe trunk on the road because the original stayed at home for safekeeping.

The next day another shout of my name sounded from across the floor. I faced its direction. Ted McRae and family of UniverSoul Circus ran toward me. Mr. Feld hired the forklift-driving daredevil to present an alligator act—from Daniel in the lions' den to T.M., the Gator Guy. The season would be his first with Ringling—his first on Big Bertha's silver slug.

Every pearly white showed. "You should see our home on the train," he said. "It's got a bedroom for both of us, and the boys have their own. The living room's tiny, but we'll fix it up."

"He has a living room?" I thought, but out loud I said, "We haven't seen ours yet. We're in a hotel until it's ready on car number 191."

The director called him away, which left a vision of his palace in my mind. Billy approached and called out. "Our room is ready." How we had looked forward to travel once again on this circus train! While we drove to it, I told him about Ted's castle, but based on yesteryear we prepared for a cubicle. The iron horse came into view, and we stopped and soaked up the scene.

"You go in first," Billy said. He didn't want to hear my explosion to a Lilliputian-size hole-in-the-wall. I sighed and got out of the truck. For the first time in two decades my hands touched the handrail and hoisted me up into the vestibule. I smiled at my husband and entered the coach. How good to be back on reclaimed ground!

A washing machine and dryer rested inside for the use of each family unit. The requirement: beat everyone to it. The second cabin down belonged to us. I gritted my teeth and slid open the door. What a pleasant surprise! Not as vast as Ted's, but a triple stateroom the dimensions of a huge bathroom in an apartment awaited—larger than both our previous accommodations combined.

It included a full-size refrigerator bolted down to prevent movement on the runs, one sink, and ample cabinet space. The double bed would serve as a table when set up, which would consume time and energy, so we'd eat on it instead. The 3' x 6' x 9'—gone.

Whoever converted train cars into mini-homes deserved a medal. We even had a stove: two electric burners covered with a glass plate built into the countertop. Formica covered everything except the refrigerator and the walls of beige aluminum—easier to clean.

I rushed from the room to the vestibule. "Billy, come and see."

After he dashed from the pickup and leapt on board, he stepped in and described the occasion, "It's like meeting an old friend."

Our walk through the car revealed two donnikers that faced two showers. Goodbye cold streams of water in secluded dungeons. After a glance here and there, Billy and I retrieved our gear from our vehicle. We didn't bring much. The smaller the space, the fewer the necessities. We unpacked and put away things, then withdrew to the truck. The 1980s surrendered to the twenty-first century as we drove away. The telltale signs of satellite dishes that pointed to the stars up and down the length of our mobile neighborhood made it so.

At the building we prepared for the road. Clowns made props and rehearsed gags. One morning the alley received assignments for production numbers and stilt walking. Youngsters reached for poles with feet and glided across the arena. I strapped on my pair of aluminum appendages, which lifted me two feet off the ground—too high. After several attempts to walk, I dismounted and trudged toward the director's office, and entered for a powwow.

"What can I do for you, Danise?"

"I have a fear of false legs."

"Did you try?"

"I gave it a shot, but my dislike of the things started a long time ago in Clown College. I've avoided them ever since."

Years had passed, yet memory of my first association with the company hung to the cobwebs of my mind. Would he mirror the instructor of the woeful trampoline during school and show no mercy? He listened and believed my plea sincere and that I was not one to finagle my way out of work.

"What do you think about pushing a scooter down the track?"

"Suits me fine."

"OK, go to the prop department and you'll be set. After you're done there, report to wardrobe."

Done deal. The replacement mode of traversing the floor carried me to the designers of fantastic spangly garb, located this time in a double-wide. Inside I glanced around the bare trailer. On the wall dangled white top hats and thin, blue, baggy jumpsuits. Next to these, sequined tailcoat tuxedo jackets. The lifeless apparel would spring to life when paired with our bodies. The costumers bade a welcome, but no head-to-toe-striptease-down-to-the-undies measurements as in the 1970s took place. Instead they asked for my proportions and left it at that. They reached for one of the lightweight, single-pieced, navy garments.

"This is your size. It's for Opening and Spec."

"Where's the glitter and the glamour?" I thought.

"You guys will strut in your agent suits for Finale."

I wondered about the term "agent suit" designated for our personal clown costumes. I didn't recall using the expression the first time on the show. Nonetheless, I transported my outfit to the wardrobe box and carried on.

One sunny afternoon Greg DeSanto asked, "What's your walkaround, Danise?"

"You mentioned on the phone I didn't need one. 'It's a new day,' you said. 'As soon as you walk through the door, they hand you a walkaround.' So I didn't bring one."

"Well . . ."

I knew better. They didn't have one for me.

"Here's a plan. My basset hound's my partner. She'll wear a tutu and dance and wave bye-bye down the track."

The idea would never leave winter quarters. My long-eared dog plodded too slow for light changes. Her replacement, a cumbersome foam barrel that hid a giant chili pepper. I would take a bite, mug "whew, too hot!" and smoke would blast from my ears, thanks to a head contraption.

Despite that setback I considered it an honor to have returned to the opus that gave rise to my libretto—a song without notes. We pressed on toward presentation night for the owner of the show. That evening we sat in front of our trunks in the open alley shared by both women and men and prepared. We separated the rest of the season. Up to that point, no one had seen my character, and quick glances shot my way when I opened the container of blue, the tube of red, and the tin of white. I slapped on the palettes and slipped into a self-sewn beige flowered skirt that draped to my calves over a white cotton petticoat. Tights covered my legs. I donned a gray wig with the bun at the back of the neck and capped it with a Sunday-go-to-meeting hat. A yellow jacket and rolled white gloves—no fingertips—topped it off. Last, but not least, my black-and-white oversized oxfords, as always in a plastic bag. They showed little damage despite the passage of time. The leather, only slightly brittle to the touch, caressed my feet. After that metamorphosis, Granny Clown emerged from behind the looking glass.

She had been my alter ego for a while and useful the second time around on *The Greatest Show on Earth*. How easy to portray age! The desire to move fast disappeared long ago. The memory of Grandmother fused with that of Aunt Roxie. Sure-footed movements would decelerate under the skirt hiked over my waistline. I looked in the mirror dimly and had become my future self.

We exited the alley and lined up. The house was dark. As in the past, fellow cast members sat in the stands to support this year's collection of those who drop their pants. One by one we walked into the spotlight, and the process of fine-tuning began. Kenneth Feld called the shots. "Good."—"No."—"Acceptable."—"Change your costume." The clown before me moved away and joined the rest on the side to see what I would do. Without a care about opinions or la-di-da, I shimmied and mugged and garnered thumbs up.

We ran back to the alley then returned to the floor to present gags. My preparation for this centered on Uncle Fred in Great Glemham and his talent with a plastic ring around his waist. In turn, I sauntered in with an enormous bag in tow and presented a geriatric versus the spinning loop for Granny Does the Hula-Hoop. My bit highlighted audience children and their fantastic wiggle skills, but only fellow troupers occupied the seats—no townies. My attempts with the hoop required the chutzpah of—ah, circus kids. The offspring of those born to make one smile grabbed the Hula-Hoop and twirled it on their waists, down to the legs, up to the neck, and raised first the right then left arms up and out for a good, long minute. The gag ended when I booted them from the ring.

The young man with the expressive face and I teamed up to showcase Greg's Tooth Fairy. He played the assistant and entered with a sack of stuff followed by me with wings on my back, a crown on my head, and a wand in my hand. We placed an oversized extracted tooth under a pillow and would exchange cash for choppers. The little, old tooth fairy, however, had a memory problem and suffered from narcolepsy.

Greg handed me the money. I stopped to remember what to do with it. When he pointed to the pillow, I fell asleep on my feet or ran out of steam in mid-stride. He then pretended to wind me up and set me in motion. Such shtick continued until the conclusion and Nurembergs closed. With time, that sketch would have developed nicely, but later it received the ax. Only Hula-Hoop and four other gags survived. The alley returned to the drawing board. Clowns made props and worked on and presented different ideas. Then Kenneth Feld delivered a stamp of approval.

Midway, rehearsals began, and the entire troupe assembled in the stands. The boss man stood in front of the microphone and welcomed everyone. Next we meandered onto the floor and dove into the business at hand without introductions around the circumference.

Phil McKinley, director for the show—who sanctioned no stilts for me—took control. "Danise, you start on number twenty-seven, then go to forty."

"What was he talking about?" I glanced downward. The length of front and back tracks revealed a numbered strip. It turned out that Ringling had adopted computerized lighting similar to UniverSoul. This version demanded precision. If not in place you performed in the dark because the lights hit each spot at specific intervals. No more improvisation here and there. I took meticulous notes to ensure each systematic position. Several cast members, used to the technique, talked on cell phones. Only one throwback held over from days gone by: sit and stand and walk and run.

In the 1970s, the funny people of *The Greatest Show on Earth* filled every nook and cranny with track gags, chases, or bits. In 2002 such diversions stayed in our trunks, but due to the professionalism of the alley, the clowns stood ready. Walkarounds still diverted attention from the crew who set trapeze nets, and Clown Car survived in the ring as a parody of Sylvia Zerbini's liberty act. Her horses were untethered, free to dance within the confines of the ring at her direction. Covered by a pink horse head attached to a rose-and-blue-colored blanket, we clowns would exit our Volkswagen Beetle and execute rhythmic steps at the commands of our clown Zerbini.

I have worked in buildings with a concrete floor and in big tops with a flap for the door; thus it didn't take long to get back into the swing of things.

The only bump in the road occurred in the first run-through. The silent footfall of the pachyderms carried them past us as we do-si-doed on our numbers. While they high-tailed it toward the curtain, an elephant left a big pile on the track.

"Hold it! Hold it!" Phil yelled. "Everybody stay in place. Get this mess out of here; it's holding up my dancers!"

Working men in black coveralls emblazoned with the enterprise's name rushed in.

"We need a shovel over here and some sawdust!" Phil instructed.

It served a welcomed break from the mundane until the man assigned the task hurried by: Billy. My heart shattered like glass.

He had held the lead alto-saxophone spot in former years. His music ability shone with the best, polished by such gigs as *The Debbie Reynolds' Show*, *Gypsy*, and more. The one called maestro had conducted a mock audition, yet the band members remained settled. Food for thought. So my life's partner plowed on. He jammed the broad blade under the mess, then lifted and dumped the smelly blob into the plastic bin held by another crew member. They sprinted out the back door, and practice continued. I don't know what transpired but my husband, who had played under the baton of Leonard Bernstein, never did that again.

Regret didn't fill Billy's spirit. He moved floats, dressed the elephants with heavy sequined blankets, and helped set up and tear down equipment in each town—strenuous work of long hours that melted weight away. He had always been a trouper. But the removal of poop? What a man surrendered proved his mettle. Bill Payne's solid-gold core enabled him to find dignity in muck and mire.

Care of the principal performer's props also rested on his shoulders. Ringling didn't present a Gunther Gebel-Williams. Instead, it highlighted Italian-born clown David Larible, billed the Prince of Laughter. Until one certain day, he shone separate from the contingent of twelve who wore greasepaint.

"Danise, I like what you're doing when the clowns sprint into position with the globe staffs for Finale," Phil said over the microphone.

"Thanks. Grannies don't move fast, so I let the others pass while I trudged."

Papa Lou had advised me long ago to do the opposite of everyone to catch the eye.

"Nice. I'm going to add something there. After the globes explode with the fireworks at the finish, continue your slow retreat. Reach the curtain last as it closes in your face. I'm going to leave you alone in the spotlight. Can you improvise at that point?"

Me by myself in the limelight? You bet. Back to places for Finale. The band started at the top. After the number concluded, folks zoomed past the fabric. I plodded toward the blue material, faced the empty three rings, and after several minutes of shtick, stopped, shrugged my shoulders, waved goodbye, and danced off to nothing but the lyrical tune of a calliope. End of show. The director's voice echoed in the building. "Fantastic, Danise!"

At the beginning of practice two days later, his words sounded from the amplifier. "Danise, we're going to add David to the jaunt in Finale—from opposite sides, of course. OK, let's go."

And so it was. Back to the top. We reached the curtain at the same time, and a competition for the spotlight resulted.

At the last rehearsal, the cast sat in the stands. I looked across the arena where David held a conversation, hands on hips, with Phil. Then Phil walked to our bleachers, climbed the steps, and knelt beside me in the dark.

He touched my knee and said, "I'm so sorry, Danise. There's been a change. We cut your bit. It was a nice way to wrap it up, especially with the lilting sound of a calliope."

"But why?"

"Well, David's going to bring it to a close up on the float."

That revelation sucked the life from me, and resentment toward the Prince of Laughter set in. I carried on in silence, for what could I say? From then on, the pitter-patter of our exodus underlined David Larible surrounded by a halo of light.

My enthusiasm didn't wane, however. On opening night at the usual call to order—"Doors!"—an electric current surged through my core.

"Come on, Sad Sack. Let's get ready." She studied every gesture.

I reached for my costume in the trunk, and the white tip of her tail wagged. On went the skirt, gray wig, and hat. My basset beckoned, "Woof!" as I slid my feet into each oversized oxford, then slipped on the jacket. She stood still for her metamorphosis: a rose-and-mustard ruffled collar, faux eyeglasses, and leash. With those in place, she moved from the alley like a tug boat with me in tow, and we entered the grand hall.

Jon Weiss, the announcer for preshow, took his stance and glanced at the top of the stands. I did the same. The audience gushed as a river over a dam. They flowed onto and covered the floor for the Three Ring Adventure that replaced come-in.

"Sad Sack, the Wonder Dog's in ring one!" he said.

Clowns worked gags within the circles of wood without the aid of music, lights, or sound effects. The gift of street performing counteracted those who made a beeline through our space for the pachyderms.

After my turn inside the circumference, my clown partner and I wandered in and out of the crowd. She growled at the adults who thought it hilarious to squirt me with rigged flowers. Bright-eyed kids ignored me, though. "Look, Mommy, that dog's wearing glasses!"

Oh, the noise and goings-on! Townies tried on old costumes and snapped photos. "Look, honey, I'm in the circus!" They posed part of a human pyramid with the Moroccan tumblers. "How many times has Dad done that, huh? Quick, take his picture!" They listened to animal facts found in an information packet from headquarters. "Elephants are excellent climbers." Another detail not taught in my zoology classes.

According to corporate the Three Ring Adventure proved good rapport and filled seats. I graduated from the old school and preferred mystique to draw spectators—curiosity about the odd. When the viewers rubbed shoulders, mystery vanished and familiarity stepped in.

New savvy geared to earn hard cash drew the people in ever-changing times. As the season progressed, we played to many turnaways. Townies loved the Adventure and swarmed us for a chance to drown the business world in a pool of fun and fantasy.

We won the house in winter quarters, and move-out arrived. Excitement of this last night in town dimmed when the boss clown called out my name to transfer trunks—a 2002 requirement regardless of gender. The chore had belonged to working men. I stepped outside the blue curtain of the girl's alley. Youth moved wooden containers that appeared to be featherweight.

I retreated into the dressing area, put my hands on a four-foot tall, mobile closet and grunted with each push and pull in the direction of the back door. My struggle with the solid boxes never repeated when merciful eyes noticed the strain. Until that time, I shoved the crates, gathered my gear, and headed out when a dancer strolled by wearing a blue helmet.

"What are you doing, Paula?" I asked.

"I help take the cable off the floor."

"Oh, cherry pie, huh?"

"What's that?"

Vernacular lost its grip on the tongue.

"Side duty for extra pay."

"No. It's in my contract. We roll it up and put it into the wagons."

I glanced into the arena, and indeed, fewer working men scurried to and fro than in 1979. What an interesting fact that young hoofers, who replaced the older showgirls seasoned with life, shed their dainty costumes; donned hard hats; and schlepped thick cable and rigging along with the balance of the crew. I stood to the side as she continued on her way.

A working man named Cowboy sat atop the Human Cannonball's cannon. He drove the massive four-wheeled, blue-silver cylinder up the ramp to a semi for transport overland.

Billy passed and said, "Hi, sweetie."

My husband had become one of those in dark coveralls. He pushed motorcycles into a metal frame, moved that up the incline, and loaded the structures into a numbered wagon.

When we first rolled into winter quarters, Billy had been heavyset. By the third town, the weight melted away, thanks to teardown and setup. The latter required his help to lift and haul cumbersome steel ramps to the flat cars, in addition to his regular assignments during the eighteen-hour day. How different from the sedentary occupation of the musician!

In the hubbub of activity, Billy and I forked over dough for two clowns to drive our truck to the next town. When the work ended, we rode the bus to the silver slug. Onboard, Billy secured loose items in our larger hole-in-the-wall for the run, and I ambled to the showers. That advantageous alteration made life simpler. I opened the door to one of our perks. But after a glance at the bathroom stall, a sick feeling rose from my feet and up my body. The coach tilted away from the drain, a bonus of the on-car privilege. As a result, the filth of the previous occupant swirled within the enclosure as a shallow sea of sewage. To return to the building was out of the question. So I stripped, wrinkled my nose, sloshed into the slimy, gray liquid, and soaped up while microorganisms in the foamy water attached themselves to my toes.

We had intended to watch our departure through the window. Exhaustion, however, drove us into deep sleep. With a jolt of the railroad cars, we were back on track with *The Greatest Show on Earth*.

We played the same towns as years before, but protocol differed. The terrorists' attacks the previous year on September 11, 2001 necessitated tight security. No one entered the buildings unless part of the show.

One day after a clown promo, we exited the bus yards from the fence that surrounded the back door. A guard with a belly that stretched the fabric of his shirt at the buttons chewed gum at the gate. He sat in a chair and yawned while we passed but stood to eyeball me dressed as Granny. We clowns sauntered into the arena and disappeared behind our sectioned-off areas, the two alleys separated by a curtain. After a moment or two, hurried footsteps broke the silence. "What's that?" I peeked out after the sprinters shot past then returned to my trunk. "Policemen. Wonder who they're chasing?" The watchmen stormed by again and zoomed into the men's alley.

Their words carried into my dressing space. "Where is she? Where is she? We're looking for someone who sneaked in with you guys."

"Who?" our boss asked.

"The little, old, black lady dressed as a clown."

Once again, the lack of women of color in a world dominated by white men created a deadlock toward acknowledgement. Caucasian women with a sense of humor stand greater in number in circuses. Until more funny sisters of my hue enter the ring, doubt about our way of life would cloud believability.

## CHAPTER TWENTY

MISTAKEN IDENTITY

We revisited the cradle of the South where the sweet scent of magnolias saturated the scene beyond the vestibule. Our train tracks crisscrossed gravel paths to broken-down cottages that once harbored horrors behind the grand houses with white columns. We settled in—the town's name has escaped me—and began another week of sawdust and glitter. During the Adventure one afternoon, an elderly Caucasian gentleman, who sported a mustache and goatee, approached. He walked with a casual gait, hands clasped behind himself. He greeted the women with a tip of his hat, then stopped to watch the children and me. The man smiled after the kids scampered off.

His southern drawl reestablished the locality. "My, my. It's nice to see you. Welcome to our fair city."

"Thanks. It's opening day for us."

My nondescript accent gave me away.

"Where are you from?"

"I've been here and there but live in California now."

"You travel with the circus?"

"What an odd thing to ask due to the garb and dog!" I thought and said, "Yes." People brushed past in a blur, but the man and I stood encased in a vacuum.

"I am glad y'all are here. We look forward to seeing this show every year." He spoke more, then tipped his hat. The conversation ended, and a breath of air escaped from my mouth. I had expected ignorance to creep from his words as phantoms out of a bygone United States.

"Thank you. We like the entire tour."

"Y'all take care, and it's nice to see you . . ." He paused and glanced at my nametag—Danise—smiled, looked me in the eye, and finished his sentence with "auntie."

The man from Dixie lived up to low expectations. I froze in place while he moved on. He saw what he wanted to see—not a young circus clown dressed as a granny but an old Negress. "Auntie" punctured eardrums of elderly, black women. Used in lieu of their names, the expression denoted no respect. The holdover from slavery days may have been a term of endearment to him, but the words *auntie*, *mammy*, *uncle*, and *boy* polluted the air with the stench of inferiority and entrapped the dignity of the African American as the 246 years of bondage had our bodies.

We left the South and received news of a trip that would render another perspective on life. "We're going to Mexico City next year!" Billy and I had played out of the country with Gerry Cottle's Circus, but a sojourn south of the border with The Big One—what an adventure!

The first few months of 2003 dragged with me the sole inhabitant in girl clown alley. Thanks to contract day during the last season, we had lost the other two and four men. I would never understand why the world of the circus didn't allow folks to stay. Nonetheless, we moved on and acquired up-to-date passports and visas. Safety precautions included animals, and Sad Sack obtained new shots and a dog license. In June the troupe filled out a personal effects/household goods form and received an inventory list of forbidden items: fruits, vegetables, plants, and poultry. I had already stocked everything on the list, plus four Cornish hens. As a result we ate three in one week and hid the fourth in aluminum foil labeled "frozen mashed potatoes."

My excitement could fuel the locomotives that chugged into my birth state of Texas. On to San Antonio, which was our last stop before heading to Mexico City. Tim Holst, performance director from yesteryear, had gained a promotion to vice president of talent and production. He informed everyone, "If you live in trailers, you will drive to Mexico City. Otherwise, personal vehicles stay here in a barn at the fairgrounds." Our truck would rest on American soil.

Billy and I headed to its sanctuary on clean roads that snaked past canals and tucked our pickup in for the duration. On the bus ride back to our living quarters, we negotiated a side street where wide-eyed tourists entered the Alamo. The day before, my husband and I had done the same and took some photos to preserve the moment. At the train, we climbed the outside steps and turned around. Performers had arrived from food stores with last minute supplies in preparation to entertain the people who had won the battle at the famous structure. We battened down the hatches, then waited.

When ready, the silver slug pulled out of San Antonio for a brief stay in Laredo. The crisp air chilled the summer's eve. Stars decorated the sky, and personnel electrified the crowded vestibules with songs and dances until *kablam!* Forward motion. The locomotives edged onto the trestle bridge over the Rio Grande. I ran to awaken my husband in our room. "Billy! We're moving!" He remained in a comatose state of sleep, exhausted from his duties of move-out. I dashed back to the party.

Our mile-long transportation spanned the dry riverbed in the middle of the night. I looked in the direction of the United States. The large, illuminated Stars and Stripes waved goodbye. Near the engines, the huge flag of the country ahead flapped hello.

At the border of Nuevo Laredo, the guards waved and smiled. "*Hola, hola. Bienvenidos a Mexico.*" (Hello! Welcome to Mexico!)

We inched onward and picked up a crew to drive us toward the land of piñatas and bullfights.

The sun rose, and down the smoothest tracks imaginable, another world rolled by our eyes, populated by beautiful shades of brown. So long, Dixie! We chugged past cinder block houses painted in brilliant hues of coral, azure, or gold as if they sprang from the mind of Frida Kahlo, the celebrated Mexican artist. We passed old men, who strained under the weight of huge bundles strapped to their backs. Wide open spaces. A rest stop for dogs to pee. Back on board. Evening. Day. Night. Afternoon. And on to the city of the ancient Aztecs.

I ran to the vestibule while we pulled into our destination. Locals gaped and lined the rails, curious about the spectacle. Several jumped onto the flat cars and helped themselves to items not secured. In the evening, however, Ringling Bros. and Barnum & Bailey Circus slumbered in peace within an abandoned, gated train station. No one dared breach our walled haven protected by guards who bore semiautomatic rifles.

The next day dawned with animal walk, which drew enormous crowds. We had witnessed the pomp and circumstance before. So instead, Billy and I strolled the neighborhood. The streets whirled with Volkswagen Beetle taxi cabs tinted the color of fresh limes and turned the city into a blender.

People scurried to business offices or to wagons filled with wares. We stopped and took in the scene, and a young man approached and extended his hand. His eyes met mine for an—albeit wrong—connection. "Cuba?" he asked.

Circus in the United States received many of its artistes from the Hispanic community, and exhibitions that catered to Spanish speakers enjoyed sold-out houses. I couldn't wait for Mexico's reaction to *The Greatest Show on Earth*.

On opening day, the performance director called "Doors!" and we sauntered onto the floor for the Adventure. What a shock! The large space dwarfed the few attendees, and it remained sparse for the entire run. Maybe culture made a difference.

Nonetheless, three children wandered up to me and Sad Sack, and I greeted with stock phrases, thanks to translations by one of the performers. "*Hola! Yo soy la payasita abuelita.*" (In English, "I'm the granny clown.")

They asked the identity of my eyeglass-wearing dog, and a childhood film about a peasant surfaced. The star had ushered in the golden era of Mexican cinema and became associated with their national distinctiveness.

I thought to bridge the gap and blurted his name: "Cantinflas." They must have been too young. They never heard of him.

The troupe carried on, ended preshow, and dressed for Opening. When Kevin Venardos, our ringmaster, blew the whistle, we bolted into place. After the lights came up and revealed that the handful of spectators had spread out, we realized we would have to draw applause

231

from an empty house. We gave it our all anyway, and our emcee pulled off the full-length performances in pre-memorized Spanish.

The lack of ticket sales blessed us with four days off each week—full pay--and the cast dispersed to see the sights. On the first time away, Billy and I moseyed to the subway and paid the equivalent of ten cents for the ride to the Zocalo, the heart of the metropolis. We exited and climbed the stairs out into the daylight where the hubbub of the main plaza reminded me of the rush of New York City. People filled the area like ants. The rhythmic thump on a drum from the center of the square caught our attention. We followed the sound of the beat to Aztec reenactor dancers, who performed for anyone who stopped for a look-see. After awhile, we plunked down a few pesos and took a breather in a cathedral that bordered the activity. We sat in the back while the faithful lit candles and knelt before semblances of saints. They gesticulated in earnest with the sign of the cross from forehead to heart, shoulder to shoulder.

We didn't pack a lunch, and soon grew hungry and searched for food. Sidewalk vendors enticed with a variety of sustenance for every palate. A woman waved us over to her stand. I glanced at her delicacies but said, "No, gracias" to the fried bugs. Down the street, around the corner, Billy and I settled on ice cream.

Two weeks into our run, the company rode one hour in a bus to the ancient site of Teotihuacan. At our trail's end, the vehicle stopped near a sky-high wall of mottled stone. We bounded off the carrier and sauntered past. On the carpet of brown grass that lay to the front, I turned back and faced the Pyramid of the Sun. A similar but shorter structure catty-cornered to this one sloped upward to pay homage to the moon.

I joined the others who began the ascent of the first edifice. We climbed the steep steps and brushed shoulders with the countless ghosts of those who spoke to gods. At the summit the Moroccan tumblers from our troupe formed a human triangle, and the top man raised his hands as if to say, "Hail! Hail!" Twilight descended, and we meandered between the ageless buildings, alone with our thoughts. That side trip south of the border highlighted our second sojourn at Ringling.

After one month, move-out from Mexico City crept in. Billy and I finished our duties at the arena and rode to the train. We secured things as usual but stopped for the barbecue—circus performers' favorite pastime—on the outside platform that ran the length of the silver slug. Until then I had avoided food bought at the Walmart across the street unless canned. But I figured on the last night, what could harm us? Billy and I gulped down ribs and hamburgers topped with lettuce and tomatoes, then turned in. Hours later when we left the station, so did a case of Montezuma's revenge. Goodbye Mexico—back to Texas that birthed the phrase, "Remember the Alamo!"

We continued, and the season ended with contract renewal in Houston. In the 1970s only those to sign made the walk. But in 2003 goodwill or humiliation took human form for every "greatest soul on earth." Footsteps approached my alley and stopped outside the blue curtain. Tim Holst called out, "Danise, come with me." I followed and entered the culling chamber. Tim sat at the table beside the assistant producer, Nicole Feld, daughter of Kenneth and granddaughter of Irvin. Jim Ragona, manager of talent and production, faced them. Tim held idle conversation and doodled on a yellow writing pad. No white paper—no contract—waited for my signature. And I remembered my dread in the 1980s.

After an uneasy silence, his eyes met mine. "Well, Danise, they're making some changes. I hope you enjoyed your two years. You can find work. I'm sure I'll see you in some production out there."

Although twenty-four years had passed, nothing prepared me for another erasure of my name, and my mind spun counterclockwise once again.

"Your character doesn't fit the next show," he continued. "Besides, we're only responsible for the signed seasons."

Nicole remained silent, but Jim Ragona spoke with arms stretched palms down across the table. "We are not obligated to keep you here."

And so it ended. My painted smile cloaked a collision of thoughts: "But I wanted to stay!" Would they cross my path again? Or would they—like these two years—fade into my scrapbook? What to do? So much for Big Bertha. Sorry Lou, no longer part of the fraternity.

After a pregnant pause, I shook their hands and left.

CHAPTER TWENTY-ONE

THIS IS MY SONG

No second thoughts if sawdust's in your blood
With homes on wheels it's all the same to us who
wallow through the mud.

—D. Payne

Billy and I sat on the floor in the hallway, and I held a cell phone. We looked each other in the eyes, then smiled. Around us troupers scurried past, others trudged. One's future with Big Bertha determined one's pace. Artistes have always needed a place to perform, so I took a deep breath, exhaled, and called Ricky Walker of UniverSoul.

"Danise! How are you? What's up?" he asked.

I ground my teeth and asked, "Can you use a lighting man and a clown again?"

"Yeah. I need a new number for the clowning. I know you can come up with something. Work on one and see you both in Atlanta, OK?"

Short and sweet. It was not over. Relief set in because we had somewhere to go.

The next day Billy and I eliminated our presence from *The Greatest Show on Earth*, a necessity because Ringling inhabited one's soul. Each step onto the wooden stool at the entrance of the coach became heavy-laden with sorrow. We removed our belongings, then stuffed them into the U-Haul trailer. We slid onto the seats in the truck, sighed, and pulled away.

In the rearview mirror, the train appeared worn and tilted to the side. The bright, silver paint had dulled, and the edges of the red banner that proclaimed Ringling Bros. and Barnum & Bailey had peeled loose. I remarked about the name. "Billy, they removed the word 'circus.'" In fact, it hadn't been there all season.

When Billy stamped on the gas, the cloud of dust veiled a pummeled dream. Twenty-four years presented many changes in the show from showers onboard to computerized lighting. The only constant, "Mr. Feld say go."

Since our possessions remained in Las Vegas, it was off to Sacramento for two months of rest and relaxation at my mother's house. Billy and I bought a new twenty-four-foot Layton Lite trailer, and after downtime, we packed, said a prayer, and climbed in with Sad Sack.

As before I leaned out the window. "I love you, Mom." The last time we had pulled away with trailer in tow, the side-view mirror framed Mom and Dad. This time her reflected image was a picture of one.

We trudged ten miles an hour up the foothills on Interstate 80, and the fuel gauge plunged. I stuck figurative pins in an imaginary effigy of the salesman who had said, "Your Dodge can pull this twenty-four-foot Layton just fine."

"At this rate, we won't make it to the top," Billy said.

His words caused havoc. "We had a full tank, and this is only Auburn, twenty-five miles out!"

We made a beeline to the first gas station and fed our guzzler. In the atlas, I reviewed the marked truck stops called Flying J that we frequented during our last barnstorm around the country. Down the road, Billy learned to pull a larger trailer, and the gas mileage improved from twenty-five miles a tank to over two hundred.

Our route covered familiar ground. We reacquainted ourselves with Steins, New Mexico—a lonely, railroad ghost town. We zoomed past Odessa, Texas, where our transmission had blown in times past. My life's song stood loud and clear after all the years. Strength of purpose overpowered the apprehension of any struggle that lay ahead. On to Mississippi, Alabama, and into Georgia.

When we approached the lot in Atlanta on the gray and dreary day, the sounds of rehearsals in process filtered through the air. We set our rig, headed around the tent, and stepped beyond the front door. My husband and I recognized a person here and there. Ricky had mentioned that ringmasters Cal and Zeke no longer worked on the show, and that he had replaced them with a man and a woman.

Billy left to find his coworkers, and I stood back while an act practiced in the ring to the rhythms of hip-hop, Soul Circus's trademark. My gaze took in Onionhead, who sat by himself in the stands. It turned out that he alone comprised clown alley. I spotted the boss man, who eyeballed the goings-on from the shadows.

In 1994 at my first encounter, he spoke with a casual ease. Ten years had passed and his face reflected time and concern. Yet at my approach, he surrendered a sheepish smile.

"Hi, Ricky. We made it and already set the trailer. How's it going?"

"Hey, Danise. It's going. I got different acts now—from China, France, and Russia." He pointed to a group. "They're from Brazil." Then he spared no words. "What do you have for me?"

"I'll portray an old woman who reviews her youth. Lunga [a young contortionist still on the show] will be my younger self."

"All right, let's see it."

I hoofed it to the trailer, retrieved my music and props, and ran back. While I handed over my tape to the sound man in the bleachers and informed him of my cue, the Brazilians cleared the space and retreated to the side, joined by the other performers.

I made my way down, into the circle of light, and called out to Ricky. "Until Lunga learns her part, this portion of the number will give you an idea."

The melody began, but something came up. Ricky changed his mind about the viewing and motioned for the rest of the cast to return. They emerged as silhouettes from the dark sidelines and climbed into the ring like spirits out of the canvas. I paused, then slinked down the ramp, made my way between the maze of trailers, and stopped at our door.

Raindrops pummeled my head and formed a puddle of water at my feet. I stamped off the mud, entered, and closed myself in. "Welcome back, Danise."

Days passed and the circus left Georgia for the road. Ricky didn't tour, so no chance existed for me to ask him to perform. Billy worked the spotlights, but time ticked at a snail's pace for me.

I searched for Onionhead, and we agreed. "We have to be part of the show. Let's dance during the Soul Train line."

UniverSoul had presented the number since 1994. The piece copied the 1970s television production of the same name, which highlighted couples' rhythmic skills sandwiched between two files of contestants.

Onionhead thought a moment, then said, "Wait a minute. I don't know about that. We don't have clearance."

Nonetheless, we planned to help with the presentation. The next evening the song for Soul Train rang out. We peeked through the curtain. Viewers jumped from their chairs and into the circle as requested. Onionhead and I sneaked up the ramp and joined them.

At our instructions, the volunteers formed two ranks and faced each other. The instrumentals enlivened the atmosphere. "Trip the light fantastic" was an old-school term for the word dance. And those in line did just that with The Four Corners, The Bump, or other rhythmic movements from once upon a time. The seated crowd egged them on.

Onionhead joined the fun. His moves received belly laughs. Unable to resist, I followed suit with the same shtick that had earned kudos from Ringling's staging director. We didn't need Ricky's approval. The audacity of the clown pushed us on.

The number progressed, and the laughs came. But a bur lodged under my saddle. A First of May in the ring took offense to the guffaws, glared at me, and stormed in my direction. She held an integral part in the show, but her name shall remain anonymous.

I weaved in and out of those present one step ahead, but not far enough. The ring curb prevented escape. Trapped. The one who resented my appearance stood two inches from my face, grabbed my shirt, and spoke vehement words, "Don't you *ever* come back into the ring!" The Johnny-come-lately then turned and carried on as if nothing happened.

In the blink of an eye, today transformed into yesteryear with bullies who taunted and belittled. "Punch them, Danise," my mother had said long ago. "That'll make them leave you alone." My former self had buried the invisible companion of childhood—the introvert. An unseen puppeteer jerked nonexistent strings, and my fingers tightened and closed one by one. My gaze followed the newcomer. "I am not going to let this happen to me." But my oversized oxfords worked like cement boots and plastered me to the floor.

The next day, I approached from the audience to avoid detection and noticed that the tenderfoot faced the curtain.

A young attendant blocked the way. "We were told never to let you on stage."

"Who is this person," I wondered, "that has such power?" I turned to the usher and said, "Don't worry. You're not in trouble." Fury formed my words. "But I'm going in anyway."

I pushed past her. The number transitioned into a game of dodge-the-onslaught. Comedy became farce. The newbie, however, succeeded in acquiring my removal from Soul Train and come-in. I never entered the ring again and wondered why Mr. Walker rehired me.

I had always wanted somewhere to plant my trunk. Barry Lubin, the instructor with the mobile eyebrows, had found his plot of land at the Big Apple Circus. For me, Ringling? No. When UniverSoul Big Top Circus rolled around, how natural—black clown, black show. But no deal.

So we tagged along from town to town. Billy continued with his duties. I joined the other artistes who received weekly paychecks for a job never done. We hovered as souls in a temporary state, neither here nor there. Limbo. I washed our laundry, shopped for food, and watched television.

During Clown College, Lou Jacobs had encouraged my talent—hence the gift of the crushed, ruby hat with a yellow band. On the road, Danny Kaye had absorbed my defense of clown. Thoughts tumbled in my head. Remembrances of the hoopla on Gerry Cottle's Circus in England battled with the humiliation of Soul Circus.

To clown was my birthright.

Intermission presented the only chance to work. My shoulders drooped, yet I swallowed my pride and trudged toward steps outside the tent one day. They led to an opening in the canvas at the top of the stands. After the climb I peered inside, drew a breath, and stepped through. I paused. In the hubbub below, spectators rushed to concessions of salty popcorn and sticky cotton candy. I clumped-clumped down the metal bleachers to interact with the audience. They pushed past, however, with vivid programs that proclaimed, "Danise Payne has come back to her home here at UniverSoul Circus."

At the conclusion of the interval, I exited the big top as I had entered. I returned to the trailer and thought, "This is ridiculous." Clown College training remained precious to me, and I valued my twenty-five year career. I pushed embarrassment and despair aside. I continued each show among the crowd that milled about while the empty stage with no beginning and no end, no left or right beckoned. Am I valid as a clown?

One day during my meet-and-greet a woman shoved her business card into my hand. I put it into my pocket and continued. The lights dimmed at the end of the fifteen minutes. Clump-clump up the stairs I went, up and out.

Our trailer was our peaceful dwelling place, our secured home. Inside I removed my jacket, and the small rectangular piece of hard paper fell from the pocket. I glanced at it. It publicized the woman's wheelchair enterprise.

My unique training for circus clowns had taught me the true art and craft of the profession. I had learned how to convey Granny Clown. She was alive and well. Legit.

Midway into the tour, the vice president of operations called. Due to this show's history of departures, a lump developed in my throat.

"Hello, Danise, this is Paula. How are you?"

"I'm fine."

She cut no corners. "Well, we're letting you go after Los Angeles. You can talk to Ricky."

What would be the point? To plead with Mr. Walker would mirror the futility of contract day at Ringling. Nonetheless, he spoke with words that hung in the air like icicles and had no explanation. After he hung up, melancholy engulfed me in a bubble, and I plopped onto the couch in our trailer. Tears pounded my black-and-white oversized oxfords like a torrent to young shoots under a canopy in a forest—my personal tempest.

I was plum tuckered out.

I raised my head and looked at the pictures on the walls of our Layton Lite. Felix Adler, Otto Griebling, and Antoinette Concello—all troupers. I had come so far: Fairytale Town, Ringling, Europe, and back again.

The agreement "no termination before end of season" should have been on paper. I would never make that mistake again. We panicked our last day at Ringling. However, with Soul Circus we had had enough. The show performed in Denver and headed toward California to play Pomona. Next, Los Angeles greeted us with its smoggy skies and turnaway houses. Finally, move-out night and no more pay for me. The crew pulled the blue-and-yellow Canobbio tent down, and the following morning everyone proceeded to Detroit. At the junction of Interstates 40 and 15, the troupe continued east on 40. Billy and I cut the umbilical cord and barnstormed north on 15. It was back to the neon in the desert while the production sure to set spirits on fire crumbled from my heart.

# # #

Everything that transpired on this unique venture—the fun and the heartache—came to mind. My belief in UniverSoul established an association that lasted the years, but disillusionment set me free from the spell of *Your Circus of Dreams*. Mr. Walker never gave an answer for the layoffs, but Billy and I learned race should never be a factor in decisions about tomorrow.

UniverSoul Big Top Circus set a precedent that African Americans can fly through the air with the greatest of ease, stroll the high wire, bend into positions that amazed, make you laugh, and own circuses on par with the rest. UniverSoul Circus also performed school presentations to instill black children with firsthand knowledge of the possibility of the impossible.

Onlookers beamed appreciation with hugs and thanks. "Child, we're so proud!" They laughed, cheered, and booed at the right places.

The enthusiasm of African American audiences stood *par excellence*. Not because we presented an unseen wonder, for circuses began long ago. The reason for the gusto, the race of the artistes. And that fueled the dream of passion.

AFTERWORD

OF BATH OIL BEADS AND ELEPHANT SMELL

Billy and I left the road, and so faded our time with elephants and unicorns. The man who hung by his knees and the woman who grasped his hands for an aerial dance; the daring soul who blasted himself out of a cannon; the mighty-mouse juggler; and Billy and I—all harbored an itch.

The circumstances that prompted our exit off the tanbark trail did not dim our love for the same. Circus was a great life. Where else could I have laughed while squashed in a tiny car with seventeen big-footed-souls! "For everything there is a season and a time for every matter under heaven": Ecclesiastes 3:1 (King James Version). It was time to take our leave.

Peggy Williams' advice, "Save your energy, Danise," helped me through the fatigue and repetition of each season. We had criss-crossed nine time zones on carbon copy roads and pulled into the same Flying J truck stops that tumbled across our paths. Yes, circus was more than a career with grafted siblings. It was our destiny. The everyday American would never understand why we froze in our vehicle and slept under blankets, or with the windows rolled down in desert-like heat, for the sake of a job. Never mind. Billy learned quickly. In my case, all proved the byproduct of a childhood with a military family—the Travellers.

243

I made comparisons while we headed to Las Vegas, and my thoughts drifted backward. My family had slumbered in open lots with each new transfer order. "Gotta get to that base," my dad had said. History repeated itself for my husband and me. We had pulled our vehicle into the train yard and plugged in the portable TV, from which came the words, "It's gonna be a long night." There, we had awaited the resonant roar of Ringling's locomotives to jolt our bones awake upon arrival.

We Wilsons had seldom eaten in a restaurant when we traveled, which spared us from the hostility of the turbulent 1960s. Instead two-day-old, wrinkled hot dogs wrapped in aluminum foil had served as manna from heaven. In contrast, Billy and I had dined on great food in restaurants such as Mrs. Wilkes's Boardinghouse (renamed Mrs. Wilkes's Dining Room) in Savannah, Georgia. De facto civil rights.

Circus and my youth interwove—a perfect patchwork of wander. A square of travel by the Wilsons stitched to the quadrangle of globe-trotting by Billy and me created our quilt of life. Our comforter included a tidbit of yesteryear's showbiz.

One day we drove on an out-of-the-way street. I woke from a stupor and peered through the window as we passed a quaint town.

"Where are we now?"

"Somewhere in Ohio," Billy said, "on State Route 716. A sign pointed to where Annie Oakley's buried in a small cemetery down that narrow road."

She and circus shared a common thread, so we executed an illegal U-turn, and backtracked. We found the forever-bed of the once lively, sharp-shooting star of Buffalo Bill's Wild West covered by its blanket of sod, surrounded by trees amongst those at rest in God's acre. In the days when variety acts carpeted the land, Little Sure Shot had aimed her gun and plugged playing cards with holes before they floated to the ground. Townies collected them as souvenirs.

Kids helped raise the big top during the heyday of living poop machines. Afterward, they reached toward the boss man for something worth more than golden words of thanks: "Here's your Annie Oakleys." The term, now part of the lifestyle's jargon, meant free passes. The lingo list from Clown College included the idiom.

During my early years, sawdust terminology seasoned the jamba-laya in the pot of fun and fantasy. The ingredients of that wonderful stew included the often-ignored working men, once known as roust-abouts. Billy in the driver's seat freed my mind to think of them—the sleazy crew with hearts of gold. Even their nicknames peppered the mix: Irish, Peg Legs, Cowboy, and Footsie.

The hypnotic effect of the open road with yesterday's lanes made me smile at our knockabout lot. I shall miss the blur of the scenery, the side trips, and the places that captivated the senses, especially the road well-traveled by Wilsons—the unforgettable Route 66. Circus—what a perfect life for a military brat who suffered from get-up-and-go!

The sun shone hotter with each mile closer to Las Vegas. The only breeze, from our vehicle that zoomed along, but I had partaken of the cold-blooded spirit of wind.

"Remember our panic heading into Palm Springs, Billy?" I asked, mostly to myself.

Strong gusts had overturned a big rig, fifth-wheel truck. Our home on wheels had swayed and prompted a prayer against the same fate. The elements clutched troupers like vise grips. The adage, the show must go on, meant it must go on through wind, rain, mud, tornadoes, and snow. We had driven through them all with our trailer in tow or on a chase for Ringling's silver slug.

Who wants to run away and join a circus? Me. Regret never bombarded the recollections while we headed away from donnikers and byways. "Have you ever thought about being a clown?" the woman asked decades ago at Fairytale Town. I had become one with no remorse and would remain so no matter what waited around the corner. The joy of my life with little people, tigers, and wardrobe trunks lifted my heart!

We turned toward tomorrow and the peaceful Mojave National Preserve. Over the state line. Into Nevada. The wasteland's sea of magenta, primrose, and sepia tones transfixed my gaze.

Oddly, my thoughts drifted to the pioneer African American performers. They enabled my entrance into the bewitching world of showbiz. In the family tree of comedy and film, broken branches sprouted Lincoln Perry, who opened the door as Stepin Fetchit. The Laziest Man in the World shuffled his feet, so I wouldn't have to. Hattie McDaniel paved the way when she covered her head with a scarf and suffered the name "Mammy" in *Gone with the Wind*, so I wouldn't have to. The Establishment demanded the stereotype. My eyes would not roll, my feet would not skedaddle, thanks to those heroes—submissive to a fault.

Billy and I stood ready for come what may. We had learned torpedoes of any color could plunge a ship. I would float, however, because of my stalwart parents. No better teachers existed than two people who lived through the slings and arrows of segregation. They had pressed on. They had ensured that I was filled with the following knowledge: "But they that wait upon the Lord shall renew their strength; they shall mount up with wings as eagles; they shall run, and not be weary; and they shall walk, and not faint." Isaiah 40:31 (King James Version). I, too, would press on.

Plow on. Plow on past the know-it-alls who had something to say: "You'll never make it to Clown College; you're too shy." Too late. Truth had rattled my bones. I knew I would succeed as a clown. As time marched forward, part of my victory was forgiveness. Eleven years passed, however, before I excused the owners of Ringling who ended my stay. I had no desire to pardon the First of May on UniverSoul who cornered me in the ring. But I moved on after having done so with my vision and self-worth in place.

My dance with an elephant on *The Greatest Show on Earth*. The melting of my heart at the words of a young British girl, "I'm brown, too!" My solo on UniverSoul. Gunther. Miss Ellen. My husband Billy. Unicycles and circus barkers. Highways and railroad tracks. These created the fun and shall always be with me. They are my bath oil beads amongst the elephant smell. I exit on a high note.

The lights of Las Vegas greeted us. With the dawn of a new day, I remained grateful to have worked at Fairytale Town, in films, and at the United Nations. More important, my heart shouted praise to my mother and father, Bob and Alma Wilson. They did not discourage me the day they heard of my plans to audition for Clown College. I pushed on indebted to the world of sawdust with its ups and downs, cramped quarters, and treks through big wide spaces. Setbacks, yes. But oh, the fun!

The years have pressed on. I have transitioned into sedentary, and my hair grows gray. But my heart still follows a wandering star. Nonetheless, I have incorporated my gifts into today. To insure that those of an ebony hue are ready for tomorrow, I have conducted "Yes, I can!" workshops at centers within black communities.

I have reconnected with my past and found my little sister from Clown College. Tina Stotts left the show in 1979 and joined The Royal Hanneford Circus for one season. She has since married and has two sons. What a pleasure to retie the binds! Las Vegas is the end of the line for many circus troupers. We get together once a month to laugh and rehash days gone by.

An event did happen, however, in 2020 that engulfed the globe and reminded us that life is precious. COVID-19 disease was a severe respiratory virus that took millions of lives. The man I called "the modern-day P.T. Barnum"—Gerry Cottle—succumbed in January 2021, one week before he was to receive the vaccination declared to save him from harm. A page of my life turned due to his show. As with the *Ebony* magazine article, Gerry Cottle also put me on the map. He had a gift to use shenanigans that enabled people to drown sorrows in that pool of fun and fantasy. I shall always miss him dearly and treasure my time on his circus.

I like to say that I was born at Ringling Bros. and Barnum & Bailey Circus. That is where the wall crumbled from around my heart, and I came into my own. So, I am most thankful to *The Greatest Show on Earth*. Performing there twice allowed me to witness its transformation. Big Bertha closed its doors, lowered the rigging, and took its final ta-dah in 2017. That news sucked the life from my spirit. Other shows have bowed, premiered, or continued to barnstorm on intact or altered.

The outcome of the world of the circus post-COVID-19 remained to be seen. One of the requirements for safety was social distancing. Would the tanbark trail remain clear or grow over with weeds? I placed thumbs up and would forever open my mouth to belt a tune in the direction of survival. I love the circus. I was born a clown, and *that* is my song.

> *First sawdust and elephant to come along,*
> *I'm back on the Tanbark Trail—gone!*
> *All slapstick props, memories, and clothes*
> *I'll pack away in an elephant's nose.*
> *Take that trunk.*
> *Billy, grab your horn.*
> *Leave monotony behind—we're circus born!*
> *The song is a gallop, extra work—cherry pie*
> *See ya down the road—our way for goodbye.*
> *I'd leave this life of townie behind*
> *Travel around for a time and a time*
> *A donniker is toilet, to disappear—pull a creep*
> *With your elbows in your ears is the only way to sleep.*
> *Miss it? You bet. Love it? Sure do.*
> *Popcorn's on the midway, they yell—ballyhoo.*
> *Load up the wagon, boys, we move out tonight*
> *Lower down the cupola and pack it up real tight.*
> *One behind the other, the jump won't be too long*
> *We'll disappear tomorrow on the wings of a calliope song.*
> *Gone,*
> *Gone,*
> *Gone.*
> —D. Payne

CPSIA information can be obtained
at www.ICGtesting.com
Printed in the USA
LVHW111047160822
726057LV00017B/364/J

9 781949 642988